FROM PLANT
TO GHET

AN INTERPRETIVE HISTORY
OF AMERICAN NEGROES

From Plantation to Ghetto *is one in a group of new books dealing with American history. The purpose of these topical histories is to present in brief compass the author's interpretation of the subject. Aïda DiPace Donald is consulting editor. The other books in this series are:*

The Reins of Power: A Constitutional History of the United States *by Bernard Schwartz*

Policy and Power: Two Centuries of American Foreign Policy *by Ruhl Bartlett*

The Sinews of American Capitalism: An Economic History *by Clark C. Spence*

FROM PLANTATION TO GHETTO

AN INTERPRETIVE HISTORY
OF AMERICAN NEGROES

by

August Meier

and

Elliott M. Rudwick

American Century Series

HILL AND WANG • NEW YORK

For
ROBERT CURVIN
and
LOUIS R. HARLAN

FIRST EDITION OCTOBER 1966
SECOND PRINTING MARCH 1968
THIRD PRINTING (FIRST AMERICAN CENTURY SERIES EDITION)
JUNE 1968
FOURTH PRINTING SEPTEMBER 1968
FIFTH PRINTING DECEMBER 1968
SIXTH PRINTING FEBRUARY 1969
SEVENTH PRINTING APRIL 1969

Manufactured in the United States of America

PREFACE

IN THIS BOOK we have attempted an analytical and interpretive history rather than a narrative account. We have assumed that the reader will have a knowledge of the basic facts of American history and have attempted to focus less on what whites were doing about Negroes than on what Negroes themselves were doing. Moreover, certain topics have been omitted altogether, and special emphasis has been placed on ideologies, institutional developments, and protest movements.

Gloria Marshall of the anthropology department of New York University very carefully read and criticized the first chapter, which greatly benefited from her suggestions. William H. Pease and Jane H. Pease of the history department at the University of Alberta kindly let us have a copy of their paper "Antislavery Ambivalence: Immediatism, Expediency, Race," prior to its publication. James M. McPherson of the history department at Princeton University very generously went through his notes and supplied us with data on the participation of Negroes in the abolitionist movement, 1861–70. We acknowledge a very special debt to the numerous individuals who, through confidential interviews, provided much of the data upon which the sections of this book dealing with class structure and the twentieth-century protest movement are based.

Over the years we have become indebted to the librarians who have facilitated our work. We especially wish to thank Mrs. Dorothy Porter of the Moorland Foundation Room of Howard University Library; Mrs. Jean Blackwell Hutson, Mr. Ernest Kaiser, and other members of the staff of the Schomburg Collection of the New York Public Library; Miss L. Zenobia Coleman, librarian at Tougaloo College; Mr. Arna Bontemps, formerly librarian at Fisk University; the staffs of the libraries at Morgan State College and Roosevelt University; and Mr. George C. Grant, librarian at the East St. Louis branch of Southern Illinois University.

Finally, we wish to acknowledge, with special gratitude, the constant help and encouragement given by two of our fellow scholars and activists, Herbert Hill, labor secretary of the NAACP, and Professor Walter Johnson of the University of Chicago.

AUGUST MEIER
ELLIOTT M. RUDWICK

Chicago
East St. Louis
December 12, 1965

CONTENTS

MAPS

I

THE WEST AFRICAN HERITAGE AND AMERICAN NEGRO HISTORY

THE NEGRO EXPERIENCE in the United States has been largely shaped by two contrasting environments. The first was the Southern staple-producing farm and plantation, on which the vast majority of pre-twentieth-century Negroes worked, in the beginning as slaves and later as sharecroppers. The second was the urban ghetto, predominantly a twentieth-century creation, which grew primarily as a consequence of the migration of rural Negroes to the cities of the South and North.

Thus Negro life and culture in America have developed within the context of a subordinate status whose leading institutional manifestations have been the plantation and the ghetto. Within these two environments, created by a dominant majority, Negroes have both assimilated the culture of the whites and also developed what many sociologists regard as a distinct, though loosely defined, subculture. On the one hand, Negroes adopted the egalitarian values of the American democratic creed and the middle-class values regarding wealth and upward mobility; on the other hand, their ideologies and institutions differed from those of the whites because Negroes had to cope with the reality that democracy, economic opportunity, and social acceptance were not extended to them.

Wishing to be fully accepted as American citizens, yet alienated from the larger society, Negroes have been looked upon, and

1

have looked upon themselves, as a separate ethnic group within that society. One facet of this ethnocentrism has been an awareness that exclusion from the mainstream of American life was related to their African origin.

1

Discussion of what the African background has meant for Negroes in the United States can be considered under two major categories. One is an analysis of the ways in which American Negroes have perceived and felt about Africa. The other is an investigation of the degree to which the distinctive aspects of the American Negro subculture may in part be derived from African ways of life.

Over the years American Negroes have displayed a broad range of views and attitudes about Africa, many of them laden with considerable ambivalence. Race prejudice and discrimination compelled Negroes to identify themselves as being of African descent, yet because the white conceptions of Negro inferiority and African savagery were absorbed by many Negroes, they displayed embarrassment over the allegedly primitive culture of the ancestral continent. At one extreme was the tiny handful of individuals who said that as Americans they had no more interest in Africa than they had in any other foreign land. At the other extreme was the minority—at times a substantial one—who rejected completely the possibility of achieving a satisfactory existence in the United States and advocated colonization, or the return of American Negroes to the African homeland. Between these existed a broad spectrum of opinions. Practically universal among articulate nineteenth-century Negroes was a pride in the accomplishments of ancient Africa, particularly Egypt. Equally universal was the view of contemporary Africa as heathen and savage. But it was generally believed that Afro-Americans, supposedly the most civilized portion of the black race, had a special duty and responsibility to assist in the uplift and moral and spiritual redemption of the homeland. Some thought of commercial ventures as playing a part in this mission, but for the most part the stress was on the role that Negro churches should play in sending missionaries to civilize and Christianize the allegedly immoral, primitive, and idolatrous inhabitants of Africa. Exclusively nationalist sentiments, looking toward the establishment of a new national homeland in Africa for oppressed American Negroes, were less common, but nevertheless existed throughout the history of Negroes in America, and at certain times flowered into highly significant and dramatic movements. From time to time eminent Negro intellectuals have espoused colonization or emigration; yet its chief appeal has been to the poorest class of Negroes—the group which has been the most alienated from society, and therefore the group most likely to identify with Africa.

Such was the range of views among nineteenth-century Negroes. These were views that had wide currency until the present generation. But as early as the turn of the century, W. E. B. Du Bois, the sociologist, historian, and noted protest leader, enunciated a new approach. Possessed of a deep emotional commitment to Africa and people of color throughout the world, Du Bois was probably the first American Negro to express the idea of Pan-Africanism: the belief that all people of African descent had common interests and should work together in the struggle for their freedom. He also appears to have been the first American author to describe the great medieval kingdoms of West Africa; and he was among the first to regard the nonliterate societies of sub-Saharan Africa as possessing complex and sophisticated cultures. Finally he was apparently the first person to suggest that the culture of American Negroes had been substantially influenced by the cultures of Africa.

Well versed in the literature produced by European explorers and historians, Du Bois' early writings on Africa were thoroughly imbued with the new knowledge that was a by-product of European penetration and conquest of the African interior in the late nineteenth century. Since then, historians and anthropologists have added greatly to and refined our knowledge of African history and culture. It took time, however, for Du Bois' picture to spread, even among Negroes. Although Carter G. Woodson, the influential scholar and propagandist for the study of the Negro's past, and founder of the *Journal of Negro History,* expressed similar ideas, few indeed were those who accepted Du Bois' suggestion that American Negro culture owed much to the African way of life. Du Bois' views on this subject were based more on mystical yearnings than on hard factual data; it was not until

Melville J. Herskovits in 1941 published his *Myth of the Negro Past,* based on extensive empirical research, that the thesis became widely debated.

The title of Herskovits' book suggests very well the viewpoint not only of whites, but also—until very recent decades—of most Negroes, in regard to the African background. Ordinarily when Negroes expressed pride in Africa they pointed to the antique past. The myth that Du Bois, Woodson, and Herskovits were bent on destroying was in their conception a dual one: 1) that the ancestral cultures of the American Negroes were primitive, with Africans making no contributions to the culture of the world; and 2) that under the slave regime practically all evidence of African culture—except perhaps for some survivals in music and the dance—had been destroyed.

Having set forth the myth, let us now turn to a brief presentation of some of the salient facts.

2

Africa south of the Sahara was known to medieval Muslims as the *Beled es-Sudan,* or "Land of the Blacks." Today the term "Sudan" is restricted to the broad belt of grassland lying south of the Sahara and north of the tropical rain forest that occupies the Guinea Coast and the Congo River Basin. The peoples who became the chief source of the Negro population in the New World resided in the forested area and in the southern portions of the western Sudan. The chief theatre of operation for the trans-Atlantic slave trade was along the West African Coast between Senegal and Angola. Some slaves came from deep in the interior, but ordinarily the range of the slave trade lay within three hundred miles of the coast. Thus the great majority of Negroes who were brought to the New World came primarily from the area drained by the Senegal, Gambia, Volta, Niger, and Congo rivers.

The theatre of much of the Sudanese cultural history we are about to relate was actually located to the north of the area from which New World Negroes came. Yet we cannot separate the history of the southern Sudan from that of the northern Sudan. Moreover the institutions of the Sudanese societies had important influences on the societies of the Guinea Coast, and some of the most important slave-trading kingdoms encompassed territory in both the rain forest and the Sudan. It therefore seems appropriate to begin our story of the American Negro's African heritage with a brief sketch of the cultural history of the western Sudan.

Modern scholarship places the western Sudan among the important creative centers in the development of human culture— along with the Ancient Near East, the Indus and Yellow river valleys, and Meso-America. In each of these places an unusually high agricultural productivity achieved during the Neolithic period sustained a relatively dense population and thus ultimately led to a profound transformation in social institutions. In each case the social complexities arising out of the increasing number of inhabitants resulted in the development of social classes, urban centers, and despotic theocratic monarchies.

The importance of the domestication of plants and animals as a catalyst for these institutional changes cannot be overestimated. It is possible that, as the anthropologist George Peter Murdock has suggested, the western Sudan was among those centers in which agriculture was an indigenous invention, thus duplicating the achievement of the inhabitants of Southwest Asia, Meso-America, and possibly other places. The staple grains of the Sudanic complex of crops, comparable to the wheat and barley of the Near East and the maize of the New World, were pearl millet and sorghum. Among the other important cultivated crops probably first domesticated in the western Sudan were okra, the kola tree (the original source of the stimulant in cola drinks), the watermelon, sesame, and cotton. Murdock's thesis, based chiefly upon plant distributions and data from historical linguistics, has not yet found support in the slim archaeological investigation thus far done in West Africa. Others insist that the knowledge and techniques of plant cultivation were not developed independently in the western Sudan but diffused into this area from Southwest Asia, via Egypt. Whatever the facts to be unearthed by the archaeologists, subsequent cultural development in the Sudan paralleled that which occurred in Mesopotamia and Egypt, in China and India, and in Mexico and Peru. By the second millennium B.C., according to Murdock, or by the opening of the Christian era, according to more conservative authorities, the Sudan had developed large-scale, complex kingdoms.

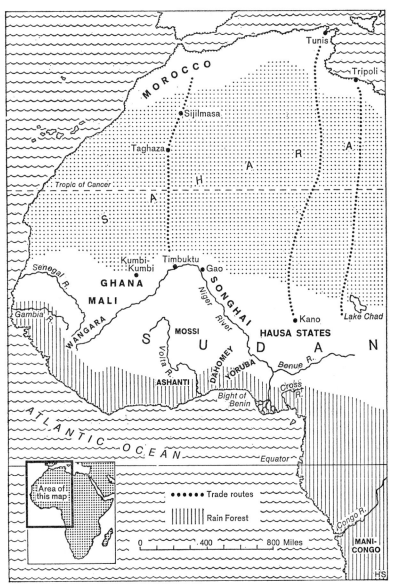

West Africa

An important factor in the proliferation of urban societies and empires in the western Sudan was the trans-Saharan trade. Though little of certainty is known about this commerce during the early millennia, it is known that the introduction of the camel during Roman times greatly facilitated it. Three major routes emerged in the western half of the Sahara desert. Of these the most important, until the end of the sixteenth century, ran from Sijilmasa in present-day Morocco to the Upper Niger River area. The prominence of this route was based on the proximity of its southern terminal entrepôts to Wangara, the gold-producing territory around the headwaters of the Senegal and Niger rivers. The principal southbound commodity was salt, an item in scarce supply in the Sudan but plentiful at the Taghaza salt mines in the Sahara desert. Lesser, but important, items in the traffic were Negro slaves from the Sudan and luxury textiles from the Mediterranean. Control of the Wangara gold fields was a leading consideration in the minds of the empire builders of the western Sudan. The significance of this, the westernmost route, is evident in the fact that the prosperity of the three most important and largest states in early West African history—Ghana, Mali, and Songhai—was largely based upon this traffic in gold and slaves, salt and cloth. Each in turn controlled the southern entrepôts of the Moroccan trade, most notably the city of Timbuktu. Timbuktu, on the edge of the desert, close to the Niger at the most northern point on its course, by the end of the twelfth century had become the major international market where the products of the Niger valley were exchanged for those of northern Africa. It also became the leading commercial and intellectual center of West Africa.

The earliest West African state of which we have any written account (and archaeological work has barely begun) was the empire of Ghana. The state was founded, probably in the fourth century A.D., by the Soninke people on the southern fringe of the Sahara, where they were in a position to benefit from the caravan trade between Morocco and Wangara. Though the exact boundaries of the kingdom have been disputed, it is generally agreed that it was located north and west of the great bend in the Niger River, the empire at its height (in the tenth century) extending as far west as the upper portion of the Senegal River. The rulers were pagan, though the capital, Kumbi-Kumbi, consisted of two towns—one pagan, which contained the fortified residence of the king and his court, and the other Muslim. Arabic was the written language of the empire, and both Muslims and pagans held high office.

For some time before its downfall the kingdom of Ghana had been threatened by the Islamized Berber peoples to the north and west, and in 1076 it was conquered by the Berber Almoravids, originally a Muslim sect in the lower Senegal valley. The Almoravid empire lasted a century, and for a brief period stretched from the Sudan almost to the Pyrenees. Though within a dozen years the Soninke peoples had regained their independence, the place of the former kingdom of Ghana was now occupied by a number of warring states. Finally, in 1240, the ancient capital Kumbi-Kumbi was completely destroyed by the rising kingdom of Mali.

Mali, which thus gave the *coup de grâce* to the history of Ghana, shared the center of the Sudanic stage with the kingdom of Songhai from the thirteenth to the fifteenth century. Both had obscure origins, dating back perhaps to the seventh century A.D. The original territory of Mali was located on the Upper Niger, west of the Great Bend. Songhai's capital was situated on the middle section of the river, east of the Great Bend. Both states were converted to Islam in the eleventh century, and the economic prosperity of both was based chiefly upon their importance as trade entrepôts. Little is known about the history of Songhai, which gradually expanded north and south along the Niger River, until the fourteenth century, but Mali had achieved prominence before the middle of the thirteenth century. Ultimately the Mali empire stretched from almost the Atlantic eastward beyond the Niger, and from the Sahara to the rain forest. It reached its apogee under the illustrious Mansa Musa (1307–32), who annexed Songhai. Even prior to this addition to his kingdom, Mansa Musa had dazzled the Mediterranean world with an elaborate pilgrimage to Mecca. His retinue of sixty thousand and his lavish gifts of gold made his name a legend among both Muslim and Christian nations.

After the middle of the fourteenth century, Mali entered into a long decline, while Songhai, which had regained its independence shortly after the death of Mansa Musa, gradually established itself as the leading power in the western Sudan. Under Askia Muhammad I (1493–1528), who acquired the remnants of the Mali empire and invaded the Hausa states to the east, Songhai, whose territories reached nearly to the Atlantic and almost to Lake Chad, became the largest empire in West African history. With Askia's encouragement of trade and learning, Songhai enjoyed an enormous prosperity, and the University of Sankore at Timbuktu became one of the great centers of learning in the Muslim world. Despite its imposing magnificence however, the Songhai empire was shattered by the Moroccan invasion of 1591, and the western Sudan was divided among several smaller kingdoms.

To the south, the inhabitants of the rain forest along the Guinea Coast followed a similar pattern in their cultural history, except that many important developments came considerably later. Since Sudanese crops were not suitable for cultivation in the tropical forest, other foods had to be domesticated, and different agricultural techniques were needed. Agriculture seems to have come to the Guinea Coast by the time of the Christian era. The staple crops were not grains but root crops—chiefly yams. Once the Bantu-speaking peoples of the Lower Niger valley had become farmers, they were equipped to cultivate the Congo River Basin. The early centuries of the Christian era witnessed the Bantu migration into central, and then eastern and southern, Africa and the displacement of the food-gathering Pygmies and Bushmen as the Bantu took over almost all of the southern half of the continent. The subsequent increase in population among the rain forest peoples had, by the second millennium A.D., made possible the establishment of despotic states modeled upon the political institutions of the Sudanese kingdoms to the north, with which they shared certain institutional and ritual forms, including the important role played by the queen-mother or queen-sister, which were unknown outside of Africa. Thus the European slave-trading nations dealt not only with coastal tribes but also with proud kingdoms like those of the Mani-Congo in present-day Congo and Angola, and of the Ashanti, the Yoruba, and the Dahomeans, whose boundaries stretched from the Guinea Coast into the southern Sudan.

3

West African societies in the slaving area ranged from small tribes to large kingdoms of a million or more; from small groups where kinship ties were the source of all authority to large states with complex political institutions. These societies were characterized by economic specialization and a monetary system based on the cowrie shell to facilitate trade. The larger ones had a system of social classes and a hierarchical territorial political organization. Interlacing and underpinning these political, economic, and social class arrangements were a deeply rooted and intricate kinship system extending from family to clan, and an elaborate web of religious belief involving the individual, the kinship groupings, and the entire society. Although these societies differed widely among themselves, their many basic cultural similarities make it possible to form some valid generalizations about the cultural background of New World Negroes. While in the discussion that follows our examples will be drawn from the larger and more complex of these societies, such as the Dahomeans, the Ashanti, the Mossi, and the Yoruba, most of what is said, except for the class structure and political institutions, applies generally to the ancestral peoples of the New World Negroes.

Throughout the entire area the economy was basically agricultural, although along the coast there was some fishing and inland poultry was raised as the main source of meat. Farming was done with the hoe, men ordinarily doing the heavy work of breaking the soil. Among the Ashanti both sexes cultivated the crops; the Dahomeans allocated this work to women, while among the Yoruba most of it was done by men. Larger, heavier tasks were performed co-operatively by the men. Among the Dahomeans, for example, fields were cleared and houses built by a voluntary co-operative male group known as the *dokpwe*. The *dokpwe* also played an important role in funeral services, and thus was an institution with both religious and economic functions.

Economic specialization involved the elaboration of a number of crafts: most notably ironworking, weaving, wood carving, basketry, pottery making, and bronze casting. The craftsmen's products often had an aesthetic function, and have been much admired by Western artists and art critics since the turn of the century. Especially notable were the bronze and brass castings made by the *cire-perdue* process. Craftsmen in most of the societies were organized into craft guilds, ordinarily along kinship lines, which set prices and often acted as mutual aid societies. Among the Yoruba the guilds of craftsmen and women traders exercised considerable political influence on the town councils.

Much of the internal commerce of each West African society was in the hands of women, some of whom were producer-traders, while other women were nonproducing middlemen. In most West African societies local and interregional trade was facilitated by the existence of complex systems of markets, held daily and periodically, in villages as well as in towns. External trade was controlled by the royal heads of state. Among the Ashanti and in Dahomey the right to trade in certain items— notably slaves, gold, and European imports—required personal authorization of the king, who levied fees for granting such privileges. The West African societies thus had an unusually elaborate economic organization for nonliterate peoples, an economic organization comparable, for example, to those of the Inca and Aztec empires in the New World.

The larger societies were characterized by specialization not only in economic pursuits but in other spheres of life as well, and there developed a degree of social stratification sufficient to lead some scholars to characterize them as possessing a class structure analogous to that in Western societies. Thus in Dahomey there was an elaborate hierarchy. At the bottom were the slaves, chiefly war captives. The children of slaves—except for those on the king's estates, where a kind of hereditary serfdom existed—were absorbed into the families of their owners. The backbone of the society was a class of free farmers and artisans. At approximately the same social level were the ordinary temple priests and diviners. The upper class consisted of the higher elements in the priesthood and the king's officials. Because members of the royal clan were not permitted to hold office, these functionaries were drawn from the ranks of the freemen. At the top stood the large but parasitical royal clan, whose members did no work, and at the apex was the monarch himself.

In general, land in West African societies was owned in

perpetuity by corporate kin groups who would alienate it only on the rarest occasions. Individual members inherited or were apportioned land for their own use, and they owned and could freely dispose of the goods they produced. In all kingdoms of West Africa the land was considered to "belong" ultimately to the paramount ruler, a consideration which signified recognition of the king's sacred authority over, and responsibility for, the kinship groupings and territorial units making up his domain.

The system of land ownership is only one indication of the importance of the family and larger kinship groupings in African societies.* Highly complex groups formed on the basis of descent and of marriage and residence were important in matters of politics and religion as well as in matters of livelihood and inheritance. And as is the case in most societies, certain of these kinship groups were the primary agents through which individuals learned the norms and values of their cultures.

Descent was usually traced either matrilineally or patrilineally. In a matrilineal society, all those males and females whose descent was traced through a line of mothers to a single female ancestor formed a descent group or lineage. In a patrilineal society, all those persons descended from a common ancestor through a line of fathers formed a lineage. Groups of lineages tracing their descent from a common ancestor formed a clan. In many cases the members of each clan believed themselves descended from a divine animal ancestor; thus in Dahomey the royal clan claimed descent from a leopard. Exceedingly important as members of all these kinship groupings were the dead ancestors. They were revered and given sacrifices. They had power to work evil or good for their relatives and descendants. The people believed that their ancestors participated intimately in the conduct and guidance of family, lineage, and clan affairs. The clan head, as a rule its oldest living male member, served as the link between the ancestors and the living, and therefore exercised considerable power over the clan's members. Among the Dahomeans he controlled the use of the communal lands of the clan,

---

* Because African kinship systems are complex and very different from those in Western societies the following discussion is somewhat technical. We thought a correct treatment preferable to an oversimplified and therefore distorted one.

could force the clan members to work the lands, was consulted in all marriages, and was treated with ritualistic respect.

   Ordinarily the West African *family* group was what anthro- √ pologists term an "extended family," comprising two or more generations of adults descended from a common ancestor, their spouses, and their children, all sharing a single residential unit, often termed a compound. A compound frequently consisted of a group of dwellings enclosing a courtyard, often with a fence surrounding the entire group of buildings. Polygyny was everywhere recognized as a suitable or preferred form of marriage. In a number of societies, such as Yoruba and Dahomey, each wife had a separate room or dwelling within the compound, living with her husband in rotation with his other wives. In patrilineal societies the *extended family* occupying a compound typically comprised a man, his wives and children (i.e., sons and unmarried daughters), his brothers and their wives and children, and his adult sons and their wives and children. Although the adult sisters and daughters of men in such a household would ordinarily have married into other extended families, they would still retain membership in their fathers' lineage, while their husbands and children belonged to other lineages. A comparable situation occurred in matrilineal societies, such as the Ashanti, except that a man and his wives often lived with, and were considered as √ belonging to, the extended family headed by his maternal uncle.

   In both patrilineal and matrilineal societies the head of an extended family was usually one of the oldest males. Typically he exercised considerable power over the members of the household. When the head of a compound died, the next younger brother, or the eldest son, or the oldest male in the household, succeeded him. When the size of a family became too large to be supported by the land resources in the compound, a younger brother or son would establish a new household in the same or a different community. This household continued to acknowledge its relationship to the parent compound, however, and the various members of the newly formed residence remained members of their original descent groups or lineages.

   Political units varied in character from autonomous villages to despotic centralized monarchies. More than any of the other societies in the West African slaving area, Dahomey resembled the European absolute monarchy. At the base of its political pyramid was the local village chief, appointed by the king but to some extent responsive to the family heads who formed the village council. The villages and towns were grouped into twelve districts, each governed by a royally appointed official with fiscal and administrative functions. The king was nearly an absolute ruler, a sacred figure, mediating between the people and the powerful royal ancestors. The king himself chose his heir from among his eligible sons. He was the highest judicial officer and had the final decision on appeals brought from cases heard by lesser officials. He appointed all of his administrators. Chief among them were the royal executioner, who exercised the power of a prime minister; the official in charge of the princely class; the governor of the coastal region, who also dealt with the European traders; the chief gatekeeper, who supervised the officers and residents of the royal palace and headed an espionage system; the commander in chief of the army; the minister of the interior who supervised markets, agricultural operations, and the ingenious system of tax collections; and the royal treasurer.

Women played an important role in the administration of political affairs in Dahomey. Each major official had a female counterpart known as his "mother," who took precedence over him at court and supervised his work. When officials reported to the king, groups of women were present, whose duty was to remember what had been transacted. Women also had an important role in the army, and, since technically regarded as wives of the king, these female soldiers were kept secluded from all men.

Dahomey was a more centralized and absolute monarchy than its contemporaries. Elsewhere the sacred rulers of the larger societies had not achieved this concentration of power. Chieftains of villages and town subdivisions were often selected by the council of local family heads from among the members of a particular lineage in which the right to this office inhered. Provincial governors and the king himself were chosen in a similar way by a council consisting of the heads of the powerful lineages in the provincial or national capitals. Often the queen-sister or the queen-mother was a powerful figure in her own right, with lands and slaves of her own and considerable influence over the king. Among the Ashanti she actually nominated the king. In most cases a king's council had at its disposal a recognized procedure by which it might depose a ruler. Among the Yoruba, when his council sent him an ostrich egg, the *Alafin,* ruler of Oyo and paramount ruler of all Yorubaland, knew he was expected to commit suicide. This limitation on the king's power, the elective nature of the office, the interregnum between the death of one ruler and the appointment of his successor, and the decentralized nature of the political hierarchy were responsible for centrifugal forces in most West African monarchies that gave them a quasi-feudal appearance. Although we lack the information to verify the hypothesis, it is likely that this characteristic had also been true of the earlier Sudanese empires, which Mediterranean travelers described as constantly threatened by rebellious vassal states.

Religion permeated West African cultures. Typically there were complex notions regarding a person's souls or spiritual attributes. Elaborate funeral services were the rule because the spirits of the dead ancestors were regarded as sacred beings, powerful in determining the destiny of kinship groups and states. Great gods, sometimes arranged in groups or pantheons, as well as numerous lesser, local deities, also had their roles in determining the course of human affairs. Elaboration of religious beliefs was carried to especially great lengths among the Dahomeans, but a brief examination of their ideas and practices will illuminate the religious life of West Africa generally.

The Dahomeans held that each individual had five different souls or spiritual attributes, one of which survived as an independent soul after a person died. Impressive ceremonies were held periodically to deify the dead ancestors. There were also annual rituals honoring and worshipping them, the rites including frenzied dancing and animal sacrifices. The yearly "custom" for the royal ancestors was an especially important occasion, since they were the guardians of the state. At these events and after the death of a king, criminals and captured prisoners of war were among the sacrifices. Like peoples in many parts of the world, the Dahomeans believed that a human being was the most valuable sacrifice they could offer to a revered and powerful deity.

The Dahomean great gods were organized into three pantheons —Sky, Earth, and Thunder. The most important deity of all was Mawu, the Moon Goddess, who presided over the Sky pantheon with her husband, Lisa, the Sun God. They were the parents of the other chief deities—including Sagbata, head of the Earth pantheon, who was responsible for bringing crop abundance, and Xevioso, head of the Thunder pantheon, with control over rain and fire, rivers and oceans. Connected with the worship of the great gods was a belief in fate. One could effect a change in his destiny by offering sacrifices to Legba, the trickster god, who relayed to the other deities Mawu's directions concerning the execution of men's destinies. Each pantheon had its own cult, its own priests, its own group of adherents. Initiation into a cult came only after a long period of training, and in the final ceremonies the initiate performed a frenzied dance, during which he was regarded as being literally possessed by the deity, who "rode" on his head and inspired his motions. Finally there was Da, the serpent, symbolizing the sentient, elusive, moving aspect of life, the dynamic element in the world, and evident in fortune, smoke, roots, and the umbilical cord.

4

As we have already noted, although Du Bois and Woodson believed that Africanisms were present in American Negro culture, it was the work of the anthropologist and Africanist Melville J. Herskovits that made this thesis a focus of controversy among students of American Negro life and culture. Not only did he insist that Africanisms existed in the American Negro subculture, but he held also that some of these cultural traits had been transmitted to the whites. Herskovits' method was basically that of making a comparative analysis of West African cultures, the cultures of Negroes in the Caribbean area and Brazil, and the patterns of life among what the sociologist Charles S. Johnson has called the "folk Negro" in the United States. Supported by impressive ethnographic field work both in West Africa and in Negro peasant communities in the West Indies and Dutch Guiana, Herskovits' work commanded attention. Scholars agree that in Brazil and the Caribbean area much of African culture has survived, and that in those countries there has been a synthesis of African and European cultural traditions. African religious and familial institutions, linguistic elements and folk tales, mutual aid societies, and musical and dance forms have had a marked effect on the life of New World Negroes south of the United States.

Haitian *vodun,* for example, is a syncretism of Catholic and African religious beliefs and practices, with various African gods being equated with Catholic saints. (*Vodun,* rendered in English as *voodoo,* is itself a Dahomean word meaning "deity.") Thus was repeated the age-old process of religious syncretism, of which Christianity, combining as it does elements of Judaism, Hellenistic philosophy, and oriental mystery religions is itself a superb example.

Controversy arises as to the degree to which African survivals are to be found in the United States, where Herskovits himself held that they were less common than in the Caribbean and Brazil. The higher proportion of whites to Negroes in the sections where slavery held sway, the absence of mountains or jungle fastnesses where escaped slaves could develop a stable community without white interference, and the generally more repressive slave codes in the United States, which made it difficult or impossible for slaves to maintain social and religious organizations of their own, all militated against the survival of Africanisms. Yet Herskovits believed he had identified numerous evidences of such survivals.

For certain items, Herskovits' claims are incontrovertible. Since Lorenzo Turner's epoch-making book *Africanisms in the Gullah Dialect* (1949), it has been recognized that the peculiarities of vocabulary and syntax among the inhabitants of the coastal Sea Islands of South Carolina and Georgia—where Africanisms are undoubtedly strongest because of the relative isolation of Negro communities—were derived from Africa and not, as was once widely held, from archaic dialects of sixteenth-century England. African influence upon American Negro music and dance, both of which have diffused into the culture of the white population, is also generally recognized and accepted. Much of lower-class Negro folklore, magic, and medicine—especially of a generation and more ago—can be traced to African origins. Much of the content in Joel Chandler Harris' Uncle Remus tales, doctored though it was for white audiences, is genuine folk material with African roots. Notable in this connection are the stories revolving around the rabbit who, as an animal trickster, is a central figure in African folklore. Herskovits also asserts that similarities between mutual benefit societies and funerary practices in the United States and those in West Africa betoken African survivals, though proof for this is more difficult to establish. Where the chief controversy arises, however, is over Herskovits' assertions regarding religion and family life.

E. Franklin Frazier, in his *Negro Family in the United States* (1939), one of the classics of American sociological literature, described what he called a matriarchal pattern that is common (though not universal) among lower-class Negro families. These are extended families in which the central figure is the mother or the grandmother. She functions as an authority figure and as a breadwinner and is the one who holds the family together. This is the kind of family life portrayed in Lorraine Hansberry's recent Broadway play and motion picture *A Raisin in the Sun*. Such families are often characterized by marital instability and desertion on the part of the husband. Herskovits held that this pattern developed out of the adjustment of African family institutions to the brutalizing conditions of Negro life in America. He referred to the importance of women in African societies, especially their economic role, not only as farmers, but even more significantly as the chief traders in the village and urban markets (a situation that exists in Haiti today). He referred also to the prevalence in African societies of polygynous family systems, and to the custom of each of a man's wives having her own dwelling. In such situations, Herskovits held, the bonds of identification and affection—even in patrilineal societies—were between the children and their mother rather than between the children and their father.

There are of course alternative explanations for the prevalence of the matriarchal or, to follow modern anthropological usage, matrifocal family patterns among lower-class Negroes. Some scholars, like Frazier, have held that they are the heritage of slavery, for if any family bonds were respected by the slave-owners, they were usually those between mothers and their young children. Psychoanalytic speculation has referred to white society's emotional emasculation of the Negro male. Whatever the origins of the matrifocal patterns and their acceptance among lower-class Negroes, the twentieth-century urban environment has served to perpetuate them. The lower-class Negro woman finds it easier than a man to obtain and hold a job. The husband, unable to fulfill the economic functions expected of a man in our society, and unable to accept the social inadequacy that his wife's superior earning power suggests, will often desert his family. Thus both authority in the family and responsibility for its economic support are often shouldered by the woman. In this view, the matrifocal family type, one in which a woman is head of the household, is to be regarded as a functional adjustment to social realities rather than any survival of Africanisms. Support for this view comes from West Indian studies. Whereas recent scholarship on American Negroes has not been concerned with testing Herskovits' thesis, recent investigations in the West Indies either implicitly or explicitly criticize Herskovits' views on the Negro family. There, family patterns appear to be well correlated with economic factors. Investigators of Negro life in the West Indies recognize the role of slavery in originating and/or perpetuating matrifocal patterns, but view their persistence in some places today as mainly dependent upon modern economic and social conditions.

As for religious survivals, Herskovits maintains that the religious hysteria characteristic of lower-class evangelical churches and pentecostal sects, among both whites and Negroes, reflects the influence of the intensely emotional and frenzied African ceremonies. The phenomenon of religious "possession," in which the enthusiast feels united with a deity, is well known to anthropologists. Its manifestations range from epileptic fits among the Arabians and the Siberian shamans, through the visions of the ancient Near Eastern Christian hermits, to trances of Hindu mystics, the fantasies induced among American Indians by starvation, self-mutilation, or drugs, to "getting religion" by the sanctified among the Holy Rollers, spiritual Baptists, and similar groups. Among American Negroes this phenomenon is especially common in lower-class Baptist and Methodist churches, the pentecostal sects, and such cults as Daddy Grace's House of Prayer for All People. Similar forms of religious possession are to be found among the white sects and cults and Baptist churches that are the counterparts of the Negro lower-class religious institutions. Herskovits, calling attention to the emotional type of religious service that came with the Great Awakening and the founding of Methodism in the eighteenth century, attributed the particular patterns of religious hysteria that developed at camp meetings and revival services to contact with slaves who attended such gatherings. His thesis is that here, as in Haiti, we find a form

of religious syncretism. Herskovits also found syncretism in the
high proportion of Negroes, perhaps as many as two thirds,
belonging to the Baptist Church. Pointing to the importance of
the river cults in West African religion, he held that the slaves
flocked to the Baptist Church because of the similarity between
West African practices and the total immersion required for
initiation into the Baptist Church, a rite to be found also among
the pentecostal sects and such cults as those of Elder Micheaux
and Daddy Grace.

Frazier, who was Herskovits' most articulate critic, regarded
such interpretations as nonsense. Most Negroes, he insisted,
became Methodists and Baptists because these were the only
churches that really proselytized among Negroes, as part of their
general interest in society's downtrodden people. Baptists especially appealed to Negroes, he wrote, because their highly
decentralized form of church organization and congregational
autonomy made it possible for Negroes to govern their own institutions and assume leadership positions without difficulty. Moreover, a functional explanation of the emotional character of
worship in most lower-class Negro churches can be based upon
the fact that the evangelical churches have always appealed
primarily to lower-class people because of the escape that "getting religion" offers from the burdens of everyday reality. Frazier
argued that every significant aspect of lower-class Negro religious
life can be explained as arising out of the social milieu in which
American Negroes found themselves, without recourse to explanations in terms of African survivals.

It can be argued of course that the aspects of African culture
which have survived in the United States are those which have
had a functional value; that the African family institutions were
modified and adapted to meet the exigencies of life for the slave
and the freedman in America; that the African forms of religious
possession fulfilled important needs for the oppressed Negroes,
and indeed for lower-class whites as well. Actually there is no
necessary contradiction between Herskovits' emphasis upon the
persistence of African cultural traditions and the functional
explanations offered by sociologists like Charles S. Johnson and
E. Franklin Frazier.

Whether the unique cultural characteristics of the Negro sub-
community are viewed as due to African survivals or to func-

tional adjustments to the specific situation in which American Negroes found themselves, this way of life is a subculture, a variety of the larger American culture; and unlike the cultures of Negro peasants and urban masses in countries to the south, what survives of African culture in the United States is relatively limited. Such Africanisms as may persist are not evenly distributed among all groups in the Negro population. They proved strongest among the rural Sea Islanders of Georgia and South Carolina, whose contact with whites was extremely limited, and in the permissive atmosphere of Latin-oriented Louisiana, where vestiges of African "voodoo" persisted until recent years. Such Africanisms as do persist are characteristic of the life of the lower classes rather than the middle and upper classes. As is true for other ethnic minorities in our society, those Negroes who have moved up the economic and social ladder have, as part of the process of upward mobility, assimilated white middle-class ways in speech, family life, religious services, and values.

Herskovits' thesis certainly remains a provocative and suggestive one. Some of his contentions are undoubtedly correct and there is no argument about them. But in its more controversial aspects, no definite conclusions can be drawn concerning its validity in explaining the existence of a Negro subculture in America.

Herskovits' ideas originally evoked a stormy response from most articulate Negroes and from most whites interested in race relations. These people were busy fighting the charges that Negroes were inferior to whites and therefore unable to assimilate white American culture and adjust to white American middle-class society. Negro intellectuals like the sociologists Charles S. Johnson and E. Franklin Frazier described distinctive patterns of life among the Negro lower classes as being responses to the social oppression and economic degradation which they suffered. During the past decade, however, Herskovits' thesis has been more hospitably received among Negro intellectuals. The rise to independence and power on the part of the new African nations has given American Negroes new feelings of identification with and pride in the ancestral continent. Prominent scholars belonging to the American Society for African Culture (AMSAC) have embraced the theory of *négritude* propounded by the international parent body, the Society for African Culture, with headquarters in France. This theory holds that the descendants of Africans everywhere in the world exhibit in their culture and in their thought certain ineradicable evidences of their African origin. The stirrings and achievements of the Negro revolution in the United States have also stimulated among American Negroes a new feeling of racial identity—of accepting themselves as Negroes rather than trying to imitate whites—and, concomitantly, a new interest in the race's past.

What then is the significance of the African—especially the West African—cultural heritage for American Negro history? Undoubtedly it contributed something to the quality of Negro life and institutions in the United States; and to some extent it provided materials which American Negroes refashioned to cope with the problems they faced in the New World. Throughout American history, Africa provided for American Negroes an ancestral homeland with which they identified in various ways and to various degrees. Not until the middle of the twentieth century, however, did the rise of African nations to independence and international influence make large numbers of Negroes genuinely proud of their African heritage. Both the changing role of Africa and the civil rights revolution gave American Negroes a new sense of identity. As a result articulate Negroes became more receptive to the idea that Africanisms survived in their way of life.

Thus changes on the world scene and in the Negro's status in the United States have made acceptance of Herskovits' thesis far more widespread among American Negroes and, for that matter, among American whites as well. We shall do well to keep his views in mind, and we shall have occasion to refer to them again. Nevertheless, the major forces shaping Negro life in the United States, from the first use of black men on the tobacco farms of Virginia to the civil rights revolution spawned in the modern cities, lay in the American environment. It is mainly to the plantation and the ghetto that we shall have to turn if we are to understand Negro history and Negro life in America.

II

NEGROES IN AGRARIAN AMERICA:
SLAVERY AND THE PLANTATION

1

THE INSTITUTION OF SLAVERY had long been known in both southern Europe and Africa, but the rise of the European traffic in African slaves was the product of two major developments in the fifteenth and sixteenth centuries: the emergence of the national monarchies facing the Atlantic and the Commercial Revolution.

Quite naturally the new nations sought wealth and empire in Africa and the New World. Once Spain and Portugal had broken the commercial pre-eminence of the Italian city-states, Holland, France, and England successfully entered the contest for a share of the African trade and empires in the Americas. Soon Africa became the major source of labor for the exploitation of the tropical and semitropical regions of the New World. Both the slave trade itself and, even more, the wealth that flowed from American staple crops cultivated by Negro slave labor created much of the prosperity and power that made first Portugal and Spain, later Holland, France, and finally England, each for a period a dominant commercial and imperial state in the affairs of Europe. Thus, the African slave trade and slavery were closely involved in the quickening of European commerce, industry, and banking, and in the shift of economic power from the Mediter-

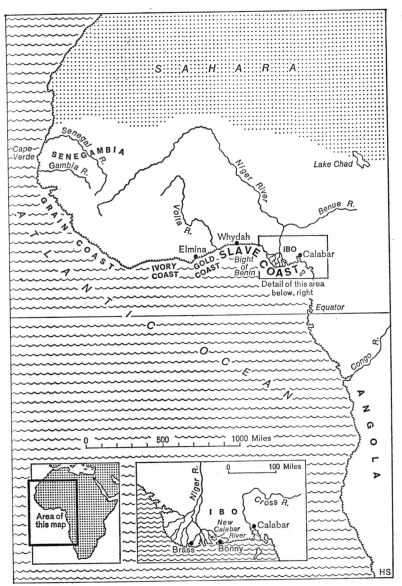

The Slave Coast

ranean countries to northwestern Europe which constituted the Commercial Revolution.

The Portuguese were the first Europeans to engage in the slave traffic with sub-Saharan Africa. The commerce developed easily and without serious opposition because slavery was an indigenous institution in both Iberia and Africa. Among West African peoples, sources of slaves included criminals, debtors who had pawned themselves as security for loans, and, most important, captives taken in war. West African slavery differed from the institution developed on New World plantations. The use of slaves as plantation laborers on the vast estates of the Dahomean kings was exceptional. Also exceptional was the small minority who, in societies like Dahomey and Ashanti, were sacrificed to the powerful royal ancestors. Usually slaves were employed as domestic or household servants. Moreover, slaves in African societies had certain rights. Among the Ashanti they could marry free people, even royalty; they could own property (even other slaves); and they could not be killed without the king's permission. In the kingdom of Benin in coastal Nigeria, slaves or their children were permitted to earn enough to purchase their freedom. Among the Dahomeans, the Ashanti, and the Ibo of the Niger Delta, slaves often achieved free status through adoption into the families of their masters. Rulers among the Yoruba and the Muslim Hausa states of northern Nigeria frequently chose slaves for high official position, and among the Dahomeans, kings sometimes selected the son of a favorite slave wife to succeed to the throne.

During the Middle Ages, gold from the Wangara area had reached Europe through Arab intermediaries trading at Timbuktu, and the origin of European trade in African slaves was subsidiary to Prince Henry of Portugal's attempt to tap the Sudanese gold marts. Thus at first the European trade with Africa resembled the older trans-Saharan traffic; not until the end of the seventeenth century did slaves become the primary object of interest. In 1441 the first cargo of gold and slaves arrived in Lisbon. By 1482 the Portuguese had explored the coast as far as Angola and erected a fort at Elmina on what later became known as the Gold Coast (modern Ghana). By the end of the century Spain had recognized Portugal's claim to exclusive trading rights in Guinea.

The Guinea Coast that presented itself to the Portuguese slavers and their successors was an inaccessible stretch of land offering few harbors. The mouths of its navigable rivers were obstructed by sand bars that proved a perennial problem to the traders. Between the area around the Senegal and Gambia rivers (Senegambia), which was the major source of slaves during the fifteenth and sixteenth centuries, and Angola, which became a leading source in the nineteenth century, lay the heart of the slave-trading belt during the seventeenth and eighteenth centuries. Europeans divided this belt into four main sections, each named after its leading export: the Malagueta or Grain Coast, from Sierra Leone to Cape Palmas, source of the grains of malagueta pepper; the Ivory Coast, from Cape Palmas to modern Ghana; the Gold Coast, a stretch of about 160 miles; and finally the Slave Coast, extending from the Volta River to the Niger Delta and beyond, and including the coastal areas of modern Dahomey, Togo, and Nigeria.

The Portuguese, like other nations later, conducted a lively trade with Africa in gold, slaves, pepper, and ivory. In the fifteenth century, substantial numbers of Negroes were brought into both Spain and Portugal. In these two countries Africans were accorded the protections which the law and the church had historically provided for slaves. There were no bars to emancipation or intermarriage, and eventually the Africans' descendants were absorbed into the general population. A few achieved distinction—the most notable was Juan Latino, who became a Latin professor and humanist at the University of Grenada in the sixteenth century. Negroes, usually as servants, accompanied many of the Spanish explorers. Estevanico, the most famous of the Negro explorers, played a major role on the expedition searching for the Seven Cities of Cibola. Subsequently Negroes were with the French Jesuit missionaries in the exploration of Canada.

After the discovery of the New World the slave trade soon became a major enterprise. Without the labor supply derived from Africa the economic development of the Americas would have been greatly retarded. The sparse Indian population in the Caribbean Islands was enslaved first, and died out under the brutal conditions. The earliest Negro slaves brought to the New World arrived at the beginning of the sixteenth century. Because of the rapid spread of sugar cultivation introduced from Brazil the slave trade grew enormously, so that as early as 1540 the annual number of slaves exported from Africa to the Spanish colonies may have reached as many as ten thousand.

Neither the Portuguese nor the Spanish monarchs permitted a competitive trade to develop. Instead, both awarded contracts to favored parties. The Spanish contract or *asiento* was a prized possession. For a century and a half the asientists obtained slaves from Portuguese traders. Ultimately in the eighteenth century the *asiento* became a valuable prize of war, awarded to France in 1701 and to England in 1713.

The French and English were relatively late as important participants in the slave traffic. Although adventurers or interlopers from these countries successfully challenged the Portuguese monopoly of African commerce during the sixteenth century, for the most part they avoided the trading in slaves as long as Spain and Portugal retained dominance over the New World markets. Then, between 1620 and 1650, the English, Dutch, and French all secured firm footholds in the Caribbean. After the introduction of sugar cultivation in these colonies during the 1640's, the slave trade expanded, and the French, English, and Dutch turned to it with zest. All three of these northern European powers sought to supply their own colonies with slaves, and to encroach upon the Spanish colonial market as well.

It was the Dutch who first really challenged the Portuguese monopoly. In 1611 they built a fort on the Gold Coast, and before the middle of the century they had driven out the Portuguese, who thereafter confined their operations to Angola. During the second half of the seventeenth century the Gold Coast became an arena of intense competition among the European powers. The peak of the slave trade came in the eighteenth century. By then the major share of the traffic had shifted from the Gold Coast to the Slave Coast, with England becoming the leading slaving power.

Like the Portuguese and the Dutch, the English and French at first conducted the traffic through chartered monopolies. The first English company to engage seriously in the slave trade was the Royal Adventurers Into Africa chartered by Charles II in 1660 and reorganized in 1672 as the Royal African Company. The company imported gold, ivory, dyewood, hides, and wax directly from Africa into England and purchased slaves for the West Indies. On the Gold Coast, where most of the company's forts were located, the trade was mostly in slaves and gold. East of the Volta, slaves were the only significant export. Most of them were sold in the British West Indies, only small consignments going to Virginia.

In 1698, following the trend among all the slave-trading powers, England ended the monopoly of the Royal African Company and inaugurated an era of free competition which brought real wealth to the country. While the Royal African Company during its prime in the 1680's transported annually about 5,000 slaves, a century later Britain was exporting a yearly average of 74,000. In addition to servicing the needs of the English colonies, British shippers had become major suppliers for the colonies of other European powers, so that during the late eighteenth century, British merchants, chiefly from Liverpool, were handling roughly half of the European slave traffic.

The dissolution of the Royal African Company's monopoly was also commercially advantageous to merchants in the English mainland colonies. Some of them had engaged in the slave traffic since early in the seventeenth century. Because the British companies chartered for the Guinea trade were interested mainly in supplying the lucrative sugar-producing West Indies, rather than in satisfying the lesser demands of the continental colonies, throughout the seventeenth century most of the slaves brought to the mainland came from the Caribbean. With the end of the Royal African Company's dominance, the number of slaves—both from the West Indies and from Africa—imported into the continental colonies increased sharply. During the last thirty years of the seventeenth century, the slave population of Virginia had grown slowly from around 2,000 to 6,000; in the first decade after the end of the monopoly in 1698, 6,369 slaves were brought into the colony.

Merchants in all sections of the mainland provinces participated in the slave trade, but pre-eminent were those from the Massachusetts and Rhode Island seaports. Rhode Island entered the slave trade much later than Massachusetts, probably around the beginning of the eighteenth century. By mid-century Newport and Providence had surpassed their rivals in Boston and Salem. From then until the official closing of the slave trade in 1808, the traffic flourished in Rhode Island and formed the basis of some of the greatest fortunes in the state.

In Africa itself the commerce in slaves developed into a relatively complex operation. Because the African rulers valued their inland monopoly, Europeans were generally confined to the coast; only in Senegambia did they penetrate far inland to trade. It was rare for Europeans themselves to engage in raids to obtain captives. Not that they had any scruples—some of the earliest traders did in fact participate in raids—but Europeans found it easier to depend for their supply upon African rulers and merchants.

European settlements, in the form of forts and sporadically occupied trading posts known as factories, were commonest in Senegambia and on the Gold Coast. At both types of establishments agents bought slaves and held them until the arrival of one or more slave ships. Along the Grain and Ivory coasts, where no forts or factories were established, the Africans used smoke signals to indicate their readiness to trade. They came out to the European ships in canoes, or sometimes waited on shore for a party from the ship. Along the Slave Coast the Africans successfully discouraged European fortifications. Near its western end was Whydah, where all the principal slaving nations of Europe maintained representatives. Here the ruler permitted only mud forts and forbade establishing them within three miles of the sea. In the Bight of Benin and in Calabar, where European forts and factories were absent, the river estuaries and the numerous mouths of the Niger provided safe places in which to conduct the traffic directly from the slave ships.

A slaving ship usually spent several months picking up captives on the shores of Africa, stopping first at one place and then another. The supply was uneven and a vessel might wait many weeks until the slaves were brought from the interior. Europeans found that a wide variety of goods was essential for trading—the almost exclusive dependence of the eighteenth-century Rhode Island traders on rum was a rare exception—and on the Gold Coast alone 150 items were required. Among the most important goods used in exchange for slaves were cowrie shells and cotton goods obtained from the East India Company, iron bars, sheets, firearms, gunpowder, brass rings which were cut into pieces to make bracelets and collars, and liquor. Since the demand for various items differed from place to place, the prudent trader selected his stock with care. Thus, iron bars were in great demand in the Gambia but useless in Angola; cowrie shells, which were used as a currency on the Slave Coast, became essential for trading there but were of limited value elsewhere.

How did the African rulers and merchants obtain the captives exchanged for these European goods? Military expeditions were always the major source of slaves. The trade was originally a by-product of war, but because of the insatiable demands of the European powers, by the eighteenth century it had become the major cause of conflict among the West African states. Villages were raided sometimes by Europeans, but more often by African rulers. Kidnapping was another significant source; lesser sources included enslavement for debts and crimes. In the Ibo area, east of the Niger River, slaves were obtained through oracles, of which the Aro Chukwu was easily the most powerful. Because political organization did not extend beyond the village level among the Ibos, the trading settlements of the Aro people, who had established colonies at river crossings and intersections along the interior trade routes, became the sites of courts where individuals and clans sought adjustment of their disputes. The Chukwu deity, serving as the highest court of appeal, levied fines on guilty parties, which were paid in slaves. The Ibos believed that these captives were eaten by the god, though actually they were sold to the coastal merchants. Where the coastal rulers did not conduct wars for slaves, merchants who dealt with Europeans bought slaves for resale at the interior markets. By whatever means they were obtained, the slaves intended for overseas trade were tied or fettered together and often marched hundreds of miles to sea. Along the Lower Niger River they were bound to the floors of canoes for the voyage downstream.

When a slave ship arrived it was first necessary to present a gift (or "dash") to the local ruler or his officials. Before commencing to trade with the African merchants, the Europeans were required to buy the king's slaves at an inflated price. The king also levied a tax (or "comey") on all slaves and goods obtained from African traders. Once the ruler's slaves had been sold, the whites could then bargain with the private traders. If there were not enough slaves immediately available, the Europeans often advanced the goods necessary to enable coastal middlemen to travel to interior slave markets. The European merchant's physician carefully examined the slaves in order to avoid purchasing ill, maimed, or elderly people. In the Niger Delta and Cross River—at Brass, Bonny, and Calabar—the slaves were immediately put on board the ship at anchor in the river estuary. In Whydah, on the other hand, where the trade was very well organized first by the king of Whydah and later by the king of Dahomey, who placed the province under a powerful viceroy, the traders were compelled to keep the slaves in the king's barracoons (temporary prisons) until the condition of the surf permitted transfer to the waiting ships. The king of course profited handsomely from payments charged for this service. In these barracoons the traders took the precaution of branding their slaves on the breast with a hot iron to prevent the king from substituting captives of poor quality.

Slaves thus obtained by the Europeans frequently displayed overt resistance. Although carefully guarded, they often jumped overboard in attempts to escape. When not eaten by sharks which nearly always surrounded slave ships, they sometimes deliberately drowned themselves if in danger of recapture by the slave-owners. Some slaves mutinied aboard ship, especially while the vessel was still anchored off the African shore. For example, on the *Nancy,* lying at anchor at New Calabar in 1769 with 132 slaves, the Negroes revolted, attacking several of the crew, whose members fired upon the slaves, killing six and wounding others. When Africans on shore heard the gunfire, large numbers of them surrounded the vessel in their canoes. Finding her poorly manned, they rescued all the slaves and plundered the ship of everything on board, leaving it a complete wreck. Slave mutinies were rarer in mid-ocean, yet a number of them occurred. For example, on the *Narborough* in 1753, some Negroes who had been given considerable freedom so that they could help run the ship obtained firearms and massacred all of the white crew except for a few, who were forced to steer the craft back to Bonny.

By far the worst part of the slave's journey was the "Middle Passage" from the African coast to the West Indies or the American mainland. This voyage generally lasted between forty and sixty days, and the overcrowded conditions were indescribable. Most eighteenth-century slave ships had two decks with the 'tween-deck space reserved for slaves. In a Newport slaver the average height between decks was three feet ten inches. Men, women, and children were each placed in separate compartments on the slave deck, the men bound together with iron ankle fetters. The slaves were made to lie with their backs on the deck, the men secured to chains or iron rods attached to the deck, squeezed so tightly together that the space allowed to each person was about sixteen inches wide and five and a half feet long. In the Liverpool ships toward the end of the century, the average height between the decks was five feet two inches. This permitted even worse crowding, for a shelf extending six to nine feet from the sides of the ship was placed midway between the two decks, and both the lower deck and the shelf were packed tightly with slaves. On the small sloops and schooners that lacked 'tween decks, the slaves were placed on a temporary platform of rough boards laid over the barrels in the hold. There are recorded instances where the space between such a "deck" and the one above was less than two feet. Most of the ships used after the trade had been out-lawed were of this type, and during this later period of great risks and greater profits, slaves were stowed closer than ever, forced to lie on their sides, back to back, "spoon-fashion." Where the space between decks was two feet or more the slaves were placed sitting up in rows, or crowded into each other's laps.

Conditions were described by eye witnesses such as Alexander Falconbridge, an eighteenth-century ship's surgeon:

> . . . In favourable weather they are fed upon deck, but in bad weather the food is given them below. Numberless quarrels take place among them during the meals, more especially when they are put upon short allowance, which frequently happens, if the passage from the coast of Guinea to the West India islands, proves of unusual length. . . . Exercise being deemed necessary for the preservation of their health, they are sometimes obliged to dance, when the weather will permit their coming on deck. If they go about it reluctantly, or do not move with agility, they are flogged. . . . The poor wretches are frequently compelled to sing also. . . .
>
> The hardships and inconveniences suffered by the negroes during the passage, are scarcely to be enumerated or conceived . . . the exclusion of the fresh air is among the most intolerable. For the purpose of admitting this needful refreshment, most of the ships in the slave trade are provided, between the decks, with five or six air-ports on each side of the ship. . . . But whenever the

sea is rough, and the rain heavy, it becomes necessary to shut these, and every other conveyance by which the air is admitted. The fresh air being excluded, the negroes['] rooms very soon grow intolerably hot. The confined air, rendered noxious by the effluvia exhaled from the bodies, and by being repeatedly breathed, soon produces fevers and fluxes, which generally carries off great numbers of them. . . . the floor of the rooms, was so covered with blood and mucus which had proceeded from them in consequence of the flux [i.e., dysentery], that it resembled a slaughter-house. It is not in the power of human imagination to picture to itself a situation more dreadful or disgusting. Numbers of the slaves having fainted, they were carried upon deck, where several of them died. . . . The surgeon, upon going between decks in the morning, to examine the situation of the slaves, frequently finds several dead, and among the men, sometimes a dead and living negro fastened by their irons together. When this is the case, they are brought upon the deck, and being laid on the grating, the living negro is disengaged, and the dead one thrown overboard.

The mortality from the bloody flux or **dysentery, smallpox,** and other diseases could be considerable. There are cases on record where whole shiploads, including the entire crew, went blind fom **ophthalmia,** first contracted by the slaves in their filthy and crowded conditions. Very sick Negroes were sometimes thrown overboard, as the underwriters would not pay for slaves who died on the ship. There were cases where two thirds and more of the slaves on a ship were dead by the time it arrived at the West Indies, and loss of half was not at all unusual.

It is impossible even to approximate the total number of slaves brought from Africa to the New World. It has been estimated, for example, that in 1768, when the trade was nearing its peak, the number taken from Africa amounted to 104,000; of these, merchants in England and her North American colonies accounted for well over half the total. It has also been estimated that between 1680 and 1786 Great Britain alone sent to her North American and West Indian colonies a total of 2,110,000. A very conservative guess placed the number of slaves who reached the New World in the three and a half centuries of the slave trade at nearly 15,000,000, about 900,000 arriving in the sixteenth century, 2,750,000 in the seventeenth, 7,000,000 in the eighteenth, and 4,000,000 in the nineteenth. One author has suggested that counting those killed in wars and raids in Africa and in the horrors of the Middle Passage the transatlantic slave trade might easily have cost Africa as many as 50,000,000 people.

Contrary to popular impression, in spite of the social disruption it caused, the transatlantic trade did not generally lead to a breakdown in West African social and political organization. In Angola, it is true, the Portuguese slave trade led to the disintegration of the extensive Mani-Congo kingdom. Because its ruler opposed the traffic, the Portuguese turned to his provincial officials, who supplied slaves in exchange for firearms that enabled them to challenge their king's authority. In West Africa, from the Gold Coast to the Niger Delta and Old Calabar, the overseas slave traffic encouraged the development of a substantial mercantile group whose fortunes were based on the slave trade. Where Europeans found strong despotic kingdoms, and rulers willing to supply their wants, the trade thrived from the start. Where these did not exist in West Africa, the slave traffic called them into being, or, as in the Niger Delta, stimulated the development of oligarchic and monarchical city-states. With the profits derived from the trade, and more particularly with the firearms obtained from Europeans in exchange for slaves, old rulers strengthened their power, and new autocratic kingdoms, such as Dahomey and Ashanti, arose. The role of firearms was crucial. Just as the Moroccans had quickly destroyed the Songhai empire in the sixteenth century because the latter lacked guns, so the strategically placed societies of the rain forest and southern Sudan were able to overpower their poorly armed neighbors.

It is difficult to ascertain with any degree of precision how profitable the slave trade was. Complete records are lacking; profits and losses fluctuated from one voyage to another, depending on the prices both in Africa and America and on the numbers surviving the transatlantic crossing. Recent research suggests that generally profits may not have been as great as they were once believed, but voyages with monetary returns ranging from one third to one half or more on the original investment were frequent. In the late eighteenth century Liverpool profits of 100 percent and more were not uncommon. Not only was the slave trade profitable in itself, but it was the base upon which the colonial industry and commerce of European powers rested. In the plantations of the New World, it supplied labor for cultivating the staple crops of sugar, cotton, tobacco, and indigo. The slave traffic was an important incentive to English industry, and to agriculture, fishing, and rum manufacture in the Northern colonies on the mainland.

The Middle Passage received its name because it was regarded as the middle leg of the system of triangular trading that by the eighteenth century became such a prominent feature of the slave traffic. From England various manufactured products—chiefly textiles, metal goods, and liquor—were exported to Africa, where they were exchanged for slaves. From the proceeds of slaves sold in the West Indies, sugar was bought and shipped to England. Each leg of the voyage was a profitable venture, and the whole business stimulated the shipbuilding, textile, and metallurgical industries. Colonial merchants also found the triangular trade exceedingly profitable. New England rum was exchanged for slaves in Africa, molasses was obtained with the proceeds in the West Indies, and in turn was manufactured into rum for use in the fur trade with the Indians, for sailors on the fishing fleets, and for further trade with Africa.

Officially the African slave traffic was outlawed by European countries during the early nineteenth century, but it actually persisted illicitly at a rate perhaps even greater than during the preceding century. In 1807 both England and the United States enacted legislation that the African slave trade would be illegal effective January 1, 1808. By 1850 other European nations involved in the traffic had followed suit, and in 1850 Brazil, the major market for African slavers, joined the list. England, the world's leading naval power, was a prime force in obtaining the co-operation of countries like Spain and Portugal, which permitted the British Navy the right to search suspicious ships carrying their flags. The African coastal waters could have been patrolled with a fair degree of effectiveness if the United States had seriously tried to suppress the trade. The United States, however, would neither give England the right to search vessels flying the American flag, nor herself dispatch enough ships to handle the matter. Searches by the United States Navy were spasmodic, and cases brought to court in the United States were often lost through legal technicalities because of sympathetic judges in both the North and South. Consequently, the United States flag came to be the most desirable one for slave traders; during the 1850's nearly all slave ships carried it.

Since slavery in the French West Indies had ended during the Revolutionary and Napoleonic eras, and England had outlawed slavery in her colonies in 1833, the principal markets for the illicit trade were Brazil, Cuba, and the United States. It is impossible to know how many were smuggled into the United States. According to one estimate 300,000 reached this country from Africa between 1808 and 1860. Undoubtedly the number veered sharply upward during the late 1850's, coinciding with the agitation of a militant group in the Deep South that demanded the reopening of the African slave traffic. There is evidence that slaves from Africa were landed on the Georgia coast in American vessels as late as 1858 and 1859.

Thus the overseas slave trade from Africa to the United States continued until the eve of the Civil War. Unquestionably it was United States policy—or lack of it—which was largely responsible, and not until 1862 when the Lincoln Administration signed a treaty giving the British the right of search and seizure was the trade destroyed.

2

The first Negroes who landed at Jamestown in 1619, probably in a Dutch warship that had seized them from a Spanish slaver, did not become slaves but were assimilated into the system of indentured servitude then existing in the colony. Not until the 1660's was a rudimentary slave code first enacted, and this fact has led some scholars to conclude that slavery could not have evolved for more than a generation after the first Negroes arrived. The data are too meager for a clear picture of the development of Negro-white relations in seventeenth-century Virginia. The colony, however, enjoyed close contact with Bermuda, which enacted restrictive legislation to control the "insolencies" of Negroes in 1623, and Virginia's inhabitants were familiar with conditions in Barbados, where a slave system flourished by the 1640's. Moreover, fragmentary evidence in Virginia indicates that no later than 1640 Negro servants occupied a status distinctly subordinate to white bondsmen.

As early as 1630 a man was sentenced to a sound whipping for having sexual relations with a Negro woman. A decade later a court case involving three runaway servants suggested that some Negroes might already have been slaves. All three received thirty lashes. The two whites were sentenced to an additional year of service for their masters and three years for the colony, but the Negro was assigned to servitude for life. In the same year the Virginia House of Burgesses specifically denied Negroes the right to bear arms. In 1643 it passed a law declaring that Negro female servants over sixteen—but not white servants—were to be included among the tithables. The House also placed limitations on the terms of indentured servants, specifically omitting Negroes. The next year, asked to determine the legal status of a particular Negro servant who had been sold as "a slave for-ever," this assembly decided that he should only "serve as other Christian servants do." But clearly he had already served an unusually long period—twenty-one years. In the 1640's inventories of estates showed that Negroes were consistently listed as more valuable than white servants, and the number of years remaining to be served ordinarily appeared in the case of whites, but no such notations were made for Negroes. Virginia court cases of the early 1650's indicate that in selling Negro servants life servitude was specified, as well as the fact that their status was to be inherited by their offspring.

By mid-century, then, court decisions were reflecting the existence of slavery. Negroes entering the colony thereafter lacked indentures, and slavery was limited to people of African ancestry. Nevertheless there were anomalies. Some of the earlier Negro indentured servants not only gained their freedom but bought Negro servants of their own and acquired considerable property. For example, Anthony Johnson, who perhaps came to the colony in 1621, appears to have been free a year or so later and by 1651 imported five servants on whose headrights he received 250 acres in Northampton County. Richard Johnson, a carpenter, imported two white servants in 1654, for which he obtained 100 acres. A third Negro was granted 550 acres after importing eleven people. Ironically, one of the earliest decisions holding a Negro bound to life servitude involved a plaintiff who sued Anthony Johnson in 1654.

Such cases were exceptional. Negroes by this time were customarily slaves. But the first legal reference to slavery was in an act of 1661, decreeing that if a white servant fled with a Negro, the former was required to make up the time missed by the latter. The very casualness of this rather incidental reference makes it apparent that Negro slavery had been the custom for some time. The following year, reversing the English common law providing that children followed the status of their fathers, the Virginia House of Burgesses enacted a statute declaring that children born in the colony would be bond or free according to the status of their mothers. Even yet, however, some doubt existed about holding Christians in perpetual bondage, and legislation settling the matter was passed in 1667. This law decreed that "baptism doth not alter the condition of the person as to his bondage or freedom."

At that time white servants still formed the backbone of the farm labor force. In 1671 there were 2,000 Negro slaves in Virginia and 6,000 white servants out of a total population of 40,000. With the development of large-scale plantation agriculture toward the latter part of the century and the ending of the Royal African Company's monopoly of the slave trade in 1698, Negro slavery rapidly took precedence over white servitude.

The evolution of Negro servitude in Maryland closely paralleled that of Virginia, but in Carolina, founded later, there was no such period of uncertainty. Negro slavery was expressly provided for in the Fundamental Constitutions of 1669 and from the beginning was actively encouraged by the proprietors. In Georgia, founded in 1733, the proprietors first excluded slavery on what they judged to be sound mercantilist grounds. Impressed by the example of South Carolina, however, the settlers clamored for slaves and permission was granted in 1750.

The characteristics of the different staple crops cultivated in the colonial South influenced the size of farming units and the concentration of the Negro population. Tobacco was the staple crop in the Chesapeake Bay colonies of Virginia and Maryland and in North Carolina. In South Carolina plantation agriculture did not really develop until the introduction of rice cultivation at the end of the seventeenth century. Indigo became a major crop following the middle of the eighteenth century. After Georgia had been opened to slavery, the cultivation of these two crops quickly spread to that colony. Of necessity, rice and indigo were concentrated in the low-lying, moist, and hot Sea Islands and coastal lands. Tobacco could be grown in the hilly back country and to a considerable extent was cultivated on small units by white farmers with few or no slaves. On the other hand, the technology of rice cultivation, with its extensive irrigation system, promoted large plantations and the use of slave labor. During the 1780's, the average size of slaveholdings in the counties surrounding Charleston, South Carolina, was about three times the average holding in the principal plantation counties of Maryland and Virginia. In 1790 the largest slaveholder in the tobacco colonies, the noted signer of the Declaration of Independence, Charles Carroll of Carrollton, held 316 chattels, while in the Charleston district one planter held 695 and five owned over 300 slaves apiece. The Negro population was chiefly concentrated in the tidewater areas of the Chesapeake colonies, South Carolina, and Georgia, where the largest plantations were located. In such counties Negroes in fact outnumbered whites, although South Carolina was the only colony where slaves were consistently in the majority throughout the eighteenth century.

With the increase in the numbers of Negroes, the fear of lawlessness and insurrection rose, leading to the passage of stringent slave codes regulating their activity. There were also sporadic attempts in Virginia and South Carolina to limit the importation of slaves (efforts often disallowed by the King's Privy Council). While the codes varied from colony to colony, generally they provided that slaves could not carry arms, own property, or leave their plantation without a written pass. Murder, rape, arson, and in some cases robbery, were capital crimes; common punishments for lesser offenses were maiming, whipping, or branding. After insurrectionary plots were discovered in the Charleston area in 1739 and 1740, South Carolina strengthened its slave code, sharply limiting the assembling of slaves and prohibiting the sale of liquor to them.

North of the Chesapeake Bay slave labor was not so economically profitable, and slavery never secured as firm a foothold. New Jersey and New York had both been familiar with slavery on a small scale during the period of Dutch settlement. Indeed the Dutch West India Company, itself a major slave-trading organization, and the Dutch government hoped to stimulate agriculture by encouraging the importation of slaves into New

Netherlands. Importations increased noticeably under the British, but in both these colonies slavery never involved large-scale plantation agriculture. In New York there was a widespread distribution of small slaveholders, Negroes forming about 12 percent of the population during the eighteenth century. In both states Negroes worked in a wide variety of occupations—as farm laborers, domestic servants, miners, and artisans (ironworkers, carpenters, coopers, tanners, shoemakers, millers). Nevertheless, the slave codes of New York and New Jersey were not very different from those of the Southern colonies; slave revolts of serious proportions in New York City in 1712 and 1741 guaranteed that the codes would be kept as severe as any in the South.

In Pennsylvania the Quakers, through their pioneering leadership in the antislavery movement, acted as a moral influence discouraging the importation of slaves. Also, white artisans and small farmers did not need slaves and feared competition with them. Though the slave code does not seem to have been too different from other colonies, contemporary reports indicate that slavery in Pennsylvania was relatively mild and the slaves were permitted considerable latitude in their activities.

The New England colonies, important though their role was in the slave trade, valued Negro labor even less than the middle colonies. There is evidence of the presence of Negro servitude in each of the four New England colonies (Massachusetts, Connecticut, Rhode Island, and New Hampshire) by the middle of the seventeenth century, but by 1700 Negroes still numbered only about 1,000 in a population estimated at 90,000. At no time did Negroes constitute as much as 5 percent of the people in any of these colonies, with the exception of Rhode Island, where Negroes were recorded in 1749 as being about 11 percent of the population. This was the one New England colony where something resembling the plantation system of the South developed. In New England, as in Virginia, the status of the first Negroes was probably that of indentured servitude. The Massachusetts Bay Colony recognized slavery in the Body of Liberties of 1641, and this law was later adopted by Plymouth and Connecticut. By 1652 Rhode Island enacted a law that limited involuntary servitude to a period of ten years, but this statute was openly violated and in 1708 slavery received legal recognition.

New England's economy was diversified and so was the Negro's work. Many Negroes were employed on small farms, but in the fertile Narragansett area of Rhode Island, they were used on the large dairy and cattle-raising estates by the local landed aristocracy known as the Narragansett Planters. The number of slaves on these farms ranged from five to forty, and although most of them were in dairying, others raised sheep and cultivated vegetables or tobacco. New England Negroes also worked as house servants and coachmen; as laborers in shipbuilding, lumbering, ironworking, cooperage, distilling, and other industries; as skilled artisans in blacksmith and carpenter shops, tanneries, and printing shops; as seamen on fishing, whaling, and trading ships; as apprentices to doctors and even as physicians themselves.

Slavery in New England was the mildest in the colonies. Legally, slaves occupied a dual status both as property and as persons. This development arose because the Puritan slave code was a modification of the Old Testament slave law. There were the limitations on the slave's behavior of course—designed as elsewhere to prevent conspiracies and robberies. They were forbidden on the streets at night after nine; they could not strike a white person; and the sale of liquor to them was prohibited. Unlike the colonies to the south, except for capital punishment for a limited number of crimes, punishment was confined to whipping; there was no maiming, dismemberment, or branding. As property, slaves were subject to taxation like other goods and chattels; they could be bought, sold, and inherited. On the other hand, they were legally regarded as persons, and masters were specifically forbidden to kill their slaves (though no master ever appears to have been executed for doing so); slaves could acquire, hold, and transfer property; they could offer testimony against whites even in cases in which Negroes were not involved (in contrast to the South and New York where this was explicitly forbidden); they were entitled to a jury trial (though they could not serve on juries). Slaves were expected to obey the sexual standards legally set for whites. Marriages were duly solemnized and legally recorded in the same manner as for whites, yet slave families were frequently broken up through sales and the settlement of wills. Masters could be as cruel in New England as elsewhere, but relationships tended to be paternalistic, as in Pennsylvania where most slaves were either household retainers or worked closely with masters in shop and field. Slaves could not vote of course, but they held mock elections in each of the New England colonies, at which a Negro "governor" was chosen amid much festivity. Apparently these "governors" exercised some control over the slaves and appointed "judges" and "sheriffs" to handle minor violations.

In New England more attention was paid to the slaves' religious conversion and education than in any of the other colonies. How many became Christians is not known, but these converts faced the usual contradictions. For example, those who were considered members of the Congregationalist Church did not vote in church affairs and sat in a rear section or in the gallery. Some Negroes were so well trained by their masters that they managed farms and stores, and had charge of ships and warehouses. Newport Gardner, a slave of Caleb Gardner of Newport, Rhode Island, received music lessons and soon became so proficient that he opened a music school and taught both Negroes and whites. A few slaves turned to literary compositions, and the most famous of these was poetess Phillis Wheatley, purchased as a young girl when she was brought from Africa in 1761 by a mistress who taught her to read and write.

Clearly slavery in New England was not of the same order as in the South or even in New York and Pennsylvania. The fact that slaves could even sue their masters not only signified a status superior to that of the slaves farther south, but helped pave the way for emancipation. In the 1760's and 1770's a number of individual Negroes successfully sued for their freedom in the Massachusetts courts. Though they uniformly won these suits, the procedure was slow and expensive. Such legal decisions applied only to the individuals who brought the action and therefore left the mass of slaves untouched. Yet these cases established a pattern, and in 1783, in the noted Quok Walker Case, the state supreme court declared slavery in Massachusetts unconstitutional.

3

Quok Walker was liberated on the grounds that since the preamble to the state constitution of 1780 declared that all men were born free and equal, slavery was illegal. To the Massachusetts Supreme Court, the ideology of the American Revolution was fundamental law and not an abstraction. Indeed, the Revolutionary era proved to be a pinnacle of antislavery sentiment and racial equalitarianism.

Negroes themselves, especially in New England, cited the principles of the Declaration of Independence in requesting an end to their servitude. In January, 1777, a group of Massachusetts slaves petitioned the state legislature, claiming a natural God-given right to freedom and asserting "that Every Principle from which Amarica has Acted in the Cours of their unhappy Difficulties with Great Briton Pleads Stronger than A thousand arguments in favours of your pet[it]ioners . . ." During the Revolutionary War many thoughtful white Americans, especially in the North, such as John Jay and Abigail Adams, were seriously concerned with the moral issue involved in slavery. Farther south, slaveowners like George Washington and Thomas Jefferson looked forward to its gradual abolition. Only in South Carolina and Georgia was support for the slavery system undiminished.

The antislavery and racially egalitarian tendencies of the Revolutionary era resulted from four converging streams of influence. One, of course, was political: the struggle for independence against English tyranny. Another was economic: slavery in the North had never been especially remunerative anyway, and in the tobacco counties of Virginia, Maryland, and North Carolina fluctuating prices and declining fertility of the land tended to make the plantation regime only marginally profitable.

Antislavery enthusiasm was also fed by two major intellectual traditions. One was the eighteenth-century European Enlightenment. Rooted on John Locke's environmentalist psychology and defense of individualism and revolution, the ideals of the Enlightenment, with its belief in human liberty, natural rights, egalitarianism, cosmopolitanism, and human progress, provided as much justification for antislavery and the cause of the free Negro as for the Revolution itself. The two leading American representatives of the Enlightenment, Thomas Jefferson and Benjamin Franklin, were both much concerned about the problems of slavery and the future of Negroes in American society.

The ideals of the Enlightenment coalesced with an older stream of religious antislavery thinking in America. The earliest opponents of the slave trade and slavery were a handful of religious thinkers, chiefly Quakers. It was primarily the eighteenth-century Quaker pamphleteers John Woolman and Anthony Benezet who brought the issues before the public. In 1754–55 the Pennsylvania Yearly Meeting of Friends decreed that persons engaged in buying or selling slaves would be expelled. In 1775 they helped to found the first antislavery society in America, and the following year ruled that all members must emancipate their slaves. Friends' meetings in the tobacco belt were drawn to the same decision, and even some substantial slaveholders among them emancipated their slaves rather than leave the church. The Quakers also exercised considerable influence in New England where, joined by a Puritan stream, the movement against slavery gained great momentum during the years prior to the Revolution.

It should be noted that antislavery men were not necessarily believers in the psychological equality of the races. Many actually accepted the notion of Negro inferiority and advocated colonization, or the expatriation of Negroes, as the only satisfactory solution to the race problem. Thomas Jefferson well illustrated the ambivalences and contradictions of many of even the most advanced thinkers on the subject. Jefferson, through inheritance and matrimony, became a large slaveholder, owning well over two hundred Negroes. To Jefferson slavery was a moral evil, unjust to Negroes and deleterious to the character of whites. From his first term in the House of Burgesses he had displayed a strong interest in facilitating the manumission of slaves. Although he recommended gradual emancipation, Jefferson did not conceive of the two races living in the same nation on an equal and harmonious plane. White prejudice, Negro remembrance of oppression, and "the real distinction which nature has made" would "divide us into parties, and produce convulsions, which will probably never end but in the extermination of one or the other race." While not dogmatic on the subject, he suspected that Negroes might be "inferior to the whites in the endowments both of mind and body," and feared the race mixture that he believed would follow emancipation. Therefore, he proposed that freed Negroes be settled in their own society in the interior of the continent, far removed from the whites. On the other hand, he was interested in evidence of Negro ability, and in 1791, as Secretary of State, appointed the Negro mathematician and almanac maker Benjamin Banneker of Maryland a member of the three-man commission which surveyed the site for the national capital. To Banneker he wrote, "Nobody wishes more than I do to see such proofs as you exhibit that nature has given to our black brethren talents equal to those of the other colours of men, and that the appearance of a want of them is owing merely to the degraded condition of their existence both in Africa and America." But to some others Jefferson took a different line, voicing a suspicion that much of Banneker's work had been produced by a white friend. Until the very end of his life, Jefferson retained his ambivalent attitudes about Negroes.

The inconsistencies that marked the thinking of Jefferson, who to this day symbolizes more than any other man the idealism of the Revolutionary era, were mirrored in the conduct of the war itself. Despite the more favorable climate, prejudice and discrimination still abounded, as the policies about the use of Negro soldiers demonstrate. All the colonies had laws excluding Negroes from militia service, but, as in crises during the French and Indian Wars, in the first battles of the Revolution in the spring of 1775 these laws were overlooked. In fact a number of Massachusetts slaves were freed to fight in the Army. By summer, however, Washington and his staff ordered the termination of Negro recruitment, and during the winter of 1775–76 both the states and the Continental Congress acted to prohibit their enlistment. The protests of free Negroes were mostly in vain. The British had no such qualms, and Lord Dunmore, governor of Virginia, promised freedom to slaves who fought alongside the British. Though the Southern slaveholders were frightened, and though large numbers of Negroes from Georgia, South Carolina, and Virginia did join the British, recent scholarship has discounted the effect that Dunmore's proclamation of 1775 was formerly supposed to have had in prompting a reversal of American policy regarding the use of Negro troops. Beginning in 1777, however, the manpower problems of raising troops compelled state after state—and in 1779 the Continental Congress—to reconsider the earlier stand. By the end of the war, both Congress and most of the states promised that slaves who enlisted would receive freedom when their military service was over. Only Georgia and South Carolina, despite urgent pleading from Congress and the military, prohibited Negro enlistments entirely.

Freedom through service in the armed forces was only one of the fruits Negroes gained from the Revolution. The movement to emancipate slaves made considerable headway in the Northern states and the Upper South. The antislavery society founded in Pennsylvania in 1775 was reorganized in 1787 with Benjamin Franklin named as president. In 1785 antislavery men founded the New York Society for Promoting the Manumission of Slaves with John Jay as president. By 1792 antislavery societies existed in each of the states from Massachusetts to Virginia. All of them attacked the slave trade and most pleaded for the eventual abolition of slavery. Some, however, agreeing with Jefferson on the future of the two races in America, advocated the deportation of free Negroes from the United States.

Moreover, Northern states took steps to free their slaves. State legislatures usually provided for gradual emancipation. Thus Pennsylvania in 1780 passed a law directing that Negroes born after that year were to be free at the age of twenty-eight, and until then were to be treated as apprentices. In 1783, as pointed out earlier, Massachusetts ended slavery by court decree. Connecticut and Rhode Island in 1784 passed acts of gradual emancipation, as did New York and New Jersey in 1785 and 1786, though the latter two states did not enact effective legislation until 1799 and 1804 respectively. In the Upper South, Virginia and North Carolina passed laws encouraging owners to emancipate their slaves. Thus in 1783 Jefferson persuaded the Virginia legislature to make it lawful for a slaveowner by will or other instrument in writing to free his slaves. Though the law held masters responsible for the support of the Negroes they freed, a wave of manumissions followed. The high-water mark in antislavery legislation was the Northwest Ordinance of 1787, which prohibited slavery in the Northwest Territory.

In that same year, however, the Constitution was written. From the point of view of American Negroes, the Constitution, coming at the close of an era of distinct improvement in their status, must be regarded as a retrogressive document. During the debates at the Constitutional Convention, opposition to slavery and the slave trade was voiced, yet because of the strength of the slave states, the framers of the Constitution gave protection of property rights in slaves higher priority than the protection of human rights. In three circumlocutory clauses that avoided the direct mention of slaves or Negroes, the Constitution clearly recognized and legitimized the existence of slavery. It provided that for purposes of direct taxes and apportioning representation in the House of Representatives, each slave would count as three fifths of a person; it prohibited Congress from stopping the slave trade before 1808; and it bound states to assist in returning fugitive slaves to their masters. Six years after the Constitution was written, Congress passed its first fugitive slave law to implement the provisions of this clause and Eli Whitney invented the cotton gin. Together the Constitution and the gin were prophetic symbols of a fateful reversal in the fortunes of American Negroes.

4

The late-eighteenth-century technological revolution in cotton manufacturing, which marked the opening phases of the Industrial Revolution in England, also strengthened plantation slavery in America. Cotton, first domesticated in Africa and an important textile in the Middle East and India, had been known to Europe for centuries. But it was the remarkable series of inventions in the spinning and weaving of cotton and the application of water, and later steam, power to the production of cotton cloth that sharply lowered the price of cotton textiles and created a great demand for the raw lint.

Cotton had been grown in the colonies, but serious interest in its commercial possibilities developed only after the emergence of the new English textile factories. The barrier in the way of cotton becoming a major staple crop was the fact that the variety grown in the United States stuck tightly to its fuzzy seeds, from which it could be separated only by laborious work. Planters began to experiment with varieties of West Indian cotton, and in 1790 a South Carolina planter harvested the first successful crop. This long-staple "sea-island" cotton was of very high quality, in every way superior to the short-staple upland cotton previously grown in the United States. Moreover it had a striking commercial advantage because its seeds could be separated easily from the lint. But climatic conditions made it possible to grow sea-island cotton only on the low-lying coast and Sea Islands of South Carolina and Georgia. Then in 1793 Eli Whitney invented the cotton gin, a simple device for separating the seeds from the lint, making the production of the short-staple cotton highly remunerative.

Although recent research suggests that on the eve of the invention of the cotton gin plantation slavery was more vigorous than had previously been believed, certainly Whitney's work fostered immeasurably the extraordinary expansion of the slave system that followed and fastened it firmly throughout the Southern states. Almost at once cotton became the staple crop in the Georgia and Carolina piedmont between the coastal plains and the Appalachians. Cotton lent itself to cultivation on small farms, though large plantations were more profitable. Coastal plantation owners staked out new lands in the piedmont, while yeoman farmers bought slaves and tried to rise into the large-scale planter class. More slave importations naturally followed—it has been estimated that in 1803 alone over 20,000 were brought from Africa into South Carolina and Georgia. After 1800 cotton cultivation spread to North Carolina, southeastern Virginia, and over the mountains into Tennessee. Then planters realized that the fertile alluvial soil of Mississippi and Alabama, and the bottom lands in Louisiana and Arkansas, were superior to the upland soils, and they streamed southwestward.

Actually the cotton gin had been introduced into the lower Mississippi Valley in 1795. Under the French, Spanish, and British, the Gulf Coast and the lower Mississippi Valley had already developed plantation economies based on the cultivation of rice, indigo, tobacco, and Creole cotton—a long-staple variety originally from Siam. In 1795, the year that Spain ceded to the United States the territory lying east of the Mississippi and north of the 31st parallel, the planters of the Natchez area, anxious to make Creole cotton commercially profitable, eagerly adopted the cotton gin. About the same time that large-scale cotton agriculture appeared on the Eastern seaboard and in the Natchez area, another major staple, sugar cane, was introduced in the delta land of southeastern Louisiana then owned by Spain; by 1796 it had proved a definite commercial success. A decade later there were eighty-one sugar estates, a number of them the property of refugees from the Haitian Revolution, who undoubtedly gave sugar production a real stimulus in Louisiana.

Ironically it was this Haitian Revolution that provided additional land for the expansion of slavery in the United States. The French Revolution of 1789 precipitated an uprising in Haiti in 1791, and after a bitter struggle the French recognized the freedom of the slaves. The leader of this revolution was Toussaint L'Ouverture, who was at the height of his power when Spain ceded the Louisiana Territory back to France in 1800. Napoleon, envisioning a grand empire in North America, with Haiti as its base, determined to overthrow the revolutionary government. Toussaint was captured, but this did not destroy the revolution. When yellow fever and the persistence of the Haitian Negroes had finally defeated the French armies, Napoleon gave up his scheme, selling the Louisiana Territory to the United States in 1803.

In the early years of the nineteenth century there was a steady growth of both the slave and white populations in the Mississippi Territory, but down to the War of 1812 the chief expansion of the cotton economy had been in the Carolina-Georgia piedmont. Thereafter as small farmers and large planters alike moved steadily southwestward, they discovered in Alabama and Mississippi two especially desirable sections for cotton cultivation. One was a strip of black soil curving from south central Alabama into northeastern Mississippi; from it came the name "Black Belt," which originally referred to the color of the soil. The other, and larger, area embraced an alluvial bottom land on both sides of the Mississippi from northern Tennessee south to the Red River. In Louisiana and Arkansas cotton agriculture was also concentrated in the rich river valleys north of Baton Rouge. After crossing the Mississippi, the cotton growers advanced into Mexico and played a crucial role in the events leading to the acquisition of Texas. This westward expansion of slavery and the cotton kingdom provided the principal focus for the sectional political controversies—the Missouri Compromise, the debate over the acquisition of Texas and the Mexican War, the Compromise of 1850, the Kansas–Nebraska Act, and the Dred Scott decision—that eventually reached a climax in the Civil War.

Although rice, tobacco, and sugar cane remained important crops in some sections of the South, cotton was indeed king.

Production rose from 13,000 bales in 1792 to 461,000 in 1817, over 2,000,000 bales in 1840, and nearly 5,000,000 bales in 1860. The states from Alabama and Tennessee westward to Texas produced one sixteenth of this cotton in 1811; they produced one third in 1820, almost two thirds in 1840, and three fourths by 1860. By mid-century nearly three quarters of the slaves were involved in cotton agriculture. This rapid expansion of the cotton kingdom was made possible by two factors: a large supply of suitable but inexpensive land, and an increasing— though never sufficient—supply of slaves. Virgin land and slaves were the most valued possessions of the rapidly advancing cotton frontier. The speed with which the cotton kingdom spread was due in part to the planter's carelessness with the land. When fertility declined after ten or twenty years, he simply moved to another plantation, often in an adjoining state. Large plantations tended to replace small farms in the fertile black belt and alluvial river bottoms. Population statistics demonstrate the prevalence of large-scale plantations. In Alabama and Mississippi slaves formed nearly half of the population in the middle of the century, and among the plantation counties of the Southwest, as in the coastal areas of Georgia and South Carolina, the proportion of Negroes in the population often surpassed 60 and 70 percent.

The rise of the cotton kingdom involved an enormous migra-tion of slaves in a generally southwestward direction. In 1820 the area which was ultimately to include the states of Florida, Alabama, Mississippi, Louisiana, Arkansas, and Texas contained about 60,000 slaves; by 1860 the region had ten times that number. Natural increase played its role, but this growth repre-sented chiefly a vast movement of slaves from the Border and Atlantic states to satisfy the insatiable demand of the expanding cotton kingdom. Many slaves were brought to the Southwestern states by Eastern planters, who either established their families on their new estates or operated them as absentee owners. But most of the slaves who populated the newly opened regions were moved through the interstate slave trade.

Virginia was the leading exporter of slaves—nearly 300,000 left her boundaries between 1830 and 1860. Maryland was also an important exporting state during the early nineteenth century. After 1830 the Carolinas and then Kentucky, Tennessee, and Missouri joined the list, and in the 1850's even Georgia was included. This geographical shift reflected not only the enormous and ever-increasing demands for slaves by the Southwestern states but also the progressive exhaustion of the soil in the tobacco and older cotton regions. As early as the Constitutional Convention Virginia slaveowners were clearly depending on the interstate slave trade to help support themselves; it was openly charged on the floor of the convention that her delegates favored the prohibition of the foreign slave trade not for humanitarian reasons but because they wanted the market value of their slaves to rise.

Slaves sold in the interstate trade were largely obtained either from impecunious planters, who disposed of them to pay off a debt, or from executors of wills settling an estate. Such transactions sometimes involved hundreds of slaves. In the largest sale on record from a single owner, the executors of the estate of James Bond, the biggest cotton planter in Georgia, in 1860 disposed of his 566 slaves for a total of over $580,000. Pierce Butler, owner of another great Georgia estate, was forced in 1859 to sell approximately 400 slaves to pay off his debts.

Though most Southern whites were scarcely likely to admit it, the commercial breeding and rearing of slaves was a common practice. Universally a slave woman's proved or anticipated fecundity was an important factor in determining her market value; advertisements and planters commonly referred to fertile females as "good breeders." Everywhere the prospect of multiplying the value of slave property through natural increase was eyed with pleasure. Some eminent Virginia citizens openly stated the economics of the matter. As the leading historian of the domestic slave trade, Frederic Bancroft, has said, slave rearing "became the source of the largest and often the only regular profit of nearly all slave-holding farmers and of many planters in the Upper South." He concluded that "next to the great and quick profit of bringing virgin soil under cultivation, slave-rearing was the surest, most remunerative and most approved means of increasing agricultural capital. It was advised and practised by the wisest rural slaveowners."

Planters who encouraged the natural increase of their slaves might regret the necessity of periodically disposing of a valuable part of their "capital," but it was, of course, an everyday occurrence. Admittedly it was considered bad form to separate families, and planters who did so often sold their slaves secretly, or only after first attempting to sell them together. Traders playing up to this desire for respectability, even the most unscrupulous ones, advertised that they did not split families. Auction records and manifests of slaves sent to New Orleans, however, prove that separation of families was the rule rather than the exception. When families were advertised for sale, they almost always included only the mother and her younger children, and often not even all of them. Youngsters of ten or twelve were generally considered single. Since even smaller children could be marketed more profitably individually than in family groups, it was not uncommon for four- or five-year-olds to be sold that way.

Slave traders ranged from itinerants, who scoured the rural counties of the Border States, to large-scale entrepreneurs operating their businesses even in the most fashionable hotels on the main thoroughfares of the principal cities. The largest and most successful had interstate operations. Franklin & Armfield owned three vessels which made fortnightly voyages between New Orleans and Alexandria, Virginia, during the trading season. Bolton, Dickens, & Company, the largest slave traders in Memphis during the early 1850's, had branch offices in Lexington, Kentucky, and St. Louis and Vicksburg. Slave traders might be "commission agents," or "auctioneers," who sold for planters on a commission basis of usually 2½ percent, or they might privately engage in buying slaves for speculation and resale. Commonly a slave trader did both. Frequently auctioneers and commission merchants were also agents for those who wished to hire out their slaves, a practice universal throughout the South. The more successful resident traders in a city operated slave prisons housing their own slaves and those of other traders as well. Slaves might make the journey to the markets of the Deep South by ship, or in the 1850's, by train, but the chief method of transporting them was overland on foot. Travelers reported seeing coffles of up to two hundred and even more, the men shackled together, marching across the countryside, and it was said that such groups could cover about twenty-five miles a day.

All the Southern states enacted elaborate slave codes, carefully defining the status of the bondsmen and enforcing their subordination in the social order. Fundamentally these codes were much alike, partly because the newer states copied their laws from the older ones and partly because the nature of the slave system determined certain types of regulations. In the years after the Revolutionary War there was a tendency toward humanizing the slave codes, but the laws became more stringent in the generation before the Civil War, particularly in the Deep South.

Basically slaves were regarded as property, and as such had no rights. They could not be parties in lawsuits, except indirectly where a free person sued for a slave's freedom; nor could they offer testimony in court except against other Negroes. They could not make contracts to buy or sell goods, and, with some minor exceptions, property ownership was forbidden. Since bondsmen could not make contracts, their marriages had no legal standing. On the other hand, the Southern states carefully guaranteed the slaveowner's rights in human property. Severe penalties were set for the theft of slaves, and when a slave was executed for a capital crime the state ordinarily compensated his master. Owners could of course sell or hire out their bondsmen. When used as security for loans slaves could be seized for the benefit of creditors. Masters writing their wills could divide their slaves as they wished, even if it was necessary to separate families or to sell the slaves to obtain cash for the estate.

Those states where slavery flourished discouraged the manumission of slaves. The Border States erected no such barriers, other than insisting that manumitted slaves must not become public charges because of age or illness. The states of the Upper South (Tennessee, Virginia, and North Carolina) insisted that manumitted slaves must leave their borders. But in the Deep South legislation on the subject became increasingly severe. Most outlawed private manumission early in the nineteenth century, the only exceptions being made by special acts of the legislature for particularly meritorious bondsmen. A master could still provide in his will that his slaves be sent to a free state and manumitted, but in the 1840's and 1850's even this practice was prohibited in several states of the Deep South. A man could always send his slaves out of the state and free them while he was still alive, but private manumissions became an increasingly rare phenomenon in the years before the Civil War.

A major part of the slave codes in all the Southern states was the provision for control and discipline. Slaves were not permitted to leave plantations without permission, and any white person finding a slave "at large" without a pass could take him to the authorities. If a slave forged a pass or free papers he was guilty of a felony. Except for a few places, bondsmen were not legally permitted to hire out their own time or to live by themselves. Slaves were not allowed to possess firearms. They could not visit whites or free Negroes, or receive them as visitors. Slaves could not assemble or hold a meeting unless a white man was present. A slave could not preach except to the slaves of his own master and on his master's premises with whites present. It was also against the law to teach slaves to read or write, or give them reading matter. Slaves were not allowed to strike whites even in self-defense; to do this, or to use insulting language toward a white man, was a crime. However, for a white man to kill a slave was seldom regarded as murder. Criminal codes were more severe on slaves and free Negroes than on whites. Slaves were subject to the death penalty for rape or attempted rape of a white woman, murder or attempted murder, revolt or attempted revolt, poisoning, robbery, and arson—and, under some circumstances, striking a white person. The death penalty was usually enforced against slaves only when whites were the victims.

Slaves, though property, were thus accountable as persons for their acts. In the colonial period, they had been tried before special courts consisting of justices of the peace and, in some states, of slaveholders. During the nineteenth century, most states provided for jury trials in capital crimes, but still the accused could not expect fairness. Those convicted were most often sentenced to a whipping since jail terms or the death penalty would deprive masters of laborers.

All of the Southern states provided for a patrol system to guard against unlawful assembly, the secreting of firearms, or insurrection. All adult white males, whether slaveholders or not, were required to serve periodically. Since slaveholders preferred to evade this onerous duty by employing substitutes or paying fines, the patrols often consisted of poor whites who were jealous of the wealthy planters and vented their hostility on the Negroes. Slaveholders constantly went to court charging that patrollers had illegally whipped their slaves. The patrol system was uneven in its implementation; in regions with many slaves, and during periods of actual or rumored insurrection, it was vigorously enforced, but otherwise the system was operated more casually.

In addition to holding slaves accountable for their behavior, Southern slave codes recognized the slaves as persons in certain other respects. Some codes regulated hours of labor and fined masters for failing to provide slaves with proper food and clothes. During the colonial period penalties for killing a slave were light. Changes occurred after the Revolution and ultimately all Southern states made malicious killing punishable as murder. By mid-century most codes regarded cruelty as an offense even if it did not lead to death. In practice, however, the courts emasculated the application of these laws, and convictions for maltreatment of slaves were extremely rare. This was inevitable, for Negroes could not testify against whites, white witnesses were naturally hesitant about appearing against other whites, and it was almost impossible to find a white jury who would convict. Thus, such slight protections as the law provided for Negroes were for the most part unenforceable.

More important than some of the legal provisions in mitigating the severity of the slave code was the fact that the laws were often ignored. Not only were petty crimes handled directly on the master's estate, but even in the more serious offenses, the owners, not wishing to lose the labor of a slave even temporarily, often failed to notify the authorities. Some masters allowed their slaves to meet together without the presence of whites, to travel at large without passes, to trade without permits, to hunt with guns, and to hire their own time. Nor was it rare for a master to teach a slave to read and write. A few owners even permitted their slaves to live independently, allowing them virtual freedom. Generally, in times when fears of slave revolt were in abeyance, there tended to be a certain laxity in the enforcement of the codes, and the paternalism of masters to favorite slaves led to violations of the strict letter of the law.

5

Despite the decline of slavery in the Northern states, the slave population more than quadrupled from less than 700,000 in 1790 to about 3,200,000 in 1850 and rose to nearly 4,000,000 in 1860. At mid-century about 400,000 of these lived in towns and cities; the majority, about 1,800,000 were cotton producers, the rest mainly used in raising tobacco, hemp, rice, and sugar cane. During the 1850's, on the southwestern frontier in Texas, the majority of the early cowboys were Negro slaves.

While the great mass of slaves were field hands, others were engaged in a variety of nonfarming occupations. In addition to the house servants and the skilled artisans of the plantations, there were skilled artisans and mechanics in the towns. Slaves were also used for many kinds of heavy labor: in the turpentine industry, in sawmills and quarries, in the coal and salt mines of Virginia, in the iron mines and furnaces of Virginia, Kentucky, and Tennessee. They worked as deck hands and firemen on river boats, as dock workers, as laborers on the construction of canals and railroads. They worked in the tobacco factories of Virginia, in textile mills from Virginia to Mississippi, in cotton presses, in tanneries, in shipyards, and in laundries of many towns.

Although the typical slave was a cotton cultivator, he did not necessarily work on a large farm or plantation. Nor did the majority of white Southerners own slaves or plantations. In the South in 1860 there were only 385,000 slaveholders in a free population of 1,500,000 families, so that only one quarter of the Southern whites had a vested interest in preserving the institution of slavery. Slaveholding families were concentrated in certain states, particularly in the belt from Georgia to Louisiana, where one third or more families owned slaves. Among them were a few Negro slaveowning plantation families, mainly located in South Carolina and Louisiana. For example, at the end of the eighteenth century one Negro resident of St. Paul's Parish, South Carolina, held about 200 bondsmen. In 1830 members of the Meytoier family in Natchitoches Parish, Louisiana, owned a total of 212 slaves, Antoine Decuire of Point Cuffee Parish possessed 70, and Martin Donatto of Plaquemine Brule Parish had 75. In the same year the two largest Negro slaveholders in South Carolina were listed as owning 84 slaves each, and the leading Negro slaveowner in Virginia, Benjamin O. Taylor of King George County, had 71.

Taking ownership of twenty slaves as the minimum for membership in the planter class, a study of the census data reveals that the great majority of Southern slaveholders could not be called planters In 1860, 88 percent of them held fewer than twenty slaves, 72 percent held fewer than ten, and nearly 50 percent held fewer than five. Most of those in the planter class owned between twenty and fifty slaves, approximately 10,000 owned fifty or more, and only 3,000 persons owned more than a hundred slaves. Yet the majority of slaves lived on plantations—over half of them on farms worked by twenty or more slaves, and a quarter of the slaves lived in units of fifty or more. At the other end of the scale, only a quarter lived on farms worked by fewer than ten slaves. Large units were more common in the Lower South, and most of the large slaveholdings were concentrated in those areas best suited for staple crops, such as the alluvial river bottoms with their fertile soil and ready access to markets. These included the Louisiana sugar parishes, the Yazoo-Mississippi Delta and the Natchez region in Mississippi, the Black Belt of Alabama, and the coastal rice lands and Sea Islands of South Carolina and Georgia. In some plantation counties, slaves outnumbered whites by more than two to one, while in other counties of the South there were very few slaves and not a single plantation.

The organization of work varied according to the crop and the size of the farm. Rice planters used the task system, where an individual slave was held responsible for a given amount of daily work which he completed at his own pace. Other staples were usually cultivated under the gang system, where slaves worked together until the task was finished. Tobacco could be grown on small farms better than the other staples, while sugar cane, which required heavy investments in refining machinery, was limited exclusively to large plantations.

On small farms, especially those with a half-dozen slaves or less, there was little or no labor specialization and in the fields the master personally directed the slaves' work. On medium-sized farms, worked by from ten to twenty slaves, there was a limited amount of specialization, with perhaps a couple of slaves trained in manual skills and one or more engaged in domestic work. On such a farm the owner did not work in the fields but confined himself to the business aspects of his enterprise, typically delegating the supervision of slaves to his sons or a slave foreman. Many of these foremen were given considerable responsibility in running the farm.

Nearly half the slaves belonged to the 25,000 planters who

owned thirty slaves or more. It was on such large plantations that the system achieved its highest complexity, specialization, and efficiency. Practically all plantations of this size had white overseers to supervise the work of the slaves or, where the owner was an absentee, to run the entire operation. Planters constantly complained of the inefficiency and incompetency of their overseers, and few stayed on the same plantation for more than a year or two. Yet the larger estates found it impossible to do without them. Beneath the overseer were one or more slave drivers, trusted slaves who were part of the system of coercion. They kept order among the field hands and were authorized to discipline them. On the larger plantations several drivers were used and were responsible to a head driver, who acted as a suboverseer. House servants were a class apart from the field hands. So were skilled artisans—blacksmiths, carpenters, and others. Some of the plantations, with very large slave forces, had full-time workers who drove wagons, cultivated vegetable gardens, tended livestock, or performed other duties.

Because there was a decline in efficiency of operations when a plantation had over a hundred slaves, planters with large slaveholdings usually owned two or more plantations. One Louisiana owner of seven hundred slaves divided his holdings into six plantations, with six overseers, two doctors, a general agent, and a bookkeeper. Absentee ownership was naturally found among large estates such as this. A few, like the Virginia and Carolina planters who preferred to live on their ancestral estates, owned plantations great distances away in the Southwest, which they visited annually but for the most part left to the care of their overseers. Planters who divided their holdings into several contiguous or nearby plantations were similarly absent most of the time, entrusting the major responsibilities to their overseers, as did urban lawyers and businessmen who were only part-time planters. On such large-scale plantations land and labor were exploited in the zeal for immediate financial returns, and these "factories in the field" differed substantially from paternalistically organized smaller units and older tidewater plantations.

Plantation slaves lived on a minimal subsistence basis. Ordinarily their living quarters consisted of a single or double row of cabins near the overseer's cottage. A humane and enlightened minority attempted to provide neat, weatherproof cabins, at times with two or three rooms, a modicum of bedding, and perhaps some other scanty furniture. But most slaves lived in rude, drafty, and leaky clapboard shacks, frequently without furniture, and quite often filthy and overcrowded. As for clothing, a standard supply for a man was two shirts of coarse cotton, two woolen trousers, a woolen jacket in the winter, and two cotton shirts and two cotton trousers in the spring. Every year he received a pair of shoes. This was scarcely enough for field hands who did rough outdoor work. For much of the year they were seen bare-footed in tattered clothes, and in the freezing winters most slaves did not have enough clothes to keep them warm. Some farmers attempted to give their slaves a varied diet and encouraged them to cultivate their own gardens, but the standard diet was hominy and fatback, with a basic weekly ration of a peck of cornmeal and three or four pounds of salt pork.

The plantation way of life evolved a complex, and often subtle, system of discipline over the slave population. Treatment varied widely, from the paternalism of some slaveholders to the sadistic cruelty of others. Acts of disobedience were most commonly punished by flogging, and few adult slaves had ever completely escaped the whip. Slaveowners who habitually used severe physical chastisement were common enough, and just about every farmer believed that slaves responded only to firm treatment and at least periodic whippings. Brutality was more frequent on the large plantations, particularly those in the Deep South operated by overseers who had no personal concern about the slaves as people or even as property. Though masters frequently condemned the harshness of their overseers and supplied specific directions about the maximum number of lashes for various violations, such instructions were usually ignored. As long as the overseer produced a large crop, the planter was ordinarily satisfied, regardless of the brutal discipline that might be used. A few slaveholders built their own jails, others used public jails, but incarceration penalized the master as well as the slave. Chains and irons were employed to control runaways, and a strong deterrent was the threat of sale to the Deep South cotton and sugar plantations.

In addition, there were several forms of indirect controls. Slaves worked long hours—well into darkness during busy seasons, especially at harvest time—and it was necessary to reward and cajole as well as to threaten in order to get the work done. Work was stopped on Sundays and sometimes all or part of Saturday, and slaves could look forward to holidays, such as Good Friday, Independence Day, "laying-by time" after the harvest, and Christmas. On these occasions passes were granted freely by many masters, and Christmas particularly was a time of celebration, slaves often being allowed considerable freedom and even the use of liquor. Some masters distributed gifts at the end of the year or compensated slaves for performing extra work or allowed them to hire their own time. Denial of weekend passes, work on Saturdays and Sundays, and confiscation of crops in truck patches were some of the milder punishments owners used.

Other indirect controls were implicit in the social stratification system of the plantation. Because of their privileged positions, slave foremen, artisans, and domestic servants showed considerable loyalty to the planters. The identification between such slaves and their owners was often so complete that they were informers in impending slave revolts and even helped to catch despised field hands who ran away. Religion was also a form of control over slaves. After it was understood that baptism did not confer freedom, and that the Southern wings of the Methodist and Baptist churches had no intention of applying their denominational egalitarianism to the temporal status of slaves, planters readily saw advantages in allowing them to attend religious services. Some owners built chapels on their plantations, but more commonly slaves worshipped in the white man's church, seated in the balcony. Of course, such religious services emphasized the quietistic, otherworldly aspects of Christianity, rather than the impulse toward social justice in the Judaic-Christian tradition, and promised salvation to those who obeyed their masters. Christianity was thus viewed as an anodyne helping slaves accept their lot in this world.

6

Modern social psychological studies have demonstrated that members of minority groups react in various ways to their subordinate status in society. They may hate and rebel against their oppressors, or they may accept the inferiority assigned them by the dominant group. They may assert social pride and emphasize the value of their own collective action, or they may attempt to assimilate the dominant group's culture and strive for acceptance in it. They may escape into religious otherworldliness. Or individuals may exhibit a paradoxical and complex amalgam of these attitudes and reactions.

Many slaves in the United States retreated into a compensatory otherworldliness; for them Christianity served the function it had so well served for the slaves among whom it first spread in the Roman Empire. Christian doctrines exalted the meek and the lowly, making a virtue of accepting without resistance the persecution that the slaves were forced to endure. Some who accommodated played the clown and told the white man what he wanted to hear. The slave elite—house servants, foremen, and skilled artisans—so valued their privileged status that they very often identified with the master class. Yet it should also be noted that a high proportion of the runaways were among those well treated by their masters. There were frequent and numerous rebellions: over two hundred have been identified. The most important were Gabriel's revolt (1800), Denmark Vesey's Conspiracy (1822),* and Nat Turner's Insurrection (1831).

It is one thing to delineate the types of responses made by slaves to their status; it is another to state with any degree of precision in what proportion each of these various reactions occurred. Historians with different theses and social biases disagree with one another on this matter, and the subject is now one about which swirls a major controversy in Negro historiography. U. B. Phillips, a Southern apologist of the early twentieth century, asserted that slaves were happy and revolts were few because of the benign, paternalistic nature of the system and the innately childlike character of Negroes. Negro sociologists like Charles S. Johnson and E. Franklin Frazier rejected the notion of inborn racial personality differences, but also emphasized the accommodating nature of the Negro's adjustment to slavery. More recent historians, like Kenneth Stampp and John Hope Franklin, have minimized the slaves' enforced accommodation and have underscored instead signs of their rebelliousness. They have held that Negroes, like other men, naturally resisted tyranny

* Recent scholarship has suggested that the Vesey plot existed only in the minds of hysterical whites. See Richard C. Wade, "The Vesey Plot: A Reconsideration," *Journal of Southern History,* XXX (May, 1964), pp. 143–61.

and oppression. Melville Herskovits, insisting that slave revolts would not have occurred if Negroes had adopted the white man's views and had lost their consciousness of group identity along with their African cultural background, accented the importance of servile rebellion as reflecting the survival of Africanisms. On the other hand, the most noted scholar on the subject of slave insurrections, Herbert Aptheker, interpreted his data in the framework of his Communist ideology, holding that oppressed classes are constantly in revolt. More recently, however, Stanley Elkins has asserted that insurrections were indeed relatively rare in the United States and accommodation the rule—but because the system was extremely oppressive. Drawing upon the experiences of inmates in German concentration camps, where there were no revolts, where few people committed suicide, where prisoners retreated into infantile behavior patterns and even admired the S.S. men as respected and revered father figures, he suggests that the picture of the "happy-go-lucky" slave, the "Sambo stereotype," contains an element of truth. Thus he concludes that the development of such a personality type and of such patterns of adjustment underscore the horror, the dehumanizing quality of slavery in the United States, especially in the generation before the Civil War.

It is true that slave revolts were more frequent and runaways more successful in the Caribbean and South America, and for this various explanations have been offered. For one, geographical factors played their part. The mountains of Haiti, for example, facilitated the cause of the Haitian rebels under Toussaint L'Ouverture. Second, African survivals are very evident in Latin-American countries and clearly contributed to some of the revolts there. Many insurrections in Bahia, Brazil, originated in Muslim religious groups among slaves from the Hausa states. The Haitian Revolution spread rapidly as drum signals transmitted news of the first uprisings from plantation to plantation, in the same way that messages were sent over long distances in Africa. Finally, as Elkins would hold, the slave system in Latin America lacked the dehumanizing, completely oppressive character of the institution in the United States. After all, revolutions do not originate among those whom conditions make hopeless; such people are generally characterized by passivity, resignation, and accommodation to the status quo. Some support is given to the Elkins thesis by a recent statistical analysis of the geographical distribution of

American slave revolts, which concludes that they tended to occur near cities or in rural areas of paternalistic traditions. On the large plantations of the Deep South where conditions were worst, slave revolts were extremely rare. Yet it is well to point out that no insurrections erupted in New England, the section of the country where the slave system was the least repressive. Clearly further research is necessary to isolate the crucial variables associated with servile rebellions.

7

Considerable illumination is cast upon the nature of the American slave system, and the patterns of race relations that subsequently emerged in the United States, by a comparison with the system of slavery historically most closely related to it: that which developed in the Spanish and Portuguese colonies of the New World. The postslavery era in the Latin-American countries proved to be one of relative egalitarianism compared to the racial system that evolved in the United States, and the roots of the difference appear to lie in the fundamental differences between slavery in the United States and in the Latin-American countries.

Three aspects of Iberian culture have been offered to account for the difference. First, there was the tradition stemming from Roman law. The Iberian Peninsula had known slavery throughout the Middle Ages, and its slave codes had been rooted in the continuing tradition of Roman civil law. This juridical tradition in its late phases, under the influence of Stoic philosophers and jurists, had done much to mitigate the evils of Roman slavery since it viewed a slave as a man with certain natural human rights and as equal spiritually with other men. The protections afforded slaves under Roman law were retained in the Iberian legal systems. Second, the Catholic Church, while recognizing the legality of slavery, insisted upon the essentially human character of slaves, their spiritual equality before God, and the importance of their religious and moral training and behavior. Third, the Iberian culture, with its lack of a middle-class or Protestant ethic rationalizing economic behavior, may have had some impact upon the character of Portuguese-Spanish slavery in the New World. The preoccupation of American slaveowners with financial profits was more likely to stifle human impulses.

Slavery could be, and often was, as cruel in Latin-American countries as in the United States, but the slaves' legal and social status was quite different. In addition to being property, a slave in Latin America was also considered a human being. He was permitted by law to testify against whites; he could bring his master to court for excessive cruelty; he could own property and engage in buying and selling. Slaves could hire themselves out, save the earnings, and purchase themselves. Nothing stood in the way of manumitting slaves. In fact, in the absence of evidence to the contrary, a Negro was considered free rather than a slave, and free Negroes had the rights of other citizens.

Both church and state interceded to protect the well-being of slaves. In Brazil and many of the Spanish colonies there was an official protector of the slaves, and magistrates were directed to make periodic investigations of the plantations to see how the bondsmen were treated. Church officials took a similar interest. Moreover, in contrast to the United States, the church required the baptism and religious training of all slaves and insisted upon the sanctity of marriage: once slaves had been joined in wedlock they were not to be separated. And the church encouraged manumission as a good deed in the sight of God. Emancipating slaves was part of an "honorific tradition," fulfilled on many occasions—on the birth of a first son, on the marriage of the master's children, on a national holiday, and at other festive times. In the United States the churches acquiesced in the slave system and religion buttressed it. It took a Civil War to emancipate the slaves here, and even then they were not really accepted as citizens. None of the Latin-American countries underwent such a traumatic experience, and in all of them, while discrimination did not completely disappear, the Negroes were generally accepted as part of the body politic.

III

NEGROES IN THE ANTE-BELLUM CITIES: MANUMISSION, ALIENATION, AND PROTEST

1

WHILE SLAVERY thrived on the plantation, it languished in the cities. From the beginning there had been significant differences between urban and rural servitude. Most urban slaves were domestic servants or unskilled workers, but a high proportion were skilled artisans. Owners often derived a regular income from hiring their slaves out by the year or for shorter periods of time, skilled slaves commanding especially high wages for their masters. Most of the slaves in the Richmond ironworks and tobacco factories, where they were used for all grades of labor from the most menial to the most highly skilled, were hired bondsmen. Though the law increasingly frowned upon the practice, some masters continued to encourage a slave to find his own job and keep a portion of his earnings for himself.

In the context of city life slaves lived under fewer restraints than in the countryside. In theory, slaves were not allowed on the city streets without passes from their masters. In practice, however, it was difficult to confine slaves to their quarters in their masters' courtyards; it was inconvenient to prepare passes every time a servant was sent on an errand about the town. Therefore, the urban slaves had considerable freedom in coming and going, simply because it was easier for their masters. Moreover, a number of slaves, especially those hiring their own time, were permitted to live out. Their wooden shanties, ordinarily in the alleys of the commercial areas and on the edge of town, were inferior physically to the quarters in the master's yard, but the added degree of freedom was highly prized. Indeed, though the number of urban slaves declined, the number of those living out rose. Also prized was the right to worship in Negro churches, which were usually mixed congregations of free people and slaves. Even some prominent white ministers defended the practice of permitting separate religious institutions for Negroes. All of these things allowed much informal socializing, not infrequently in illicit dramshops run by white saloonkeepers. Although the public feared that such gatherings were seedbeds of revolt and crime, attempts to circumscribe this sort of activity largely failed. "A city slave is almost a free citizen," declared Frederick Douglass, with pardonable exaggeration, when he compared his experiences in Baltimore during the 1830's with his earlier life on Maryland's Eastern Shore. "He enjoys privileges altogether unknown to the whip-driven slave on the plantation."

In the two decades before the Civil War the size of the urban slave population was falling, apparently because young Negro males were being sold to the countryside, where prices for prime field hands were rising extravagantly. At the same time, however, the number of free Negroes, who were in the main an urban group, increased substantially. Divided roughly equally between the North and South, their numbers rose from about 60,000 in 1790 to half a million in 1860. The chief areas of concentration were: tidewater Virginia and Maryland; the Virginia and North Carolina piedmont, where there were numbers of Negroes who owned small tobacco farms; the Southern coastal cities of Baltimore, Washington, Charleston, Mobile, and New Orleans; and the Northern cities of Boston, Cincinnati, New York, and Philadelphia.

In the Northern states emancipation laws effected the liberation of all slaves before the middle of the nineteenth century. The free Negro population there had been augmented through natural increase and through the arrival from the South of fugitives and Negroes manumitted and sent North by their Southern masters.

In the South, the free Negro population was descended mainly from slaves who had been emancipated by their masters either because of faithful personal service or because of close kinship ties. Accordingly, a relatively high proportion of the free Negroes were of mixed racial ancestry. Some were the offspring of free Negro women cohabiting with white men or, more rarely, of white women cohabiting with Negroes. Interracial unions were especially prevalent in the Southern cities. Occasionally slaves were emancipated by legislative act for some particularly meritorious service to the white community, such as reporting slave conspiracies or performing heroic acts in serious fires or epidemics. In the Border States in the East a substantial number of slaves had gained their freedom during the peak of antislavery enthusiasm in the 1780's. In the last decades of the slave regime, thousands of superannuated Negroes, who had been put off Maryland plantations, crowded into Baltimore. A number of skilled slaves, especially in the cities, had purchased freedom by securing permission to hire themselves out and keep a share of the earnings. Though after 1830 it became more and more difficult—and in most states practically impossible—for slaves to obtain freedom legally as a gift from their owners or by self-purchase, the number of free Negroes in the United States continued to grow by the excess of births over deaths.

2

With the possible exception of certain New England states, the status of free Negroes deteriorated in the course of the nineteenth century. At best, the ante-bellum free people of color could be described, in John Hope Franklin's words, as "quasi-free Negroes."

In the South, of course, free Negroes had never enjoyed many rights. As time passed, legislation grew more restrictive, and their status became increasingly similar to that of the slaves. Throughout the region laws required that the free Negro carry on his person a certificate of freedom, and without this document he might be claimed as a slave. Because his movements and activities were subjected to surveillance and regulation, many local jurisdictions demanded that his name be registered with the police or court authorities. Migration to another Southern state was severely restricted if not completely prohibited by the

1830's. Maryland, Tennessee, and North Carolina, the only three Southern states that had accorded the franchise to free Negroes, had, by 1835, amended their constitutions to deprive them of the right to vote. In the courtroom the free Negro could neither serve on juries nor give testimony against whites. If convicted, he was liable to punishment more severe than that imposed on white men. He might be whipped prior to imprisonment or even sold into slavery.

The Southern free Negro's right of assembly was also proscribed. Evening activities were subject to a curfew in many parts of the South, and meetings of benevolent societies and churches frequently required the presence of a respectable white person. Toward the end of the ante-bellum period, police often forbade attendance at lodges, dramatic societies, or charitable organizations. As a potential insurrectionist, the free Negro was discouraged from entertaining slaves. Since his motives were questioned, he could not own a gun or a dog without a special license. As an additional safeguard, Georgia, Florida, and Alabama required him to have a white guardian. Able-bodied Negroes not holding steady jobs might find themselves classed as vagrants and sold into servitude for months or even years.

Turning to the North, a distinction should be made between the original states of the Union and those carved out of the old Northwest Territory. Inequalities before the law existed in the Northeast, but they were far more pervasive in the Old Northwest, where many white Southerners had settled, and which retained strong commercial links with the lower Mississippi Valley, especially before the building of the Erie Canal. Ironically, despite the Northwest Ordinance's prohibition of slavery, it was in this area that, next to the South, free Negroes found the most hostile reception.

The Black Laws regulating the behavior of free Negroes in the Old Northwest were in fact based upon the slave codes of the Southern states. For a period the legislatures of Illinois and Indiana evaded the antislavery prohibition of the Ordinance by enacting laws placing Negro youths under long-term indentures. Thus was perpetuated in modified form the practice of Negro slavery known previously in the Northwest Territory when it had been under French and British rule. The Illinois constitution of 1818 expressly provided for the hiring of slave labor at the saltworks near Shawneetown. Nowhere in the Old Northwest or in the newer Western states could Negroes exercise the right to vote or serve on juries. They could not testify in cases involving whites in Ohio, Indiana, Illinois, Iowa, or California. Most of the Western states also banned intermarriage. The Northwestern and Western states attempted to discourage Negro settlers by requiring them to register their certificates of freedom at a county clerk's office and to present bonds of $500 or $1,000 guaranteeing that they would not disturb the peace or become public charges. Toward the end of the ante-bellum period, Illinois, Indiana, and Oregon excluded Negro migrants entirely. Only Ohio, after a long battle, repealed its restrictive immigration legislation in 1849. Though such anti-immigration statutes were only erratically enforced, nevertheless they intimidated Negroes. In 1829 an attempt to enforce an 1807 law requiring a $500 bond precipitated a race riot at Cincinnati and a mass Negro exodus to Canada.

In the Northeast, none of the states provided by law for discrimination in the courtroom, and Negro testimony was admissible in cases involving whites. Social custom, however, barred Negroes from sitting on juries, except in Massachusetts where a few Negroes served just prior to the Civil War. Negroes enjoyed the same voting rights as whites in all the original Northern states for a generation after the American Revolution. Then, one by one, between 1807 and 1837, five of them—New Jersey, Connecticut, New York, Rhode Island, and Pennsylvania —enacted disfranchisement provisions. The laws of Connecticut and Rhode Island did not disqualify those already on the rolls, and in Rhode Island the prohibition was repealed in 1842.

The movement for disfranchisement in the Northeast was usually related to the increasing political power of urban white workingmen and the enactment of universal white manhood suffrage. Negroes tended to vote Federalist, and later for the Federalists' heirs, the National Republicans and the Whigs. This Negro tie with the aristocratic parties was no accident. In New York, for example, where Negroes had been servants in the homes of the wealthy, the paternalistic relationship helped to bind Negroes to the Federalist Party. More than this, prominent Federalists like John Jay and Alexander Hamilton were active in the antislavery movement and in charitable work among free

Negroes. Both *noblesse oblige* and partisan advantage prompted such men to champion the cause of Negro suffrage. In opposition was the Democratic Republican Party (by 1828 known as the Democratic Party), representing the interests of the white working classes, who viewed the Negroes as economic rivals. Their prejudice was reinforced by partisan zeal, since most Negroes voted for what was generally conceived to be the party of privilege. At the New York constitutional convention of 1821, the Federalists favored a franchise based on property qualifications without race discrimination, but the Democrats, who were in the majority, secured the adoption of universal white manhood suffrage; Negroes could vote only if they owned a freehold estate worth $250. In Pennsylvania also the Democrats agitated for the elimination of Negro suffrage. There race riots and other forms of intimidation practically ended Negro voting in Philadelphia even before the state constitutional convention of 1837 legalized disfranchisement. In Rhode Island, those Negroes still voting in 1841 were a factor in defeating a new constitution that provided for universal white manhood suffrage. The following year the victorious conservatives rewarded their Negro supporters by repealing the earlier racial restrictions.

The legal restrictions imposed upon Negroes by the Northern states generated a steady stream of protest and agitation. Conventions and mass meetings passed resolutions, issued addresses to the public, and sent petitions to governors and legislatures. In campaigning for the franchise, for equal treatment in the courts, for guarantees of civil liberties, and in the Old Northwest, for the abolition of the Black Laws, Negroes emphasized that they were simply asking for basic citizenship rights. First and foremost, therefore, they appealed to the democratic principles upon which the nation was founded. They advanced other arguments as well to support their claims. They denied the existence of innate racial differences, stressed the presence of a thrifty and industrious class of Negroes, and on occasion even enumerated at length the substantial property holdings that free Negroes had acquired under unfavorable conditions. They returned again and again to the theme that Negroes were native Americans, loyal to the nation that oppressed them. Fortified with these persuasive arguments, they agitated for the repeal of the Ohio Black Laws, and after achieving that goal, attempted to secure the right to vote.

They unsuccessfully fought to stem the tide of disfranchisement in New York and Pennsylvania and were still propagandizing on this issue in both these and other states on the eve of the Civil War.

Most of their efforts ended in failure. It is difficult to see how it could have been otherwise. Evidences of thrift, sobriety, and economic achievements, and the hortatory phrases of even the most skillful writers could scarcely influence a public that was fundamentally hostile, or at best indifferent, toward them. A minuscule proportion of the electorate even where enfranchised, possessing only a few champions of equal citizenship rights among their abolitionist friends, Negroes lacked the power essential to convince whites of the fairness of these often humble requests. To protest against disfranchisement by refusing to pay a modest poll tax, as two Negro retail merchants did in San Francisco in 1857, was an act both courageous and rare. In view of their situation, Negro leaders could do no more than protest by respectfully petitioning for the redress of their grievances, and continue to hope that some day moral virtue and the acquisition of property would win the respect of their white fellow citizens.

Besides legal restrictions in voting rights and the courts, there were other forms of oppression. In Northern cities the most extreme of these was mob violence. During the 1830's and 1840's riots occurred in Philadelphia, New York, Pittsburgh, Cincinnati, and other places. More continuous and pervasive were the patterns of segregation and employment discrimination.

The Jim Crow or segregation laws were largely a product of the late nineteenth century. Segregation by custom, however, and even occasionally by statute, was already common during the ante-bellum period. In the South segregation developed as one of the devices to control the urban free Negroes and the slave population. Separation in jails and hospitals was universal. Negroes were widely excluded from the public parks and burial grounds. They were relegated to the balconies of theatres and opera houses and barred from hotels and restaurants. The New Orleans street railway maintained separate cars for the two races. Sometimes these practices were codified in law: as early as 1816 New Orleans passed an ordinance segregating Negroes in places of public accommodation. The legal codes of Savannah and Charleston excluded free Negroes from public parks, Charleston,

Baltimore, and New Orleans were among the cities legalizing segregated jails and poorhouses.

In the North, Negroes were not legally segregated in places of public accommodation, nor, except for schools, in publicly owned institutions. Custom, however, barred them from hotels and restaurants, and they were segregated, if not entirely excluded, from theatres, public lyceums, hospitals, and cemeteries. Even in abolitionist Boston, the Negro was considered a pariah in most circles. In 1846 Frederick Douglass wrote William Lloyd Garrison from Ireland:

> I remember, about two years ago, there was in Boston . . . a menagerie [that] I had long desired to see. . . . I was met and told by the doorkeeper, in a harsh and contemptuous tone, *"We don't allow niggers in here."* . . . Soon after my arrival in New Bedford from the South, I had a strong desire to attend the Lyceum, but was told, *"They don't allow niggers in here."* On arriving in Boston from an anti-slavery tour, hungry and tired, I went into an eating house near my friend Mr. Campbell's, to get some refreshments. I was met by a lad in a white apron, *"We don't allow niggers in here!"* On attempting to take a seat in the Omnibus [to Weymouth], I was told by the driver, (and I never shall forget his fiendish hate,) *"I don't allow niggers in here!"*

Traveling by public conveyance was difficult for Negroes. In Boston there were signs: "Colored people not allowed to ride in this omnibus." In New York City Negroes were refused streetcar seats except on a segregated basis. Philadelphia Negroes were restricted to the front platform of these vehicles. Long-distance travel was even more of a problem. On stagecoaches Negroes usually rode on an outside seat, and on the early railroads they often occupied filthy accommodations in a separate car. Steamboats offered the worst conditions, since Negroes were almost invariably excluded from cabins and required to remain on deck even in cold weather. On the all-night trip from New York City to Newport, Rhode Island, they usually had the choice of pacing the deck or sleeping among cotton bales, horses, sheep, and pigs.

Southern Negroes were unable to protest such treatment in their section of the country, nor were Negroes of the Old Northwest in a position to do much. Northeastern Negroes did protest vigorously, though without much success except in Massachusetts. Some Negroes simply boycotted local omnibuses.

Others—such as David Ruggles, the New York Underground Railroad leader—frequently tried to occupy seats reserved for whites but were usually thrown into the street. On one occasion in 1841 when Ruggles sought a first-class ticket on a steamer bound from New Bedford to Nantucket, he was beaten up by the ticket seller for refusing to accept deck accommodations.

When the early Massachusetts railroads provided separate racial accommodations, Negroes like Frederick Douglass were forcibly dragged from the white coaches for defying segregation. Aided by leading white abolitionists, Negroes petitioned the legislature for remedial action. In 1842 Charles Lenox Remond, a noted anti-slavery lecturer, testified before a legislative committee of the Massachusetts House of Representatives: "The grievances of which we complain, be assured, sir, are not imaginary, but real—not local, but universal—not occasional, but continual, every day matter of fact things—and have become, to the disgrace of our common country, a matter of history. . . ." He added that a white man's "social rights" guaranteed free choice of personal friends but did not justify violating the Negro's "civil rights." Sensing a change in public opinion, the Massachusetts railroads abolished the separate coach for Negroes in 1843.

Another method of protest involved legal tests of segregation practices. In 1854 a Negro woman sued after being forcibly ejected from a New York City streetcar. The lawsuit was handled by the Legal Rights Association, a Negro group, which engaged twenty-four-year-old Chester A. Arthur as attorney. Although she was awarded damages, Negroes continued to face discrimination on the streetcars. In 1856 when a minister was removed from a vehicle, the judge upheld the transportation company on the ground that its business would suffer if Negroes could sit anywhere they pleased. This decision was interpreted to apply to omnibuses, hotels, and other public facilities. Five years later a Philadelphia court also ruled in favor of a transportation company's right to bar Negroes by force if necessary.

Recent scholarship has found residential segregation and the origins of the modern ghetto in the ante-bellum city. Actually, before the Civil War urban Negroes generally resided in racially mixed neighborhoods. The homes of the more prosperous free Negro artisans and businessmen were often scattered throughout various parts of the city, singly or in small clusters. There was a tendency, however, for Negroes to be concentrated in certain neighborhoods or wards, but within close proximity to whites. In the Southern towns the slaves who "lived out" tended to move to the edges of the city, where they formed neighborhoods predominantly, though not exclusively, Negro. In Baltimore and Philadelphia there were Negroes living in the alleys between the main streets on which fashionable whites resided. The most impoverished Negroes were the most segregated, often in vice districts controlled by white overlords. New York Negroes were heavily concentrated in a few wards, where poor whites also resided. In Philadelphia the worst slum consisted of a few densely populated blocks inhabited by incredibly poverty-stricken Negroes living in unheated rooms, garrets, and tiny wooden shanties lacking even the most modest comforts. In Boston, Providence, New Haven, Cincinnati, and other seacoast and river cities, Negro slum neighborhoods, with names like "New Guinea," developed first along the wharves. Later the Negroes tended to shift to outlying sections known by such names as "Nigger Hill." As discrimination increased all over the North, even the more prosperous colored men were often drawn to predominantly Negro neighborhoods.

3

One reaction to the discrimination and segregation imposed by whites was the formation in the late eighteenth and early nineteenth century of free Negro community institutions. In part this development also resulted from the growing number of free Negroes in the urban centers, and their tendency to concentrate in certain neighborhoods. Thus racial separation became even more deeply imbedded in American life.

The institutional organization of the Negro community took two forms: the church and the fraternal or mutual benefit organization. Historically, the two were closely interrelated. The distinction between the sacred and the secular was not closely drawn. In a period when there were hardly any ordained ministers, it was natural for the mutual aid society to perform both religious and secular functions. Moreover, leaders were few in the relatively small urban Negro communities, and where there were ministers it was natural that they would play an important role in all Negro affairs.

In Newport, Rhode Island, the mutual benefit society preceded the church by many years. The African Union Society formed there in 1780 recorded births, marriages, and deaths and provided for decent burials. The organization also assisted members in times of distress and apprenticed Negro youths to skilled artisans. In 1808 it merged with the African Benevolent Society and established a free school. In 1824, under the auspices of the Society, the first Negro church in Newport was formed. This pattern was not uncommon, although in some communities the mutual benefit society and the school followed, and were outgrowths of, the church and its activities.

The independent church movement stemmed from prejudicial treatment in white-dominated churches. In Southern and Northeastern cities, free Negroes were admitted to membership in white churches but generally were seated in galleries, "nigger pews," and "African corners." Racial distinctions developed in other aspects of church life, such as separate Sunday school classes, communion services, and baptisms. Talented Negroes were sometimes invited to preach and occasionally even to be the pastor in a white church. One of the most celebrated examples is John Chavis of North Carolina, who ministered to a white Presbyterian congregation until the state prohibited Negroes from preaching in 1831. Generally, however, Negroes were required to assume an inconspicuous demeanor. Deeply resenting these racial restrictions, they usually responded by attempting to form their own congregations within the predominantly white denominations or to secede completely and establish independent denominations.

Most Negroes were either Baptists or Methodists. Various reasons have been offered to explain this fact, but one factor must have been that originally, during the eighteenth century, these two churches, appealing to the poor and downtrodden, accepted both Negroes and whites on a basis of relative equality, even in the South. Here and there, Negroes ministered to white or mixed Baptist congregations, and early in the nineteenth century a Negro Baptist minister was elected first moderator of the Louisiana Baptist Association, which, except for himself, was composed of white clergymen. By the 1790's, however, overt discrimination was becoming the more typical pattern in all of the churches.

The origins of the African Methodist Episcopal (AME) Church illustrate Negro response to this change. Its leading figure and first consecrated bishop was Richard Allen, a former Maryland slave who had been converted to Methodism. Allen in turn converted his master, who subsequently permitted Allen to purchase his freedom. Moving to Philadelphia, Allen became a circuit preacher and began attending the predominantly white St. George's Methodist Church in 1786. Allen gathered a group of Negroes for prayer meetings at the church. Realizing that Negroes would not be able to achieve positions of true leadership at St. George's, he suggested establishing a separate place of worship. The response of most of the Negroes was not enthusiastic. Allen's forceful personality was drawing ever larger numbers of Negroes to St. George's, however, much to the annoyance of the trustees, who stopped his prayer service and ordered Negro communicants to sit in the rear of the gallery. When Allen and another Negro leader, Absolom Jones, took places toward the front of the gallery, they were peremptorily directed to change seats in the midst of their prayers. Accordingly, Allen and Jones departed from St. George's with their followers.

Several months earlier, in April, 1787, the two men had already founded the Free African Society, a mutual aid organization which experimented with nondenominational religious exercises conducted along Quaker lines. However, the silent prayers and meditation were satisfying to neither Jones nor Allen, who soon differed with each other on doctrinal matters. Jones led his band of followers to establish the first Negro Episcopal Church in America while Allen organized the Bethel African Methodist Episcopal Church in 1794. For many years he retained affiliation with the white Methodists, who ordained him a deacon in 1799.

Parallel developments were occurring elsewhere. In Baltimore, during the late 1780's, after both races had worked side by side in creating two interracial Methodist churches, discriminatory practices evolved. One group of Negroes agreed to become the "African Branch" within the parent body, and with financial support from the whites, opened the Sharp Street Church in 1792. For many years whites continued to pay some of the bills and supply a minister, who gave inadequate attention to the needs of the congregation. Another group of Negro Methodists in Baltimore seceded completely, for a while meeting in each other's homes for religious services. In the early 1800's they engaged Daniel Coker, a former slave, as their pastor. Finally, in 1816, representatives of the various African Methodist churches in Pennsylvania, New Jersey, Delaware, and Maryland met in Philadelphia to form a national body. Coker was first elected bishop, but before he could be consecrated, charges of scandalous behavior were circulated and Coker withdrew in favor of Richard Allen.

If there were schisms and rivalries within the AME Church from its very beginning, there were other differences that prevented all of the Negro Methodists from joining under one roof. Some Methodists, like the members of the Sharp Street congregation in Baltimore, preferred to form separate congregations within the predominantly white denomination. Meanwhile, contemporary with the developments in Philadelphia and Baltimore, a comparable evolution was taking place in New York, leading to the organization of the AME Zion Church in 1821. Throughout the ante-bellum period the New Yorkers and Philadelphians were rivals for leadership of the free Negro community, and this competition was apparently at the root of the failure to form a united denomination.

Negro Baptists also established their own churches. The two earliest recorded instances were in Georgia and Virginia during the Revolutionary War. Then, between 1805 and 1809, separate Negro Baptist churches appeared in Boston, New York, and Philadelphia. In Philadelphia Negroes were disturbed because the predominantly white church had employed a succession of Southern ministers who encouraged the congregation to regard the slavery issue as a political question outside the concerns of the church. The Negro Baptists were also sensitive to the more frequent manifestations of race prejudice that accompanied the growth of the city's nonwhite population through migration from the South. In Boston the dissatisfaction of Negro Baptists led Rev. Thomas Paul, a recently ordained clergyman, to establish a congregation as a gesture to "independence and a more congenial atmosphere." He also aided a group of New Yorkers whose reasons for favoring separation included the fact that "the col-

ored Methodists and Episcopalians had made similar proposi-
tions to their respective churches with success. . . ." For a few
months Paul went to New York and filled the pulpit of what later
became known as the Abyssinian Baptist Church. Other Baptist
congregations followed in Northern and border cities.

Unlike the Methodists, the separate Negro Baptist Churches
for years remained tied to the white Baptist conventions. The first
independent Negro Baptist conferences were the Providence Baptist Association in Ohio, formed in 1836, and the Wood River
Baptist Association in Illinois, formed in 1838. Not until 1853
was a larger regional body, the Western Colored Baptist Convention, created, and not until the 1890's was a truly national
Baptist organization of Negroes formed.

Both the Negro Methodists and the Negro Baptists encountered considerable difficulty in pursuing their work in the South.
Southern fears that gatherings of Negroes were hatching places
for rebellion sharply limited the work of the Negro denominations. Travel restrictions imposed on free Negroes prevented
several clergymen from the Lower South from attending the
founding meeting of the AME Church, and the AME Zion
Church did not establish itself in the South until 1864. The most
noted AME congregation in the South was that organized in
Charleston, South Carolina, by Rev. Morris Brown. Despite
police efforts to discourage the attendance of free Negroes and
slaves, membership tripled in the next five years, but the hysteria
surrounding the Denmark Vesey Conspiracy in 1822 forced the
closing of the church and Brown's flight from Charleston. From
then on, the AME denomination was suppressed in most of the
South.

Southern white Baptist ministers and board members closely
supervised the work of the colored churches and the "colored
branches" of white congregations. After the Nat Turner Insurrection of 1831, laws were enacted to circumscribe the activities of
Negro preachers and guarantee white domination of all churches.
The Negro ministry in North Carolina was completely silenced.
During 1832–33 Virginia and Alabama forbade Negroes to
preach except in the presence of trustworthy whites. After 1834
Georgia required Negro preachers to secure a certificate from
ordained white ministers as a first step in applying for a license.

Negro Baptist congregations in the state continued at the sufferance of whites and largely became wards of the white churches. In many Southern communities curfews prevented Negro congregations from meeting in the late hours of the evening. Clergymen who accommodated themselves to these restrictions, however, managed to attract large congregations. In Mobile, when a trusted Negro preacher was found, the white elders of the First Baptist Church allowed Negroes to leave the congregation and form the African Baptist Church. In a number of other communities, whites were installed as the spiritual leaders of the African Baptist churches. Apparently only in the Upper South—in parts of Maryland, Virginia, and the District of Columbia—did some Negro Baptist congregations obtain the right to direct their own affairs.

Among the Presbyterians and Episcopalians, separate Negro congregations emerged but retained affiliation with the parent bodies. The Presbyterian officials sought to avoid conflicts in ecclesiastical government by providing that when presbyteries and synods were held, delegates from Negro churches should receive equal rights and privileges. In contrast, the Episcopalians maintained the attitude of a colonial power dealing with natives. In Pennsylvania diocesan conferences Negro churches were completely denied representation. In 1852 Philadelphia's Church of the Crucifixion, a Negro congregation with white vestry and clergyman, asked permission to send white delegates to the Episcopal Convention. Since this request might have given Negroes some slight indirect influence, it was denied. In the New York Episcopal diocese, only delegations from white congregations participated in church government until shortly before the Civil War. Furthermore, Bishop Benjamin T. Onderdonk refused to admit Negroes as regular students in the General Theological Seminary. In 1834 Onderdonk forced Peter Williams, a Negro clergyman in the diocese, to resign his office in the newly formed American Anti-Slavery Society. The bishop suggested that affiliation with abolitionists was un-Christian. Despite these discriminatory practices, the Negro upper class of New York and Pennsylvania tended to affiliate with the Episcopal Church, and, in fact, identified closely with the aristocratic white Federalist and Episcopal elite, which often took a paternalistic interest in Negro affairs. For example, when Bishop Onderdonk barred Alexander Crummell from the seminary, William Jay arranged for the young Negro to secure his training in Boston and England.

Articulate Negroes protested against church discrimination in many ways. Sarah Douglass, a Philadelphia teacher, simply ceased going to Quaker meetings, although her mother regularly attended, sitting alone on "a whole long bench." Frederick Douglass abruptly walked out of a New England Methodist Church because Negroes were denied participation in a communion service until all the white communicants had received bread and wine. In 1848 Douglass suggested another method of dramatizing grievances. He urged Negroes to enter white churches, take the first available seats, and remain limp while white deacons and clergymen pulled them to the street. The New York *Colored American* in 1837 told readers to combat discrimination by conducting a "stand in": "Stand in the aisles, and rather worship God upon your feet, than become a party to your own degradation. You must shame your oppressors, and wear out prejudice by this holy policy."

The most characteristic form of Negro protest, however, was the withdrawal from white churches and the formation of their own congregations. Only a handful of Negroes consistently opposed this kind of action. One of them was Frederick Douglass. He solemnly warned Negroes that although their segregated churches were created because of exclusionary practices of whites, "complexional distinctions" in houses of worship or in other social institutions were wrong and self-defeating. The race church, said Douglass, benefited Negro-haters by compounding misunderstandings between blacks and whites and therefore making racial equality harder to attain.

Like the churches, the mutual benefit societies, whatever their possible origins in slavery and ultimately in Africa, helped the free Negroes adjust to a hostile urban environment. Occupying marginal jobs, many Negro families lacked the financial resources to cope with periodic crises such as serious illness and death. In the late eighteenth century leaders urged Negroes to avoid reliance on charity and establish beneficial societies. They believed that the mutual aid organizations would encourage thrift, industry, and morality, provide a method for upward mobility, and prove to whites that Negroes were self-respecting citizens deserving equal treatment before the law. These societies also offered members companionship, recreation, recognition, and prestige, which to some degree compensated for the racial proscriptions facing them. The most extensive organizational development appeared in the North, at least partly because Negroes there were allowed greater freedom of movement.

The earliest recorded Negro mutual aid organization was the Free African Society formed at Philadelphia by Absolom Jones and Richard Allen in 1787. Through the Society, members pooled their resources to "support one another in sickness, and for the benefit of their widows and fatherless children." Shortly after its founding, the leaders persuaded influential whites like Dr. Benjamin Rush, a pioneer antislavery leader in Pennsylvania, to support an application for land in potter's field for use as a Negro cemetery. Survivors of members received financial aid, and the Free African Society educated children not admitted to a free school. Some attempts were also made to find apprenticeships for orphans. Members were required to pay one shilling monthly for distribution to the needy, "provided this necessity is not brought on them by their own imprudence." This middle-class, moralistic tone pervaded other organizational rules, such as one denying membership to those unwilling to lead "an orderly and sober life." Free African societies soon spread to Newport and Boston.

Benevolent societies multiplied all over the North. By the 1830's in Philadelphia alone there were one hundred organizations averaging about seventy-five members each. Many of course were connected with churches, and some operated on an occupational basis, such as the Coachman's Benevolent and the Humane Mechanics societies. The Philadelphia Library Company of Colored Persons maintained a well-furnished room with several hundred volumes and scheduled public debates on moral as well as literary topics. The Phoenix Society of New York City, whose president was Bishop Christopher Rush, one of the founders of the AME Zion Church, established a library and school for Negroes and sought to encourage the study of morality, literature, and mechanic arts.

In the South Negroes also formed mutual aid associations, although their activities were limited after white fears of slave insurrections resulted in laws curtailing the assembling of Negroes. In 1790 a group of light-skinned Charlestonians established the Brown Fellowship Society, specifically providing that black men were not eligible. The following year the Free Dark Men of Color organized their own association, which evidently flourished until after the 1820's when its activities were curtailed by the fear of slave insurrections. The Brown Fellowship Society, however, continued to function because of the connections its artisan members maintained with influential whites, and because of the fact that the organization's bylaws prohibited discussions at meetings of such controversial issues as slavery. Baltimore was the Southern city with the largest number of benevolent societies. By 1835 there were more than thirty, with membership rolls ranging from 35 to 150. As in other communities, several associations were organized by trades, such as calkers, coachmen, and mechanics, with a number maintaining savings accounts in local banks. Many other communities had similar mutual benefit and burial societies, which frequently had to operate clandestinely. Even in Washington, in 1855, police arrested twenty-four "genteel coloured men" during a meeting of one of these societies. When apprehended, they had in their possession a Bible, two volumes on morality, the constitution of their benevolent organization, and a document indicating their interest in buying the freedom of a female slave. The police judge ordered one prisoner, a slave, to be whipped, four free Negroes to be sent to jail, and the others to be fined.

More elaborate were the secret fraternal orders. With their rituals, ceremonies, and regalia, they gave members even greater prestige and also performed some economic functions of mutual aid. The Masons and Odd Fellows were the two oldest Negro orders; both obtained their charters from England because of exclusion from white American orders. The founder of Negro Masonry was Prince Hall, a soapmaker and a part-time Methodist preacher and active leader in the Free African Society of Boston. In 1775 Hall and other Negroes had been initiated into a military Masonic lodge by British soldiers on duty at Boston. Hall sought to establish a Negro lodge but was rebuffed by the white American Masons. Applying for a warrant from England, which he received in 1787, he formed an African Lodge in Boston and was instrumental in bringing Negro Masonry to Philadelphia a decade later, where the organizers were Absolom Jones, Richard Allen, and James Forten, the wealthy sailmaker.

About the same time a lodge was also founded in Providence, Rhode Island. The organization spread rapidly throughout the North and reached California with the Gold Rush in 1849. Restrictive legislation made it more difficult for the Masons to organize in the South. Nevertheless, as early as 1825 lodges thrived in Baltimore and in the District of Columbia. The only other Southern cities in which the Masons established a foothold were Louisville and New Orleans, where lodges were organized at mid-century.

The Negro Odd Fellows formed their first lodge in the United States in 1843, shortly after whites rejected the application of the Philomathean Institute of New York and the Philadelphia Library Company and Debating Society. Peter Ogden, a ship steward who already held an Odd Fellows membership card from Liverpool, obtained British authorization to found the Philomathean Lodge in New York. The Negro Odd Fellows also organized in neighboring states, though their most flourishing period did not come until the first part of the twentieth century.

Between the founding of the Odd Fellows and the start of the Civil War, a number of other national, quasi-religious fraternal orders came into being, but most of them had only limited influence until after the Civil War. As in the case of the smaller mutual benefit societies, Baltimore spawned a number of these organizations, including the Galilean Fishermen, the Nazarites, the Samaritans, and the Seven Wise Men.

While the independent churches and the mutual benefit societies contributed to the separation of the races, they were also refuges from white supremacy. While they functioned in part as an accommodation to the realities of American race prejudice and discrimination, they were also an assertion of Negro independence and racial self-respect. To Negroes whose ambitions were crushed by caste, they offered opportunities for self-expression and leadership development. Prominent figures in the churches and fraternal societies were from the beginning ardent advocates of equal rights and abolition. In the generation before the Civil War they provided leadership both in the separate Negro Convention Movement and in the interracial abolitionist societies. Prior to the rise of militant antislavery they had also made a significant contribution to Negro education.

4

The history of Negro education before the Civil War can be divided into three rather distinct, though overlapping, stages: 1) white philanthropy, 2) Negro self-help, and 3) public support. With a few conspicuous exceptions, the general pattern was always a segregated one. During the eighteenth century, religious organizations such as the Episcopal Society for the Propagation of the Gospel, which worked in both North and South, and the Society of Friends had undertaken rudimentary education of slaves and free Negroes to enable them to read the Bible. Some antislavery societies formed during the Revolutionary era also offered free Negroes an opportunity for elementary education. The New York Manumission Society in 1787 opened the African Free School, which was so successful that six additional ones were added in the city by 1834. Ultimately they became part of the public school system.

Under the auspices of the Negro churches and mutual benefit societies emerging at the end of the eighteenth century, free Negroes maintained their own schools. Even where white philanthropic support was solicited, the initiative came from Negroes themselves. In Newport, Rhode Island, a white Episcopal rector established a school for Negroes in 1763. In 1807, eight years after the school had closed, the leaders of the Negro community reopened it through their newly organized African Benevolent Society. The institution was operated with varying degrees of success until the city took over. At Boston Prince Hall led a group of Negroes in 1787 in petitioning the Massachusetts General Court for a school, since Negroes "receive no benefit from the free schools." According to some authorities, a few Negro children did attend the public schools with whites at the end of the eighteenth century but most withdrew because of ridicule and mistreatment. In 1798 some Negro parents, supported by white friends, opened a private school in Prince Hall's home. Seven years later the institution moved to the African Meeting House. Not until 1820, however, was a Negro public school opened, and within a short time Negroes lost their right to use the white schools. Early in the nineteenth century several

Philadelphia Negro ministers organized schools in their churches, and the Bethel AME Church founded the Society of Free People of Color for Promoting the Instruction and School Education of Children of African Descent. In 1812 the New York Society of Free People of Color established a school for orphans.

In the South during the ante-bellum period, Negro education never went beyond the second stage. By the beginning of the nineteenth century a substantial number of free Negroes, having achieved a degree of economic security as mechanics and tradesmen, were financially underwriting their own schools. In the Deep South the Brown Fellowship Society of Charleston as early as 1790 provided educational facilities as part of its mutual welfare program. Two decades later the Minor Society was organized to educate indigent and orphaned children. In 1829 one of the youth trained by the Minor Society, Daniel Alexander Payne, opened a school of his own for Negro children. In New Orleans the Roman Catholic Church educated some Negroes, but that city's prosperous *gens de couleur* provided financial support for several schools of their own, sent their older children to France for instruction, and in 1840 established the Ecole des Orphelins Indigents for the education of lower-class youth. As the Southern race system grew harsher in the course of the nineteenth century, the education of free Negroes was restricted but never completely eliminated. In 1823 Mississippi forbade groups of Negroes larger than five to study together. In Charleston, beginning in 1834, it became legally mandatory that a white person attend each class meeting. Though Payne closed his school and moved to the North, where he became a distinguished AME bishop, some of the free Negro schools continued. In many other parts of the South private classes were sometimes held, even by philanthropically minded whites, often in violation of state or city regulations.

In the Border States there was no such interference by public authorities, but neither did they actively assist Negro schooling. The first two schools that Negroes established in Baltimore were in existence by the beginning of the nineteenth century. One was under the auspices of the all-Negro Sharp Street Methodist Church and the other was conducted by Daniel Coker, the pioneer AME minister. Other Negro churches were soon operating educational institutions, and during the 1820's even adults received instruction at night in various subjects including Latin and French. Some white philanthropists also contributed time, money, and teachers to supplement these efforts. The first school for Negroes in Washington was formed in 1807 by three illiterate colored men, two of whom worked in the Navy Yard. They constructed a small frame schoolhouse and employed a white teacher. Beginning with the educational institution opened in 1818 by the Resolute Beneficial Society, Washington's Negroes were not without at least one well-administered school, and in their efforts they obtained the co-operation of certain dedicated whites as well. Not until 1862 did the municipal authorities undertake to create schools for Negroes.

In the North free public education for all white youth was the rule by the 1830's, but the fruits of Horace Mann's famous crusade for the common school left Negroes pretty much out of the picture. In Ohio, Michigan, Wisconsin, and Iowa Negroes received no public school funds until the middle of the nineteenth century, and in Illinois and Indiana not until the eve of the Civil War. Even where schooling was provided for Negroes, it was generally separate and unequal. Segregation was simply the custom in most places, but in some states it was legislated. A New York statute specifically gave school boards the option of establishing segregated institutions. Pennsylvania and Ohio required separate schools wherever the number of Negro pupils exceeded twenty. Where Negroes attended integrated schools they usually found themselves placed in special seats and subjected to other indignities. Segregated institutions ordinarily operated on as skimpy a budget as possible. An 1859 New York *Tribune* editorial noted that "the school houses for the whites are in situations where the price of rents is high, and on the buildings themselves no expenditure is spared to make them commodious and elegant. . . . The schools for the blacks, on the contrary, are nearly all, if not all, old buildings, generally in filthy and degraded neighborhoods, dark, damp, small, and cheerless, safe neither for the morals nor the health of those who are compelled to go to them, if they go anywhere, and calculated rather to repel than to attract them." In city after city, Rochester, Philadelphia, Hartford, and New Haven, the same gloomy picture was evident—overcrowding and limited supplies and equipment.

The tactics which Northern Negroes employed in dealing with public school discrimination in the generation before the Civil War varied with the conditions in local communities. During the years in which Illinois and Ohio refused to provide for colored youth the educational opportunities offered to white children, Negroes raised money among themselves and opened schools that supplemented those financed by the white abolitionists. At the same time Negro state conventions appealed to the legislatures to provide public education for members of the race. In certain cities, like Rochester and Hartford, where Negro children were insulted in the mixed public schools, colored citizens successfully appealed for separate schools during the 1830's. Thus a segregated school system might be inaugurated by the white authorities, or might be requested by Negroes because it would be preferable to no schools at all or to a mixed system where their children were mistreated. In either case, once a separate system had been introduced, Negroes petitioned for greater financial support. Their complaints sometimes led to school improvements. For example, a memorial from Hartford Negroes in 1846 resulted in the erection of a new building. New York Negroes, led by abolitionist Charles B. Ray, formed a Society for the Promotion of Education Among Colored Citizens, which in 1857 submitted a detailed analysis of the "caste" schools in the community. Subsequently one institution was renovated and another constructed to replace a school that had been torn down.

Some thus worked to secure adequate training for their children, but accepted separate schools as a necessary evil. Others insisted on a direct, frontal attack on the system of segregation. Negro newspapers and conventions constantly agitated on the issue, and numerous petitions were sent to the public authorities appealing for an end to the discrimination. Robert Purvis, of Philadelphia, in 1853, refused to pay the school tax and publicly announced that school segregation violated "my rights as a citizen, and my feelings as a man." During the 1850's Frederick Douglass led a successful attack against the separate school system in Rochester.

Probably the most notable desegregation campaign occurred in Boston during the 1840's and 1850's. By then, integrated schools existed in many Massachusetts communities, among them Cambridge, New Bedford, Worcester, and Lowell. In the early 1840's Negro and white abolitionists of Boston sent many petitions to the Primary School Committee, but these were dismissed on the grounds that neither law nor custom could efface inherent distinctions between Negro and white children. In 1849 Benjamin Roberts sued the Committee for excluding his daughter from the school in her neighborhood and compelling her to pass five white institutions on her way to the Negro school. Roberts, who was represented by the white lawyer Charles Sumner and the Negro lawyer Robert Morris, lost in the courts. The state supreme court upheld the legality of segregation, justifying it with the first recorded use of the separate-but-equal doctrine. Hundreds of Negroes and whites petitioned the Massachusetts legislature, and in 1855 it enacted a law requiring public schools to admit students without regard to color. Elsewhere, in spite of all efforts, when the Civil War began, segregation prevailed for the overwhelming majority of Negroes attending public schools. Northern white private schools which admitted Negroes experienced opposition—even mob violence—from local citizens.

At the college level some private institutions accepted Negroes, and the first two to receive their A.B. degrees graduated from Amherst and Bowdoin colleges in 1826. Two all-Negro collegiate institutions were developed during the 1850's: in 1854 Presbyterians organized Ashmun Institute in Pennsylvania, later known as Lincoln University, in order to train Negroes for missionary work in Africa; in 1855 the Methodist Episcopal Church, North, founded Wilberforce University in Ohio, transferring it in 1862 to the AME Church.

5

Because of white prejudice and discrimination the overwhelming majority of free Negroes were unskilled laborers. Negro entrepreneurs found it difficult to obtain capital, since lending institutions considered them poor risks. White businessmen were reluctant to employ Negroes in skilled or white-collar work. Where employers were willing to hire a Negro, white workers often refused to work with him. The Negro skilled artisan faced greater obstacles in the North than in the South. The New York Manumission Society complained that many students leaving the

African Free School in the 1820's were idle because they could neither enter trades nor find jobs, and that the educated young Negroes often had no alternative except to become sailors, cooks, waiters, coachmen, servants, and laborers. After Frederick Douglass fled from Maryland to New Bedford, Massachusetts, in 1838, a sympathetic shipowner hired him as a calker, the trade he had learned as a slave in Baltimore. When the other calkers would not accept Douglass, he was forced into common labor and took a succession of jobs sawing wood, digging cellars, collecting rubbish, and loading ships.

Nevertheless, in the face of all these obstacles a minority made a comfortable living and a few founded modest fortunes. The successful free Negro entrepreneurs catered principally to well-to-do whites and were concentrated in the service trades. There were many Negro barbers, hackmen, draymen, and owners of livery stables. Others were blacksmiths, grocers, fashionable tailors, restaurateurs and caterers, proprietors of coal and lumber yards, and occasionally hotel owners. Negroes were also engaged in the shoemaking and building trades in a number of cities, especially in the South. Baltimore had many slave and free Negro ship calkers. In Philadelphia sizable numbers of Negroes were carpenters, tailors and dressmakers, brickmakers, shoemakers and bootmakers, and cabinetmakers. A handful of colored men created and dominated the fashionable catering business in the city until the end of the nineteenth century, making Philadelphia catering famous over the country. At the end of the eighteenth century James Derham was a highly respected physician, friend of the distinguished Dr. Benjamin Rush. James Forten, one of the city's principal sailmakers, employed over forty white and black workers, and by the 1830's had acquired a fortune of $100,000. William Still, the Underground Railroad leader, was the proprietor of a successful coal and lumber yard. In Charleston, as in certain other Southern cities, Negroes monopolized barbering, practically controlled the building trades, and were prominent among the shoemakers and butchers. The more outstanding carpenters or contractors employed both white men and slaves. For a number of years, the leading hotel proprietor was a free Negro named Jehu Jones. In 1850 New Orleans, with its Negro architect, five jewelers, four physicians, eleven music teachers, and fifty-two merchants, exhibited an even greater occupational diversity. Most of the really wealthy Negro artisans or retail merchants invested their money in real estate. George Thomas Downing, the prominent caterer of New York and Newport, and Thomy Lafon, the New Orleans merchant, each acquired several hundred thousand dollars in this manner.

In the course of the nineteenth century the position of the Negro artisan-entrepreneur deteriorated. As the white working class grew in numbers in the Southern cities, its members made determined efforts to exclude Negroes from the better-paying occupations. Savannah ordinances of 1822 and 1831 barred both slave and free Negroes from most of the skilled trades. In 1845 Georgia made it a misdemeanor for a Negro mechanic to make a contract for the repair or construction of buildings. By the 1840's the colored draymen had largely disappeared from New Orleans. Yet even after the Civil War the South provided more opportunity than the North for the Negro entrepreneur.

In the Northern states in fact the arrival of nearly 5,000,000 immigrants in the generation prior to the Civil War posed an alarming threat to the Negroes' already meager economic opportunities. By the early 1850's Douglass observed, "Every hour sees the black man elbowed out of employment by some newly arrived emigrant whose hunger and whose color are thought to give him a better title to the place." Most of the newcomers who settled in the cities came from Ireland. Possessing no marketable skills, they became the Negroes' implacable competitors for the heavy laboring and menial jobs. The Irish, who experienced discrimination from other white Americans, vented their aggression upon the "Nagurs," attacking them around docks, railyards, and coal mines. Gradually many Negroes were displaced as laborers in these areas and in other occupations, such as hod-carriers, waiters, barbers, even porters and bootblacks. Negro women, who could count on a degree of economic security even when their husbands could not, began losing positions as maids, cooks, and washerwomen. On the waterfront, economic competition and hostility between the two groups was exacerbated when employers, playing one race against the other, hired Negro workmen as strikebreakers. In New York City this policy produced among the predominantly Irish longshoremen an intense animosity that came to a violent climax in the bloody race riots of 1863.

6

There was enough economic differentiation among the urban Negroes to provide the basis for a social class system. However, it should be pointed out that because of the limited occupational opportunities open to Negroes and the high proportion of them in the most menial job categories, their criteria for social class membership diverged sharply from those of whites. Among the slaves in the Southern cities there were distinctions based upon color, occupation, and the prominence of one's master. Among free Negroes the chronically unemployed unskilled laborers formed the lowest class. Those who had regular employment, especially if the job involved a degree of skill, formed a middle class. In the North this group included even domestic servants. Such middle-class persons were likely to be regular churchgoers and members of the mutual benefit societies. The upper stratum included independent artisans and businessmen. While the occupational distribution among elite Negroes varied from city to city, broadly speaking it can be said that at the top were the successful entrepreneurs, particularly the barbers, restaurateurs, caterers, tailors, and contractors patronized by fashionable whites; the house servants of the most socially prominent white families in Northern cities; and the handful of well-educated professional people in law, teaching, medicine, and the ministry. In the South it included a tiny slave-owning Negro aristocracy.

Occupation and wealth were the most important criteria of class affiliation. There were also more subtle distinctions based on skin color, education, church membership, and family background. A long history of free ancestry was treasured, especially if one's forebears included distinguished white people. The middle and upper classes stressed home ownership, thrift and hard work, and moral respectability. The upper-class Negroes dressed conservatively, practiced an elaborate and formal etiquette, cultivated the arts, and, in short, led lives characterized by gentility and refinement. From this elite came the majority of the race's important protest leaders.

1) adaptation of thought
social accommodation and nationalism
2) protest and accommodation
3) assimilation

7

The racial ideologies of the free Negroes—both before and since the Civil War—can be analyzed from various points of view. One can examine how the Negroes adapted to their needs various elements in American social thought, such as belief in political democracy, advocacy of thrift and industry, and faith in the efficacy of education. One can describe how in some situations and in certain periods Negroes have protested against their status, while in others they were compelled to accommodate to it. Finally, one can describe Negro social thought as ranging along a continuum of ideologies from assimilation to nationalism.

At one end of this continuum have been the advocates of complete biological amalgamation and cultural assimilation with members of the dominant society, and the complete disappearance of Negroes as a racial group. At the other end have been those who advocated complete withdrawal from American society and the creation of independent Negro states. Between these two extremes have been a great variety of philosophies recognizing the Negro as an American citizen, yet emphasizing his distinctiveness as an ethnic group. This intermediate category has included the advocacy of attaining constitutional rights through self-help and racial solidarity, an insistence upon racial equality combined with preference for separate clubs and churches, and even espousal of the creation of all-Negro communities within the United States. This ethnic dualism, this ambivalence, which has been produced by the contradiction between the values of American democracy and the facts of race discrimination, was best articulated by W. E. B. Du Bois. In an essay written early in this century, he said: "One ever feels his two-ness,—an American, a Negro; two souls, two thoughts, two unreconciled strivings; two warring ideals in one dark body, whose dogged strength alone keeps it from being torn asunder. . . . He simply wishes to make it possible for a man to be both a Negro and an American, without being cursed and spit upon by his fellows, without having the doors of Opportunity closed roughly in his face."

In no case have Negroes, even those completely favoring integration and assimilation, been able to forget their connection with an oppressed group. From this very alienation came the desire for separate institutions operated without white interference, such as the church and the mutual benefit society. The gap between ideal and practice in American society meant that Negroes not only wanted to be a part of that society, but that they also found it desirable to develop their own group life within it. Thus, ironically, the establishment of the separate Negro church and fraternal organization was both a form of protest against American racism and yet an accommodation to it.

It should be emphasized that the whole subject of the Negro's response to discrimination and his search for freedom and human dignity is a highly complex one, not easily condensed into a few pages. For one thing the diverse ideologies delineated above have been combined in a bewildering variety of ways. Both protest and accommodating leaders have advocated thrift, industry, and economic accumulation. Usually these values have been associated with the idea of Negroes gaining acceptance in American society by assimilating American middle-class ways. These economic ideas have also been combined with the advocacy of race pride and race solidarity to stimulate Negro support of Negro business and, by thus achieving material success, to gain acceptance in American society. Finally, certain highly nationalist movements, like the modern Black Muslims, have combined the Puritan ethic with complete rejection of American white society.

Negro thinking has varied under the impact of changing conditions. Gunnar Myrdal described the situation perceptively. Noting that to a large degree Negroes are "denied identification with the nation or with national groups," he observed:

to them social speculation, therefore, moves in a sphere of unreality and futility. Instead of organized popular theories or ideas, the observer finds in the Negro world, for the most part, only a *fluid and amorphous mass of all sorts of embryos of thoughts. Negroes seem to be held in a state of eternal preparedness for a great number of contradictory opinions*—ready to accept one type or another depending on how they are driven by pressures or where they see an opportunity. Under such circumstances, the masses of American Negroes might, for example, rally around a violently anti-American, anti-Western, anti-White, black chauvinism of the Garvey type, centered around the idea of Africa as the mother country. But they might just as likely, if only a slight change of stimulus is provided, join in an all-out effort to fight for their native country . . . for the Western Civilization to which they

belong, and for the tenets of democracy in the entire world. . . .
Or they might develop a passive cynicism toward it all.

Keeping the foregoing observations in mind, we shall now turn
to an examination of the changing programs proposed by Northern Negro leaders to achieve freedom for themselves and for the
slaves. Having previously indicated the nature of Negro protest
against specific kinds of discrimination, in the following pages we
will focus primarily on the Negro Convention Movement and on
Negro participation in the antislavery movement.

8

As already noted, the deteriorating status of free Negroes in
the North following the adoption of the Constitution was a prime
factor in the formation of separate community institutions. The
leaders of these organizations, despite their alienation from
American society, retained their faith that in God's plan the
slaves would be freed and Negroes accorded equal rights in
America. Along with the more successful businessmen, they led
the early Negro agitation against both slavery in the South and
discrimination at home. On behalf of the bondsmen Northern
Negroes held meetings and passed resolutions, listened to spirited
orations commemorating the legal closing of the slave trade in
the United States in 1808, and sent respectfully worded petitions
to Congress. There was something ritualistic about much of this
activity. Whites were aware of but little of it, and most of what
they perceived they ignored. Quite naturally, therefore, the
Negro leaders tended to concern themselves mostly with something they could hope to accomplish more readily: the elevation
of the Northern free people of color.

A very few exhibited an even greater degree of estrangement
than had the creators of the separate community institutions,
and, giving up all hope of a decent future in this country,
advocated colonization or emigration to Africa. As early as 1789
the Free African Society of Newport went on record as favoring a
return to Africa. In 1815 the prosperous New England Negro
shipowner, Paul Cuffe, took thirty-eight free Negroes to Sierra
Leone at his own expense. Cuffe, while interested primarily in
Christianizing the Africans and destroying the slave trade, also
believed that emigration would relieve the oppression of Ameri-

can Negroes. His case is of particular interest because during the Revolutionary era he had been an ardent advocate of protest. But the subsequent erosion of the free Negroes' status had disillusioned him.

Actually, interest in colonization was much less common among Negroes than among white antislavery advocates. The antislavery movement had flourished in the Border States after the passage of emancipation laws in the North. Colonization was espoused both by humanitarians who thought that free Negroes would fare better in a land of their own and by Southern slaveholders who considered the free Negroes a dangerous element. In December, 1816, a group of prominent Americans, including Henry Clay, then speaker of the House of Representatives, established the American Colonization Society. While claiming to be motivated by humanitarianism, the colonizationists not only refused to oppose racist laws and customs, but many actually supported and justified such barriers in order to make the condition of the free Negroes so humiliating and debasing that, by comparison, the prospect of being transported to Africa would seem inviting. Although colonizationists stated that the establishment of an African "homeland" would ultimately encourage slaveholders to liberate their slaves in the United States, actually some founders of the Society suggested that the exodus of free Negroes would strengthen the institution of slavery. Nevertheless, until after 1830 most of the white antislavery advocates coupled their interest in the slave with support for colonization as a solution of the American race problem.

Before the Colonization Society was launched, those responsible for initiating it had consulted with Paul Cuffe, and there were other Negroes who subscribed to its program. This was especially true in Maryland, where the largest and wealthiest of state colonization societies existed. Daniel Coker of Baltimore sailed for the Society with about ninety free Negroes in 1820. As a Negro colonization convention in Baltimore in 1826 stated, since Negroes were strangers in the United States and could never enjoy full rights there, emigration to Africa was the only way to obtain freedom.

In the main, free Negroes were suspicious of the motives of the American Colonization Society and strongly opposed it. Within a few weeks after the formation of the organization, Negro leaders in Philadelphia—among them Bishop Richard Allen, Rev. Absolom Jones, and James Forten—drew a large crowd to the Bethel Church for a vigorous protest against the colonizationists. The Philadelphia Negroes reminded America that in past wars, colored people had "ceased to remember their wrongs and rallied around the standard of their country. . . . Whereas our ancestors (not of choice) were the first successful cultivators of the wilds of America, we their descendants feel ourselves entitled to participate in the blessings of her luxuriant soil, which their blood and sweat manured; and that any measure or system of measures, having a tendency to banish us from her bosom, would not only be cruel, but in direct violation of those principles, which have been the boast of this republic. . . ." They declared that their cause could not be divorced from their brothers in bondage—with whom there were ties not only of color but "of suffering and of wrong," making it impossible to "separate ourselves voluntarily from the slave population in this country . . . and we feel that there is more virtue in suffering privations with them . . ."

During the following years, free Negroes in Northern cities sponsored numerous protests against the American Colonization Society. In 1827 a group of New Yorkers founded the first Negro newspaper, *Freedom's Journal,* edited by Samuel Cornish and John Russwurm. The paper attacked the Colonization Society, declaring that the organization's true motives were not to end slavery but to rid the nation of its free Negro population. Cornish soon resigned, and in 1829, after Russwurm joined the colonizationists, *Freedom's Journal* folded. The Boston agent for the paper had been David Walker, a clothing dealer who in 1829 published an incendiary pamphlet, *Walker's Appeal, in Four Articles.* His hatred of slavery and the American Colonization Society brought him to the conclusion that if whites refused to grant emancipation voluntarily, Negroes should break the "infernal chains" by an armed rebellion.

The influence of the Colonization Society and its local branches was shown in extreme form by the Cincinnati riot of 1829. Cincinnati's Negro population had increased substantially since the early 1820's, causing special concern among the unskilled whites, who demanded that the new arrivals be expelled. This anti-Negro hostility acquired respectability through the activities of the Cincinnati Colonization Society, which, since its founding in 1826, had attracted the city's most prominent citizens. These influential leaders encouraged local newspapers and ministers to agitate against the community's free Negroes, and the Society's propaganda provided justification for the campaign to drive Negroes from the city. During the summer of 1829, Cincinnati's officials attempted to enforce the Ohio Black Laws, which required Negroes to post $500 bonds guaranteeing "good behavior." While ghetto leaders petitioned for a legislative reprieve, white mobs attacked. More than half the Negro population fled to Canada and other parts of the United States.

The Cincinnati riot dramatized, as had no previous single event, the exposed and defenseless position of the free Negro in American society. Fearing that it was the precursor of similar outbursts elsewhere, Negro leaders called a conference for September, 1830, in Philadelphia, the first effort within the race to effect unified action on a national scale. Bishop Allen presided over this convention of Negro leaders, which was attended by representatives from Rhode Island, Connecticut, New York, Pennsylvania, Delaware, Maryland, and Virginia. Repudiating the principles of the American Colonization Society, they urged those Negroes unable to endure further oppression in the United States to consider settlement only in Canada.

To the Negro delegates at the Philadelphia conclave, it had been a source of frustration that many sincere whites in the antislavery movement supported the Colonization Society. Among these men were Gerrit Smith, one of New York State's wealthiest landowners; Arthur and Lewis Tappan, prominent New York merchants; and Benjamin Lundy, a coeditor of the *Genius of Universal Emancipation*. This antislavery newspaper had recently suspended publication because of the outspokenness of its other editor, William Lloyd Garrison. The year before the 1830 Negro convention several Baltimore Negroes had been instrumental in converting Garrison from his former sympathy with colonization. Among them was William Watkins, "A Colored Baltimorean," who had ridiculed the organization in a letter published in the *Genius* in 1828. He and the other Negroes failed to modify Lundy's attitude toward colonization projects, but in 1829 when Garrison arrived in Baltimore they held extended talks with him and brought him around to their point of view. In a biography of Garrison his children recalled: "Garrison was slow to discover [the society's] real animus. . . . Some of his colored friends in Baltimore were the first to point out to him its dangerous character and tendency, and its purpose to strengthen slavery by expelling the free people of color."

Garrison also read *Walker's Appeal* with its condemnation of colonizationists, and although considering the call for a slave rebellion "injudicious," he found the pamphlet "warranted by the creed of an independent people." Impressed by the abilities of men like Walker and Watkins, Garrison became furious with the Colonization Society for seeking to convince the nation that Negroes were too degenerate to profit from American civilization. Subsequently, Negro antislavery men in Philadelphia, such as James Forten and his son-in-law, Robert Purvis, impressed him with their refinement, their fervent belief in emancipation, and their hatred of colonization. He addressed the second national Negro convention (1831) in Philadelphia, and the following year published *Thoughts on African Colonization,* containing a copious selection of "Resolutions, Addresses and Remonstrances of the Free People of Color," demonstrating all too clearly the long-time opposition to the Society from the race it was ostensibly aiding.

Before long, other influential whites such as the Tappans and Gerrit Smith also renounced the organization. For helping to enlist these white allies, the Negro leaders gratefully acknowledged their debt to Garrison, but on occasion they reminded whites that, as Rev. Charles Gardner, a Philadelphia Presbyterian minister, said at the 1837 convention of the American Anti-Slavery Society, free people of color had held numerous meetings opposing the American Colonization Society when Garrison was still a schoolboy.

9

The Negro Convention Movement, which had begun in 1830, continued to function until the end of the century, but its most important work was done during the ante-bellum period and Reconstruction. National conventions were held annually from 1830 to 1835; subsequently, they were held irregularly as the occasion seemed to warrant. No permanent organization was effected. Usually a concerned group would issue a call to convention, and self-constituted *ad hoc* organizations in other cities would send representatives, if they desired, to the state and national conclaves. The movement was a Northern phenomenon until after the Civil War, for the participation of Southern Negroes in such gatherings would have subjected them to danger at home. The importance of the Convention Movement derives from the fact that it was led and attended by the most distinguished leaders of the race—prominent ministers, physicians, lawyers, and businessmen, and, after the Civil War, politicians. More than any other source, the conventions provide illuminating insight into the thinking of articulate Negroes in regard to the problems facing the race.

The early conventions protested against slavery, and at greater length against the indignities facing the free people of color. Besides condemning race prejudice, the convention leaders sought to convince lower-class Negroes that they could do much to elevate themselves despite adverse circumstances. If Negroes would only try hard enough they would attain "the standard of good society"—temperance, industry, thrift, and learning. The race was urged to stress schooling, good moral character, and economic accumulation. An important part of this economic program was a concern with training Negroes for the skilled trades. For the most part shut out from apprenticeships, free Negroes had little or no opportunity to learn these crafts, and therefore lacked an important means of becoming independent and self-supporting entrepreneurs. Negro leaders therefore eagerly seized upon the proposal, put forth by white abolitionists and reformers, that manual labor schools would be valuable for the lower classes, both white and Negro. Such schools would teach not only a trade with which to earn a living, but, by paying students for their work, would inculcate the habits of thrift and industry. Negro leaders fervently believed that training for the trades would free many members of the race from menial, low-paying jobs. Unfortunately, the attempt sponsored by white and black abolitionists to establish such a manual labor school for Negroes in New Haven failed because of the hostility of local whites.

After 1835 there was no formal National Negro Convention Movement until 1843. In part it had foundered on the rivalry between the New Yorkers and the Philadelphians. And in part its suspension was due to a feeling that there was a serious contradiction involved in advocating integration and equal rights by means of an all-Negro or "caste" convention. After the appearance of the American Anti-Slavery Society in 1833, it seemed to many that in view of substantial white interest, all-Negro conventions were no longer necessary or advisable.

Pennsylvania Negroes like Purvis and William Whipper, a lumber merchant, admonished the race to participate with whites in all antislavery activities. Believing that the Negro Convention Movement was especially self-segregating, they sought to change its direction. In 1834 these Negro Garrisonians formed the American Moral Reform Society for Improving the Condition of Mankind, an organization that dominated the Negro conventions of 1834–35 and ultimately replaced them. The Moral Reformers, who held annual conferences until 1841, had little influence except in Philadelphia and Boston. They sought to turn Negroes away from parochial racial interests to a concern for uplifting "the whole human race, without distinction as to clime, country, or complexion." In their dedication to a broad humanitarianism, Whipper and other members even scorned such terms as "Negro," "colored," and "African," urging their elimination from the names of churches, schools, and other institutions. Whipper and his associates identified themselves as "oppressed Americans" rather than "colored people." They subscribed to the view that as the entire society was regenerated, Negroes would naturally share in the moral elevation along with everyone else.

Opponents of the Moral Reformers pointedly noted that for all the talk about integration, the organization had been unable to attract white members. Much of the criticism came from New York, where many gibes originated in the *Colored American,* a newspaper edited by Samuel Cornish. Commenting on their use of the term "oppressed Americans," he insinuated that the Moral Reformers lacked race pride. He contended that they were being too visionary in talking of solving the nation's problems without special attention to Negroes, the most deprived segment in the population. He insisted that discrimination forced Negroes to rely upon themselves to chart a program that would topple racial barriers. In pressing for a stronger racial consciousness and solidarity, the New York leaders laid the groundwork for the revival of the National Negro Convention Movement in 1843.

One reason for this appeal to racial self-help and solidarity, and for the renewed interest in a national convention, was the growing feeling, especially strong among New Yorkers, that white abolitionists were guilty of race prejudice and of monopolizing power within the antislavery movement.

10

The American Anti-Slavery Society, founded in 1833, had merged two rather distinct antislavery traditions. One was the Garrisonian wing, with its supporters largely in Puritan New England and Quaker Philadelphia. The other was centered mainly in New York State and the Old Northwest; its roots lay in the evangelical revivalism, led by the Presbyterian Charles Grandison Finney, which had swept western New York and the Old Northwest in the 1820's. Its leading apostle was the dynamic antislavery agitator Theodore Dwight Weld; its key financial supporters were the brothers Lewis and Arthur Tappan. In contrast to earlier antislavery advocates, both groups demanded "immediate abolition" of slavery, both were anticolonizationist, and both gave at least rhetorical support to the ideology of racial equality. The two groups, however, split in 1839–40. In part due to the irascible nature of Garrison's personality, the schism also involved important tactical and ideological issues. Garrison insisted on relying only on "moral suasion," and opposed political action because slavery was recognized in the Constitution, which he denounced as a "covenant with death and an agreement with Hell." Garrison also insisted on militantly championing other reform issues, including women's rights. The Weld-Tappan faction was also interested in women's rights but felt that the slavery issue was of such transcendent importance that it should take precedence over everything else. They maintained that if antislavery societies advocated other reforms, they would alienate many potential supporters. They also concluded that propaganda or moral suasion would not of itself overthrow slavery, that political action was necessary. In the split of 1839–40 most Negro leaders went with the Weld-Tappan group into the American and Foreign Anti-Slavery Society. A minority, chiefly in Boston and Philadelphia, remained loyal Garrisonians.

Exactly what role did the Negro abolitionists play in the

organized antislavery movement, and what was the nature of their relationship with the white abolitionists? Historians of the American Negro have generally stressed the importance of their role, while the historians of the antislavery movement and the biographers of its leaders have usually written as if Negroes played only a minor and incidental part. Some recent scholars, quoting from speeches and letters of antislavery leaders, have engaged in a spirited debate as to whether or not the white abolitionists were genuine racial egalitarians. It would appear to us that the fundamental question to be raised is, How did Negroes actually function in the abolitionist movement?

We have already discussed evidence suggesting that Garrison's attack on the American Colonization Society stemmed from his contacts with Negro leaders. Negroes were especially appreciative of the support given their cause by the new immediatist antislavery newspapers established in Boston and New York. Garrison's *Liberator,* founded in 1831, might have died without the financial help of Negroes, who constituted nearly 90 percent of the subscribers during its first year and held meetings in several cities urging support for the publication. James Forten purchased thirty-seven subscriptions before the *Liberator* was a month old. The paper's financial crises were recurrent and three years later Negroes, then constituting about 75 percent of the subscribers, helped save "our paper." In its pages Garrison published their articles, essays, letters, and reports of their meetings. They passed the paper from hand to hand and showed it to sympathetic whites. In Carlisle, Pennsylvania, a Negro barber shared his copies of the *Liberator* with J. Miller McKim, who later became a prominent abolitionist leader. Another newspaper which attracted substantial Negro support was the *Emancipator,* founded in 1833 by a committee of New York abolitionists. The Underground Railroad leader David Ruggles and other Negro agents enthusiastically built up the paper's circulation.

Although Negro churches and mutual benefit societies as well as the National Negro Convention Movement had engaged in antislavery agitation over the years, it was the white leaders who seized the initiative in creating a national network of abolition societies. It was in a Boston Negro church that Garrison and a small group of white friends met to organize the New England Anti-Slavery Society in 1832. Only after the plans had been formulated were Negroes invited to participate. When the Society's constitution was approved, about one fourth of the seventy-two signers were Negroes. Among the local auxiliaries was the Massachusetts General Colored Association, a fraternal and anti-slavery organization founded in 1826, which affiliated with the New England Anti-Slavery Society in 1833. Some Negroes always attended annual conventions of the New England Society, and ordinarily a few shared the platform with the white speakers.

Only three Negroes were listed on the official roll of the Philadelphia conference that created the American Anti-Slavery Society in December, 1833. The three men, James G. Barbadoes of Boston, and Robert Purvis and the dentist James McCrummell of Philadelphia, were also among the sixty-two signers of the Society's Declaration of Sentiments—a document which Garrison drafted at McCrummell's home. Published accounts of the Convention suggest that Negro participation in debates and motions was minimal. On one symbolic occasion Negroes had a prominent role. On a motion to praise antislavery editors, the convention resolved itself into a committee of the whole with McCrummell in the chair, and Robert Purvis was among those lauding Garrison. Yet when Purvis made a forceful speech, "impassioned, full of invective, bristling with epithets," criticizing the cautious and equivocal passage on colonization which the conferees had substituted for Garrison's indictment, the convention failed to heed him. Six Negroes were appointed to the seventy-two-man Board of Managers, including the three named above. One of the others was the Episcopal minister Peter Williams of New York, who resigned before serving on it because of pressure from Bishop Onderdonk. Purvis was named to the nominating committee. Nevertheless, when it came to policy-making positions, Negroes were conspicuous by their absence. There were no Negro officers, not even among the twenty-six vice-presidents, and none among the original nine-man Executive Committee.

In addition to its interest in abolition, the American Anti-Slavery Society publicly opposed race prejudice and undertook to advance the status of free Negroes in the North. The delegates asserted that since all men were "of one blood," Negroes and whites should share equally in "civil and religious privileges." To help Northern Negroes achieve their potentialities, the conference recommended a program of moral elevation similar to that adopted by the Negro Convention Movement. In 1834, the first annual report of the Society declared that the way to bear witness against race prejudice was to invite more of "our colored brethren" into active affiliation with the organization. Two New York Presbyterian ministers, Samuel E. Cornish and Theodore S. Wright, received places on the twelve-man Executive Committee, and James Forten and William Watkins were among the fifty-eight vice-presidents. Nine Negroes were named to the Board of Managers, constituting about 10 percent of its membership. Although Cornish and Wright remained on the Executive Committee, after 1834 no Negroes were named as vice-presidents of the Society for several years, and beginning in 1837 there was a sharp reduction of Negroes on the Board of Managers to half a dozen or less a year.* Throughout the decade, only a handful of Negroes attended the Society's annual meetings.

The American and Foreign Anti-Slavery Society, with an Executive Committee twice as large as that of the American Anti-Slavery Society, appointed a somewhat larger number of Negroes, usually four, but sometimes only two, to that body. They included Cornish and Wright, Bishop Christopher Rush, Dr. James McCune Smith, who had been educated at the University of Glasgow, the Congregationalist minister J. W. C. Pennington, and Charles B. Ray, Presbyterian minister, noted Underground Railroad leader, and sometime editor of the New York *Colored American*. During the 1850's Ray and Smith each served as recording secretary, though the more powerful position of corresponding secretary always remained in the hands of a white man. After the loss of Cornish and Wright, Negro participation at the top levels of the American Anti-Slavery Society declined. Robert Purvis was a perennial vice-president, however; Charles Lenox Remond served on the Executive Committee of twelve for five or six years beginning in 1843; and between 1849 and 1852 Remond and Frederick Douglass were among the three dozen men who sat on the Board of Managers. From time to time men like Purvis, Remond, Douglass, and William Wells Brown sat on convention committees and occasionally addressed or presided over a convention session. A similar pattern prevailed during the 1860's. No Negroes appear to have had important positions in

* The Board of Managers was an unwieldy and honorific group; for example, it numbered 131 in 1839 and 63 in 1841.

the American Anti-Slavery Society during the Civil War, and only three, including Robert Purvis, held any but honorary posts in the same organization during the period 1865–70.

Negroes occupied prominent positions in some of the state and local auxiliaries. Among the Garrisonians, Margaretta Forten was secretary of the Philadelphia Female Anti-Slavery Society and Purvis for years presided over the Pennsylvania Anti-Slavery Society. A tiny handful of colored men worked as paid agents and lecturers for the national societies. Though Negroes also participated as speakers at annual meetings, though Negro delegates did contribute to the discussions on the convention floor, and though Purvis, Wright, and others presided over business sessions and public meetings, there is no evidence that their role was other than a symbolic one. This conclusion receives further support from the paucity of letters to and from Negroes in the papers of white abolitionist leaders; only Gerrit Smith seems to have corresponded extensively with them. As Douglass said in 1855:

> Our oppressed people are wholly ignored, in one sense, in the generalship of the movement to effect our redemption. We are a poor, pitiful, dependent, and servile class of Negroes, *"unable to keep pace"* with the movement . . . not even capable of *"perceiving what are its demands, or understanding the philosophy of its operations!"* Of course . . . we cannot expect to receive from those who indulge in this *opinion practical recognition of our Equality.* This is what we . . . must receive to inspire us with confidence in the self-appointed generals of the Anti-Slavery host, the Euclids who are *theoretically* working out the almost insoluble problems of our future destiny.

In view of the attitudes of some abolitionists it might be deemed surprising that Negroes received any positions at all in the affairs of the antislavery societies. At the beginning at least, some of the auxiliaries excluded Negroes entirely. Shortly after the Junior Anti-Slavery Society of Philadelphia was founded in 1836, a motion to accept members without regard to color was passed by only two votes. In the same year the New York women's antislavery society adamantly refused to admit Negroes. When the Fall River, Massachusetts, Female Anti-Slavery Society urged Negro women to affiliate, the organization was nearly torn apart. In 1837 the Convention of the Anti-Slavery Women of the United States took cognizance of the matter, and declared, "Those Societies that reject colored members, or seek to avoid them, have never been active or efficient," but took no steps to expel such auxiliaries. Because of these attitudes, Negroes in places like Albany, Rochester, New York, Nantucket, and Lexington, Ohio, formed segregated local auxiliaries. In the published lists of auxiliaries, the American Anti-Slavery Society often designated these by the word "colored."

Although men like Weld, Garrison, and the Tappans discountenanced such exclusionist policies on the part of white auxiliaries, and the practice certainly was not typical, Negroes were concerned that the white antislavery workers were not completely unprejudiced. Even the most prominent white abolitionists were criticized. For one thing, Negroes were disappointed that, in spite of the rhetoric of the 1833 Declaration of Sentiments and of the many addresses by white abolitionists, few of them actively participated in the fight against the discrimination faced by free people of color in the North. On the floor of annual conventions Negroes repeatedly tried to make the white abolitionists more conscious of this discrimination. For example, at the 1849 meeting of the American and Foreign Anti-Slavery Society, the famous abolitionist orator and Congregationalist clergyman, Rev. Samuel Ringgold Ward, who was known as the "Black Daniel Webster," told of racial exclusion in a medical college and in churches. The following year Ray complained of discrimination in the churches, and of how Negroes, "compelled by self-respect to rent or purchase churches for themselves," had encountered obstacles to making even this type of accommodation. Theodore Wright, speaking before the New York Anti-Slavery Society in 1837, expressed alarm over the "constitutions of abolition societies, where nothing was said about the improvement of the man of color! They have overlooked the giant sin of prejudice. They have passed by this foul monster, which is at once the parent and offspring of slavery."

The dissatisfaction ran deeper than this. Militant Negroes made numerous references to the insincerity of "professed abolitionists." They reported that many white abolitionists refused to admit colored children to their schools or to employ colored men in their businesses other than in menial capacities. Wright, in his speech before the New York Anti-Slavery Society, denounced the sort of abolitionist who would invite a Negro clergyman to his home but serve him dinner in the kitchen and fail to introduce him to his family. "Our white friends are deceived," the New York *Colored American* declared in 1837, "when they imagine they are free from prejudice against color, and yet are content with a lower standard of attainments for colored youth, and inferior exhibitions of talent on the part of colored men." Eighteen years later Douglass charged that abolitionist businessmen "might employ a colored boy as a porter or packer, but would as soon put a hod-carrier to the clerk's desk as a colored boy, ever so well educated though he might be." At the 1853 convention of the American and Foreign Anti-Slavery Society white abolitionists were openly attacked for failing to employ Negroes in the antislavery offices or in their places of business, and Arthur Tappan himself was criticized for using Negroes only as menials in his department store.

The Negroes were right about the prejudice within the white antislavery groups. Although the abolitionists were a distinct improvement over their colonizationist predecessors, and far in advance of the public opinion of their age, at the same time they were, in fact, ambivalent in their relationships with Negroes. One must therefore distinguish carefully between their egalitarian rhetoric and their paternalistic and prejudiced actions. They spoke feelingly of the "sins of caste," but they were highly sensitive to charges that they advocated social equality and intermingling. They spoke of the importance of opposing discrimination against free Negroes, but even where they fought for civil rights they usually did so under prodding from their Negro colleagues. In fact, much of the activity on behalf of free Negroes consisted of exhorting them to assume the responsibility for their own elevation by acquiring wealth and education and exhibiting good moral character. Due to Negro pressure, in 1838 the Executive Committee of the American Anti-Slavery Society praised Negroes for seeking advancement beyond unskilled jobs and urged abolitionists to offer employment to colored people—but employers affiliated with the Society were unmoved by this appeal.

The Anti-Slavery Society itself had at first bypassed Negroes when hiring lecturers. The so-called "Seventy," recruited by Weld for antislavery speaking, were all whites. Not until 1839 did Weld suggest the names of several Negroes as lecturers, saying, "They would do more in three months to kill prejudice . . . than all our operations up to now." At the outset of his antislavery career Weld had helped establish schools for Cincinnati's Negroes and frequently visited their homes and churches. He believed that "persons are to be treated according to their intrinsic worth irrespective of *color*" but felt that this principle sometimes required "modifications"; a sincere abolitionist must ask himself if mingling with Negroes in public would be "a *blessing* or a *curse*" to them. He regarded public association with Negroes as often "an ostentatious display of superiority to prejudice," which could hurt the antislavery movement as well as create mob violence against Negroes. Weld even justified his own exclusion of a Negro delegate from an antislavery convention in Ohio on the ground that if the man sat in the convention, mobs would make renewed attacks on Ohio Negroes.

The Tappan brothers displayed a comparable attitude. As in Weld's case, it is difficult to ascertain to what degree their ambivalence and paternalism were blended with genuinely tactical considerations. Lewis Tappan, for example, was disturbed at the failure of the arrangements committee to invite Theodore Wright to speak at the 1835 convention. The committee did allow Wright's church choir to participate, but some members of the Society complained about "race amalgamation" because a white chorus sang from the same platform. They charged that the "choir mingling" had later helped to cause mob rioting. Tappan believed that this accusation was merely a mask to cover race prejudice. All the same, he himself did not want to be regarded as advocating socializing with Negroes; to Weld he confided that aside from the "choir mingling" incident, the only time he had ever attempted to "mix up the two colors" involved occasional dinners with a few Negro gentlemen in the course of business conferences. Like his brother, Arthur Tappan also condemned "caste usages," but yielded to social pressures. On one occasion he was severely criticized for inviting Samuel Cornish to share his pew at church. Tappan called that action the only effort at "amalgamation that I remember," and he vowed not to associate publicly with Negroes until white citizens became more enlightened. The influential abolitionist James G. Birney, candidate for President on the Liberty Party ticket in 1840 and 1844, argued that granting "social privileges" to Negroes should be postponed until they had attained "civil privileges." In his judgment the failure to establish clearly such a system of priorities jeopardized the entire antislavery movement, since the enemies of the Negroes used the social equality issue to defeat the cause of abolition.

The paternalism of abolitionist leaders toward Negroes was most evident in the case of William Lloyd Garrison. Actually Garrison could not work with anyone except on his own terms, but he portrayed himself as unselfishly seeking to encourage Negroes to become independent, self-assertive citizens. As the founder and editor of the earliest and the most celebrated of the abolitionist newspapers, financed at least in the beginning almost entirely by Negro subscriptions, Garrison's chief personality difficulties with Negroes quite naturally involved Negro editors. Although in the early 1830's he had urged the development of a Negro press to vindicate the rights of the race, when Negroes decided to become editors, Garrison discouraged them. In 1837 when Samuel Cornish sought support for his proposed *Colored American,* one of the earliest Negro newspapers, Garrisonians opposed the venture. After Cornish had gone ahead, Garrison sometimes criticized the *Colored American*'s policies and at other times acted as if the paper did not exist. The editors of the *Colored American* were not intimidated. In a pointed blast at Garrison, the paper criticized those white abolitionists who "outwardly treat us as men, while in their hearts they still hold us as slaves." Years later when Cornish died, the *Liberator* carried no obituary.

More celebrated is the experience of Frederick Douglass. Garrison discovered Douglass at an antislavery meeting at Nantucket in 1841, when the fugitive slave told an audience about the world from which he had escaped and what freedom meant to him. On the platform Garrison was so moved that he asked the crowd, "Shall such a man ever be sent back to slavery from the soil of old Massachusetts?" The spectators arose shouting, "No, No!" Afterward the Massachusetts Anti-Slavery Society engaged Douglass to lecture on his experiences as a slave. During the passing months he was intellectually "growing and needed room," and wanted to share with audiences the ideas of his "reading and thinking," rather than simply mechanically perform his stage role as a slave. Officials of the antislavery society, however, discouraged his striving toward manhood and independence. Instead of applauding his intellectual progress as an illustration of Negro potentiality, they preferred to exhibit him publicly in his frozen status of fugitive slave. Garrison told him, "Tell your story, Frederick." Others admonished, "We will take care of the philosophy. . . . Let us have the facts." As Douglass continued to acquire self-confidence and literary skill, members of the Society complained that he seemed "too learned": "People won't believe you ever were a slave, Frederick, if you keep on this way. . . . Better have a *little* of the plantation manner of speech than not."

Douglass went his own way. Within the next four years, he had published his autobiography and lectured in England. He returned to the United States, grateful for the help of abolitionists but ambitious for greater independence and the opportunity to edit his own newspaper. Over the objections of Garrison and his friends, Douglass moved to Rochester and founded the *North Star*. At the time he was still a Garrisonian in his ideology, but after coming into contact with the political abolitionists of western New York, he was gradually converted to their way of thinking. In 1851 he frankly told a meeting of the American Anti-Slavery Society of his new views, whereupon Garrison declared, "There is roguery somewhere." Later Garrison denounced Douglass as "destitute of every principle of honor, ungrateful to the last degree and malevolent in spirit."

Probably nothing could better illustrate the essentially peripheral, almost superfluous role in which whites sought to cast Negroes than the two anniversary celebrations of the American Anti-Slavery Society in 1853 and 1863. While the published proceedings of the twentieth anniversary reported in infinite detail the speeches of many white delegates, the comments of the Negroes received perfunctory attention. In two instances the original remarks themselves were evidently short, but in the only other case so distinguished a person as the noted antislavery and feminist orator Sojourner Truth rated only one sentence: "Previous to the calling to order, Sojourner Truth (formerly a slave in the State of New York) sang a plaintive song, touching the wrongs of the slave, and afterwards spoke of the wrong Slavery had done to herself and others." Ten years later the American

Anti-Slavery Society held its thirtieth-anniversary meeting. By then the Emancipation Proclamation had been issued, Negroes were accepted in the Union Army, and the abolitionists felt a pardonable pride in their accomplishments. Delegates like Garrison, McKim, and Lucretia Mott, who had attended the founding convention, reminisced about the early days. Several of the surviving signers of the historic Declaration of Sentiments were present, among them Robert Purvis and James McCrummell. Yet neither was invited to speak, and in fact the only Negro addressing the convention was Frederick Douglass, who pointedly told the abolitionists that their task was unfinished until Negroes were accepted in American society. If, as one participant said, an abolitionist aim was to "vindicate the ability" of Negroes, the fact that neither Purvis nor McCrummell was asked to speak does seem strange. Purvis especially had made significant contributions to the cause during the three decades.

Judging from these important anniversary celebrations, Negroes, in the abolitionist cast of characters, were regarded as bit players or even as extras shunted off in the background where they would not detract from the stellar performance of the whites spotlighted downstage center. The evidence suggests that this limited participation was due to the ambivalence of white abolitionists in their relationships with Negroes. The whites appeared not to have encouraged Negroes to seek other than a few symbolic roles in the antislavery societies. While Negroes received token representation in the offices of the American and the American and Foreign Anti-Slavery societies, there is no indication that they were influential in shaping the strategy and tactics of the organizations. Despite their reiterated declaration that improvement of the Negro's status in the North was "a most effectual means of promoting the abolition of slavery," the white abolitionists concentrated on the single issue of converting other whites to antislavery. Since Negroes recognized the reservations among the white leadership, they organized much of their protest activities outside of the antislavery societies. It was no wonder that in the late 1850's J. Mercer Langston felt it advisable to form a separate, black antislavery society in Ohio. And it was also no wonder that the only Negro to achieve a position of real influence in antislavery councils was Frederick Douglass, a man so Olympian in stature that he compelled recognition. To be of influence even he had to establish himself as essentially an independent force outside either of the two major antislavery organizations.

Yet Negroes did play a vital role in antislavery activities. To them must be given the chief credit for running the Underground Railroad. And from among the fugitives the antislavery societies found some of their most effective lecturers and propagandists.

11

Contrary to popular impression, and Southern fears, the Underground Railroad was not a well-organized institution and white abolitionists did not play a commanding role in it. The work of the white abolitionists of course should not be minimized —some, like Levi Coffin of Newport, Indiana, and later Cincinnati, were of great assistance to the runaways—but the most arduous and dangerous part of the fugitive's journey was in the South, where there was seldom anyone to help him. And once the fugitive did reach the North, it was usually the free Negroes who took the initiative in aiding him. Individual Negroes opened their homes to runaways. Even more important was the work of the organized Vigilance Committees in several Northern cities, which elicited support from sympathetic whites but were founded and essentially run by Negroes.

Slaveholders charged that whites on the Underground Railroad were invading the South to lure away their bondsmen. Their view was distorted. John Fairfield's activities in bringing slaves out of Alabama and Kentucky and John Brown's abduction of slaves from Missouri were exceptional exploits that sprang from the urges of daring personalities. More often than not such "conductors" were Negroes who had escaped from the South and returned to take others North. Harriet Tubman, called the Moses of the race because of the large number of trips she made to bring "passengers" to the promised land, was the most celebrated of them. Her journeys from the South usually began on Saturday night, giving the fugitives more than a day before their owners discovered their departure and sounded the alarm for their return. She is reported to have thus helped three hundred slaves to their freedom. Less famous was Josiah Henson. Henson escaped from Kentucky "after a youth full of good deeds to his master." Making his way to Canada, he later returned South to help the family of another fugitive to escape, and thereafter made other trips, carrying away scores of bondsmen.

Only a small percentage of the slaves who attempted to escape actually were able to reach the North. Armed with courage and ingenuity, guided by the North Star, some began their tortuous journey by stealing supplies from their masters, "borrowing" canoes or skiffs along the way, and finding lodging with other slaves or free Negroes. William Wells Brown, later an agent for the American Anti-Slavery Society and the first American Negro novelist (*Clotel; or the President's Daughter,* 1853), escaped in 1834. He later recalled that his constant fear of recapture forced him to travel only at night, and to choose between stealing food or going hungry. Although determined "not to trust myself in the hands of any man, white or colored," he did receive assistance from Ohio abolitionists and an Indiana Quaker. Finding employment as a steamboat workman in Cleveland, he aided other fugitives en route to Canada, and upon moving to Buffalo opened his home to runaway slaves. On occasion Brown helped rescue runaways in danger of being recaptured by slave traders. Brown had thus received only minimal help from white abolitionists, extended after the major risks were taken. Frederick Douglass, like Brown, later became a leading agent in the Underground Railroad, an active participant in the Rochester depot. Unlike Brown, in the course of his own escape from Baltimore in 1838, Douglass received no help at all from whites. Using a method frequently employed by slaves escaping from Southern seaports, he borrowed a free seaman's "protection" papers. When he was unable to find a job in New York City, he finally revealed his plight to a sailor who notified David Ruggles, a Negro printer-bookseller and secretary of the New York Vigilance Committee. Ruggles supplied temporary lodging, later sending Douglass to New Bedford, where he stayed with a Negro family and started a new life "as a free man."

The Vigilance Committees arose in the middle 1830's. The New York Vigilance Committee—under the direction first of Ruggles and later of Charles Ray, who was also secretary of the New York State Vigilance Committee—collected pennies and nickels, mainly from Negroes, to feed, clothe, and shelter fugitives arriving from the South. Some were helped to settle in New

York, while others like Frederick Douglass were sent to other cities. Even runaways who had lived in the North for years were always in danger of arrest. Because the fugitive slave laws were designed to help masters, it was even possible for free Negroes to be kidnapped and taken South. The Vigilance Committees attempted to prevent these kidnappings and made numerous propaganda appeals to protest them. In New York Ruggles was always on guard against slave agents, and even compiled a Slaveholders Directory listing the names and addresses of lawyers, law enforcement officers, and others who "lend themselves to kidnapping."

In other communities, such as Boston or Philadelphia, although whites collaborated with Negroes on the Vigilance Committees, most of the work was actually performed by Negroes. In Philadelphia Robert Purvis was president of the Vigilance Committee, while William Still, the corresponding secretary, was the one who co-ordinated the rescue work. In Syracuse, New York, the Committee depended on the AME Zion minister J. W. Loguen to shelter many runaways. In Rochester Frederick Douglass and many other colored men in the community assisted fugitives. Douglass, "superintendent" of the Underground Railroad station there, used his home as its headquarters and equipped his office with a trap door and secret stairway for hiding fugitives. He spent many hours raising money to transport them to safety in Canada.

That the work of aiding the fugitives was largely done by Negroes rather than whites was attested to by abolitionists of both races. James Birney, writing in 1837, described how slave escapes were facilitated by other Negroes: "Six weeks ago, a young married woman escaped from N. Orleans by steamboat and was successfully concealed here [Cincinnati] by her colored friends. Yesterday, her husband arrived, and at 5 o'clock in the afternoon they were both in the Stage on their way from this place to Canada. Such matters are almost uniformly managed by the colored people. I know nothing of them generally till they are passed." In the 1830's Theodore Wright complained that members of antislavery societies had not taken sufficient interest in helping fugitive slaves or protecting Negroes from kidnappers. Wright, among the founders of the New York Vigilance Committee, appealed to whites to make the work of the Committee a basic objective of the American Anti-Slavery Society. While limited aid was ultimately given by such leaders as the Tappans, Weld, and Gerrit Smith, fugitive rescue work did not receive the kind of support that Wright and his Negro colleagues sought. The New York Vigilance Committee had emphasized that the institution of slavery could not be destroyed unless large-scale efforts were undertaken to alleviate the plight of its victims in the North, but the antislavery societies did not allow fugitive aid to detract from the basic goal of abolition.

After the passage of the Fugitive Slave Law of 1850, however, more whites became sufficiently aroused to help the Vigilance Committees, or at least to give tacit support. In 1851 two publicized cases demonstrated how Negroes aided brethren whose liberty was threatened and how white juries were sympathetic toward such activities. In Christiana, a southern Pennsylvania town not far from the Maryland line, a slaveholder searching for runaways died in a gun battle waged against a group of free Negroes who had armed to protect the home of one of their fellows. Thirty-eight were charged with treason and confined in jail to await a court trial. A jury deliberated only a few minutes before finding the first "traitor" not guilty, and the government's case collapsed completely. In Boston a Negro crowd entered the courthouse where a fugitive from Virginia named Shadrach was held in the custody of a United States marshal during proceedings preparatory to a return to slavery. On signal the Negroes seized Shadrach, spiriting him away to Canada. Several alleged conspirators were prosecuted, but a divided jury failed to find them guilty and the case was dismissed.

An important contribution of Negroes who had escaped was their work as abolitionist propagandists. As already noted, during the first years of the American Anti-Slavery Society the leadership failed to make much use of Negro lecturers. In the 1830's the first Negroes to speak before local antislavery groups were Theodore Wright, James Forten, Robert Purvis, and Charles Lenox Remond, but all of these men were free Negroes who had never been slaves, and although they eloquently discussed the peculiar institution, their presentations lacked dramatic impact. Former slaves, many of whom were fugitives, were eventually asked to lecture. By the 1840's Frederick Douglass, William Wells Brown, Samuel R. Ward, Henry Bibb, Lunsford Lane,

Harriet Tubman, Sojourner Truth, and many others spoke to antislavery audiences all over the North. Their activities probably constituted the Negroes' most important contribution to the abolitionist movement. In their speeches, and also in autobiographical narratives, Negroes provided the most compelling propaganda against the institution of slavery, the fugitives serving as a constant reminder of the millions of slaves who had not been able to run away. Audiences flocked to hear these speakers describe the whippings administered by overseers, the separation from loved ones sold down the river, and the often hectic efforts to get beyond the reach of slave catchers and bloodhounds. In the most personal terms they told exactly what slavery meant to them, and, speaking of what they had seen and experienced, they were deeply convincing.

Henry Bibb moved audiences to tears with a recital of how his wife, naked and bound, had been brutally whipped by an intoxicated slaveholder. Bibb's listeners would burst into cheers, laughter, and applause a few moments later as he described ways in which slaves outwitted their masters. Another crowd pleaser was Henry "Box" Brown, who recounted his escape from Richmond in a shipping box, which he later used as a prop on antislavery tours. Though white audiences felt entertained, they usually also came away impressed by the resourcefulness and indomitable will to freedom which these lecturers demonstrated. The sense of momentary aloneness and apprehension many runaways felt when they "crossed the line" to freedom was vividly portrayed by Harriet Tubman: ". . . I was free, but there was no one to welcome me to the land of freedom. I was a stranger in a strange land. . . ." Recounting the tale of her escapes, she affected listeners with a profound faith in God and in herself.

For the many thousands of whites at these antislavery meetings who identified themselves with the sufferings of these speakers, there was often an opportunity to purchase their personal narratives, which were widely circulated. For example, the autobiography of Frederick Douglass received extensive distribution and the narratives of William Wells Brown and Josiah Henson sold thousands of copies. This body of literature became an important propaganda force in the struggle to win converts to the antislavery position and was supplemented by biographical and autobiographical sketches of thousands of slaves published by abolitionists. The printing presses kept turning as more fugitives arrived in the North and more whites joined the antislavery ranks.

Abolitionist writers heavily edited the bulk of these sketches, but there is no doubt that Douglass, Brown, Bibb, and others did their own writing. From the printed pages emerged a black hero whose aspirations for freedom and self-fulfillment represented a variation of the American dream, and in this sense a lesson in racial equality which aroused the interest and respect of many white Northerners. A contemporary reviewer of Douglass' *My Bondage and My Freedom* commented: "The mere fact that the member of an outcast and enslaved race should accomplish his freedom, and educate himself up to an equality of intellectual and moral vigor with the leaders of the race by which he was held in bondage, is, in itself, so remarkable that the story of the change cannot be otherwise than exciting."

12

The achievements of men like Douglass intensified Negro resentment of the patronizing attitude of the white abolitionists who determined organization policies and made little effort to treat Negroes as equal co-workers. Negroes were also dismayed by the deteriorating economic situation and the futility of most of their protests for equal rights. Later, they grew alarmed over the threat to their very safety raised by the stringent Fugitive Slave Law of 1850. Many concluded therefore that Negroes must band together and help themselves. Critics might blast "a caste convention to abolish caste," but advocates of a separate convention held that Negroes should be less subservient to white friends, and should act independently to avoid the impression that they merely echoed the words of white abolitionists. As Douglass was to say in 1855, "It is well known that we have called down upon our devoted head, the Holy (?) horror of a certain class of Abolitionists, because we have dared to maintain our Individualism." Welcoming the growing recognition of the fact that "OUR ELEVATION AS A RACE IS ALMOST WHOLLY DEPENDENT UPON OUR OWN EXERTION," Douglass maintained that while allies were useful, history had demonstrated that no oppressed group had achieved its deliverance without taking "a prominent part in the conflict," rather than being used merely to do "all the incidental drudgery of the warfare."

The new spirit was manifested in several ways. One was the revival of the Convention Movement in 1843. A second was a serious discussion of the advocacy of violence and slave rebellions. Another was an experiment with an independent Negro political party. There were also proposals for economic co-operation along racial lines. Finally there was a dramatic upsurge of interest in colonization.

The National Convention Movement was revived with a conference at Buffalo in 1843, and thereafter it continued an active life through the rest of the ante-bellum period. Those pressing for separate meetings denied any desire to eliminate joint activity with whites in the antislavery societies or in a political organization such as the Liberty Party. The 1848 National Negro Convention urged members of the race to "act with the white Abolition societies wherever you can, and where you cannot, get up societies among yourselves. . . . We shall undoubtedly for many years be compelled to have institutions of a complexional character, in order to attain this very idea of human brotherhood. We would however, advise our brethren to occupy memberships and stations among white persons, and in white institutions, just so far as our rights are secured to us."

The 1843 convention was famous for the heated controversy aroused by Rev. Henry Highland Garnet's speech entitled "An Address to the Slaves of the United States of America." Garnet, a Presbyterian minister with a white congregation at Troy, New York, urged the bondsmen to kill any master refusing to liberate them. Douglass, Remond, and others argued that approval of Garnet's address would create further hardship for free Negroes in the slave and Border states. A resolution endorsing the speech failed by only one vote as the convention declared that "a righteous government" would destroy slavery.

At the next national convention, four years later, Garnet's Address was discussed again and aroused far less disapproval. Indeed, during the late 1840's, the use of violence to destroy slavery was being widely discussed by Northern Negroes. After the Address was printed in a special volume with *Walker's Appeal* in 1848, a group of Ohio Negroes made plans to order five hundred copies. Some Negro delegates at a Maine convention suggested that the race was morally obliged to provide aid in a slave rebellion, and at a Negro meeting in Boston there was considerable sentiment favoring a fugitive's right to kill in order to save himself from capture. In 1849, when Douglass reminded a white Boston audience of their grandparents' militance in the American Revolution, he declared, "I should welcome the intelligence tomorrow, should it come, that the slaves had risen in the South." The following year, shortly after Congress passed the Fugitive Slave Law, Douglass suggested that "the only way to make the Fugitive Slave Law a dead letter is to make half a dozen or more dead kidnappers. . . . The man who takes the office of a bloodhound ought to be treated as a bloodhound." Negroes in several state conventions attacked the law and counseled militant resistance. Men like Henry H. Garnet carried a pistol, and Samuel R. Ward asserted that although the law might try to enslave every Negro in New York there was still "one Sam Ward—who will never be taken alive."

Negroes were divided as to the proper course to take in regard to political action. The 1843 convention voted overwhelmingly to endorse the Liberty Party, though it was done only over the strenuous opposition of Frederick Douglass and Charles Lenox Remond who, as loyal Garrisonians, warned that all political parties were inherently corrupt, and that only moral suasion could free the slaves from bondage. State conventions in the late 1840's and 1850's agitated more on political rights than on any other issue. In actual fact Negroes found political action particularly frustrating just because they were barred from voting in so many states. For those who were entitled to vote the question of which political party to support was fraught with difficulties. By backing a minor abolitionist party they would be throwing their votes away, but by voting for one of the major parties they would be compromising their principles in supporting an organization that took only a mild antislavery stand. Some backed the Liberty Party in the 1840's and its offshoot, the Radical Abolitionist Party of the 1850's, but others regarded it as a tactical error to support such a weak third party. Many supported the Whigs during the 1840's, as the better of the two major parties. Others, including most of the delegates to the National Colored Convention of 1848, endorsed the Free Soil Party, despite their well-justified skepticism about the attitudes of its leaders on the question of Negro suffrage. Similarly, the Republicans, by calling merely for the exclusion of slavery from the territories and remaining silent on the matter of voting rights, placed Negroes in a dilemma. Only reluctantly did most of them support the Republicans as the best practical choice. In desperation some New York State leaders turned toward independent political organizations. At a convention in 1855 they established a New York State Suffrage Association with Frederick Douglass originally endorsing it and acting as chairman. Intended as a Negro political party for the state, the Association hoped to be in the position of serving as a balance of power in close elections. It did not run candidates of its own, but threw its weight behind the Republicans in 1856, 1858, and 1860. Nevertheless its existence symbolized the Negroes' estrangement from the mainstream of American politics.

Delegates to the Negro conventions of the 1840's and 1850's agreed that the race should seek respectability and wealth through mechanical trades and agricultural pursuits and through the cultivation of thrift, industry, and good moral character. Discouragement with the political scene, as well as fears aroused by the inroads of immigrants into the unskilled and menial jobs traditionally performed by Negroes, led the noted Rochester Convention of 1853 to place strong emphasis on racial solidarity and economic advancement. The delegates repeatedly asserted that as American citizens they were entitled to equality before the law, in schools, and in churches. But they also took a more nationalistic position than any of the earlier conventions by emphasizing the necessity of tightening the bonds of racial unity. The conclave created a national council to supervise a highly organized system of racial uplift. Negroes were told that survival depended on using each other's economic services whenever possible and plans were made to establish a national register of race businessmen, mechanics, and laborers. At the urging of Frederick Douglass, the convention also went on record as approving the creation of a manual labor school. To encourage race pride, a national Negro museum and library was also envisioned. While this comprehensive program was never carried out, the 1853 convention was significant because it clearly showed increasing support for an ideology of self-help and racial solidarity in the face of the ever more critical situation in which Northern free Negroes found themselves during the decade before the Civil War.

Another manifestation of this disillusionment and frustration and consequent stress upon racial unity, or what can be called Negro nationalism, was the rising crescendo of support for emigration to Africa and tropical America. There was a growing interest in the subject beginning with the late 1840's. In 1854, 1856, and 1858, Negro colonizationists held their own national conventions. Among themselves they differed as to what would be the best site. Some opted for the Caribbean area, especially for Haiti, whose ruler encouraged their aspirations. Several preferred Lower California and the Far West of the United States. But the most popular place was Africa. A few leaders even made their peace with the American Colonization Society. All agreed on the hopelessness of continued agitation for equal rights in the United States. They agreed also in articulating a nationalist ideology which insisted that Negroes had made a contribution to world civilization in the past, and that by destroying the slave trade and redeeming and Christianizing Africa, they were to make one in the future. Episcopal clergyman Alexander Crummell, who had received a degree from Cambridge University before going to Africa on behalf of the American Colonization Society, summed it up best when he described Liberia as "this spot dedicated to nationality, consecrated to freedom, and sacred to religion."

The leading emigrationist during the 1850's was the Harvard-educated physician Martin Robison Delany. Delany's mind oscillated between Africa and Central America as the most appropriate place for colonization, but he consistently denounced the American Colonization Society, which he regarded as "anti-Christian in its character, and misanthropic in its pretended sympathies," its leaders "arrant hypocrites seeking every opportunity to deceive" the free Negroes. Better than anyone else during the ante-bellum period Delany exemplified the dual ethnic loyalties of the American Negro. On the one hand he believed, "We are Americans, having a birthright citizenship—natural claims upon this country—claims common to all others of our fellow-citizens." Yet Delany was pessimistic about the Negro ever achieving the full rights he deserved as a citizen. The only real solution lay in emigrating and establishing "a national position for ourselves." In 1859 he led an exploring party up the

Niger River, where he signed a treaty with the Yoruba granting him a tract for settlement by American Negroes. As he had written to Garrison several years before, "Heathenism and Liberty before Christianity and Slavery!"

During the 1850's probably most of the Negro leaders at least toyed with the idea of colonization. Some, like the Ohio lawyer J. Mercer Langston, who was later a congressman from Virginia (1890–91), espoused colonization only briefly. Others, like Henry Highland Garnet, Martin R. Delany, Alexander Crummell, and Samuel Ringgold Ward, substituted a long-term advocacy of emigration for their earlier intense absorption in the campaign for equal rights. In 1858 a group of prominent New York Negroes founded the African Civilization Society for missionary and colonization work. Even Frederick Douglass, discouraged by the Republican Party's moderate stand on slavery in the election of 1860, and disillusioned by Lincoln's temporizing with the white South after he entered office, became more open-minded toward colonization. He had no intention of emigrating himself, but on the eve of the Civil War he was preparing to visit Haiti in order to investigate its possibilities for settlement by those American Negroes who wished to leave the United States. The Confederate attack on Fort Sumter in April, 1861, dramatically altered the situation.

The outbreak of the Civil War and the momentous events of the succeeding years dissipated colonizationist sentiment. The War and Emancipation were to renew the Negroes' faith in the vision of a racially egalitarian and integrated American society. But once again the American conscience, only temporarily aroused by a wartime crisis, would fail to destroy what black and white abolitionists alike described as the "sins of caste."

IV

A DREAM BETRAYED: NEGROES
DURING THE CIVIL WAR AND
RECONSTRUCTION

FOR NEGROES the Civil War was, from its beginning, inextricably bound up with their future and their freedom. They saw it first of all as a war for the emancipation of the slaves. Beyond this, they believed that at stake was the recognition of their rights as men and citizens.

Neither the Administration at Washington nor white public opinion generally regarded the war in this light at the start. To them it was emphatically a war to preserve the Union, not to end slavery, much less to obtain for Negroes the rights of citizens. Yet as the hostilities dragged on, the Union was ineluctably drawn toward incorporating emancipation and the recognition of the Negro as man and citizen into the goals of the war and the postwar settlement.

1

At the outset of the war Negroes and white abolitionists raised two crucial issues: the emancipation of the slaves and the right of Negroes to bear arms in defense of the Union. The free Negroes hoped that by fighting for the Union they would contribute to the liberation of the slaves. Indeed in the evolution of Union policy these two issues were closely intertwined.

When Lincoln issued his call for volunteers, Negroes promptly offered their services as soldiers. A mass meeting of Boston Negroes declared, "Our feelings urge us to say to our countrymen that we are ready to stand by and defend the Government . . . with 'our lives, our fortunes, and our sacred honor . . .' " But all offers were rejected.

It was the slaves themselves who brought about the first shift in Union policy. In May, 1861, three runaways appeared at Fortress Monroe in Virginia. General Benjamin Butler, upon learning that they had been helping to build Confederate fortifications across the Chesapeake Bay, declared them contraband of war. News of this action spread quickly; by the end of July nine hundred Negroes had arrived at the fortress. Butler interpreted the word "contraband" loosely. In fact, no one who came was turned back. The first "contrabands" were put to work unloading vessels and storing provisions, but by July Butler decided to employ them on the erection of fortifications. Using contrabands became very popular. For Northerners, not prepared to grant Negroes freedom or allow them to fight against slavery, the use of contrabands was a convenient formula for depriving the South of its labor and employing that labor itself, without any commitment to emancipation. In August Congress passed the first Confiscation Act, providing that slaves used on Confederate fortifications were forfeited. In September Gideon Welles, Secretary of the Navy, authorized naval officers to use fugitive slaves even in fighting, though they were to have a rating no higher than "boys" at a pay of ten dollars a month. But the national Administration was evasive and noncommittal on employing fugitives, and therefore the practice of field commanders varied widely. Many refused to receive the contrabands and even allowed slaveowners to reclaim those who had entered Union lines.

If the North hesitated, the South had no qualms about employing Negro labor. From the start Negroes were used in building fortifications. Slaves were also vital to the Southern war effort both as food producers and industrial workers, particularly in the coal and iron mines. In early 1862 the Tredegar Iron Works in Virginia advertised for a thousand slaves. In 1865 three fourths of the four hundred workmen at the naval works in Selma, Alabama, were Negroes.

Some free Negroes volunteered to fight in the Confederate

Army. Among them were the New Orleans Native Guards, composed of proud Creole Negroes, whose predecessors had served in a free Negro regiment during the War of 1812, winning the unstinting praise of Andrew Jackson for their role in the Battle of New Orleans.* There has been considerable speculation on why free Negroes offered their services to the Confederacy. Fear or the desire to curry favor undoubtedly played a part, and a number of free Negroes in the Charleston and New Orleans areas were substantial slaveowners themselves. In any event the volunteers hoped to obtain better treatment by demonstrating their patriotism. Such offers were turned down, however, as they had been in the North. It was only in the final agonizing months of the war that the Confederate government in desperation finally decided to enlist Negro soldiers and emancipate slaves willing to fight.

Everywhere, as the Federals approached, slaves ran away from the plantations. Except in the most isolated areas, they were well posted on the progress of the war, and regarded the arrival of Federal troops as the harbinger of their freedom. Many a trusted servant, even some who had managed the plantations during the war, departed at the first opportunity—to the surprise of their former masters. By the end of 1861 both the Union Army and Navy were employing contraband laborers, cooks, and servants on a fairly large scale. In addition to the labor they performed, runaways were also useful to the Union forces as sources of information regarding Confederate movements, positions, and occasionally even plans. Others served as scouts and sometimes as spies. A few escaped slaves were valuable as pilots on expeditions up the narrow, treacherous, meandering channels of the coastal rivers. The most famous of these was Robert Smalls who, one night in May, 1862, as the pilot of *The Planter,* a former cotton boat converted into a Confederate armed vessel, steered her with a party of sixteen past the fortifications in Charleston Harbor to the Union naval force outside.

Despite the contributions of the fugitives, their legal status was a problem for Lincoln's Administration. To have freed them would have alienated the Border States and pro-Union slaveholders in the South and would have aroused the opposition of

* During the War of 1812 Negro sailors had also played a major role in the Battle of Lake Erie.

Northern workingmen who feared an influx of Negroes into Northern cities, where they would be serious competitors. But the abolitionists, both Negro and white, were agitating for emancipating the slaves. In August, 1861, the antislavery general John C. Frémont, facing rebel guerrillas in Missouri, declared martial law, confiscated all the property of rebels, and freed their slaves. Lincoln promptly rescinded the order.

With the President unwilling to do anything to encourage emancipation, the abolitionists shifted their goal toward securing the employment of Negroes as soldiers. Because of the suggestion of racial equality that this idea carried, it was strongly opposed. Therefore the Administration moved haltingly, and then only under considerable pressure.

Toward the end of 1861 Union forces occupied several of the South Carolina Sea Islands. The planters hurriedly departed before the arrival of the troops, and the slaves were assigned to cultivating cotton under the supervision of the United States Treasury Department. In May, 1862, General David Hunter declared these slaves free and impressed the men into the Army. Hunter created a furor with his First South Carolina "Volunteers," both because the Administration regarded the general as exceeding his authority and because the treasury agents and missionaries in the Sea Islands complained that without warning the Negroes had been seized in the fields while they were working and forced into army duty. Lincoln angrily countermanded Hunter's emancipation order, believing that it jeopardized his own plan of compensated emancipation for the Border States. The general disbanded his South Carolina Volunteers on August 10, but already one company of the unit had seen action on the Georgia coast.

By the summer of 1862, with the war going badly, Northern opinion veered toward accepting the idea of arming the slaves, an idea that Negroes and white abolitionists had been urging since the beginning of the war. In March Congress had passed an act forbidding officers to assist in capturing runaways and returning them to their masters. On July 17 Congress passed the second Confiscation Act, which emancipated all slaves who had escaped from rebel masters and gave the President discretionary power to use Negro troops.

Two weeks later General James H. Lane began to recruit

Negro companies openly in Kansas. In Louisiana, where Butler had captured New Orleans in May, 1862, caring for the large number of contrabands proved a heavy responsibility. Since many of the planters had taken an oath of allegiance to the Union, Butler directed that the fugitives return to the plantations. But on August 22 he called for the recruitment of Negro troops. Sensitive to the views of those who were reluctant to arm the slaves, Butler technically simply activated the free Louisiana Native Guards, but slave enlistments were accepted from the beginning. Neither Lane nor Butler was acting on authorization from Washington, and as late as August 6 Lincoln stated publicly that he did not favor the use of Negro troops. Yet less than three weeks later, on August 25, Secretary of War Stanton personally directed General Rufus Saxton to recruit a Negro regiment in the Sea Islands. Undoubtedly, Lincoln had approved of this step. The First South Carolina Volunteers was reconstituted and placed under the command of the Massachusetts abolitionist Colonel Thomas Wentworth Higginson, whose book, *Army Life in a Black Regiment,* later became a minor classic.

By the time Stanton authorized the First South Carolina Colored Volunteers, Lincoln had already decided to issue the Emancipation Proclamation, and on July 21 announced that fact to his cabinet. While it cannot be said with certainty what Lincoln's precise views were during the summer, it is quite likely that in his mind the decision to arm the slaves was closely linked with emancipation. Yet, though sentiment and pressure for freeing and arming the slaves was rising, Lincoln did not show his hand. When, in a New York *Tribune* editorial in August, Horace Greeley denounced Lincoln for subserviency to the slavery interests, and urged emancipating the slaves and enlisting them in the armed forces, Lincoln replied that his duty was to save the Union and that whether he freed all the slaves, or none of them, or some and not others, depended on what seemed best calculated to achieve that goal. It was the last of the alternatives mentioned in this politically shrewd document that Lincoln was going to use. The preliminary proclamation of September, 1862, stated that as of January 1, 1863, slaves in areas held by rebels would be freed.

Originally, Lincoln's plan for emancipation was twofold: compensation for the slaveowners and colonization for the Negroes.

Only in this way did he feel that Union men, especially in the Border States, would accept freeing the slaves. In March, 1862, he sent Congress a message urging gradual emancipation and proposing that the federal government assist states initiating such a plan. Congress concurred and passed a supporting resolution. In April, 1862, Congress also abolished slavery in the District of Columbia with compensation up to $300 per slave. Lincoln advised the Border States to follow, but they ignored his warning that if the war continued, slavery would be abolished in any case and without compensation.

Lincoln's attitude toward Negroes was essentially a conservative one, reflecting the racial biases of the vast majority of American whites. It is doubtful that Lincoln believed that the races were equally endowed; like Jefferson he thought it unlikely that Negroes and whites could live peacefully with equal rights in the same country. He had long been an admirer of colonization. Early in the war the Liberian and Haitian governments had indicated an interest in attracting American Negroes and ex-slaves to their countries and in fact employed agents for that purpose. Lincoln, however, cherished the notion of settlement in Colombia's Chiriquí Province (now in Panama). A speculative, fraudulent company had sold Lincoln on the idea that a Negro colony in Chiriquí could engage in coal mining and supply the United States Navy with fuel at half the usual price. Free Negroes attacked the proposal, and the scheme collapsed when the nature of the company's operations became clear. Later, presidential interest in a similarly unsound colonizing venture on an island off the Haitian coast only led to tragedy for the migrants. Many of them died under the unhealthy conditions and the survivors returned to the United States.

Lincoln had hoped to sweeten emancipation with colonization, and Congress even appropriated money for it. Although his Chiriquí dream failed, the President went ahead with his plan for emancipation. Negroes and white abolitionists were jubilant when on January 1, 1863, Lincoln finally issued the Emancipation Proclamation. Abolitionists—and popular tradition since—magnified the significance of this act far beyond what it actually accomplished. Although it declared free those slaves still in rebel hands and authorized the use of Negro troops for certain purposes, it is hard to see that it did more than the second Confiscation Act. For the slaves still in the Confederacy, freedom of course depended upon the further progress of the Union armies. Since the proclamation did not even claim to free the slaves of the Border States, or those working on plantations in areas like the Mississippi Valley (where many slaveowners had taken an oath of allegiance and pledged their "loyalty" to the national government), from a legal point of view, it was really the Thirteenth Amendment, approved by Congress in February, 1865, and ratified in December, that actually emancipated all the slaves. Practically, of course, slavery as an institution disintegrated with the end of the war. Thus the importance of the Emancipation Proclamation was chiefly symbolic. It rallied the North through an idealistic appeal, encouraged the Negroes to escape and take up arms, and supported the hand of antislavery friends abroad in their efforts to prevent diplomatic recognition of the Confederacy.

After the Emancipation Proclamation the recruitment of Negro troops was gradually accelerated by the national government and some of the states. Massachusetts' antislavery governor was enthusiastic, but New York's Democratic governor refused to request authorization for Negro troops. In fact, though the use of Negroes was welcomed as a relief to the battle-weary white troops, sentiment in New York and many other parts of the North was still highly prejudiced.

An important source of conflict continued to be rooted in economic competition. Stevedores and longshoremen in all the major inland and coastal ports attributed the failure of strikes to Negro strikebreakers. In July, 1862, the employment of Negro stevedores on Ohio river boats precipitated the burning of Cincinnati's Negro section. Not until Negroes retaliated and burned several homes in the Irish neighborhood did the mayor seriously attempt to restore order in the community. Violence and race riots erupted in other Northern cities, but the worst outbreak occurred in New York in July, 1863. The traditional hostility against Negroes had been further inflamed when the conscription law was passed four months earlier. On July 13, the day after announcement of the names drawn for the first draft, a crowd raided the draft headquarters, looted stores and set fire to warehouses, and clubbed and lynched Negroes. For four days the riot continued. People employing Negroes were attacked and their properties sacked. A mob even burned down the Colored Orphan Asylum on Fifth Avenue. After the riot subsided, businessmen raised over $40,000 as a relief fund, and when in March, 1864, the first New York colored regiment departed for the front, its members were feted by the city's most distinguished citizens. The New York *Times* congratulated the community upon a "prodigious revolution" in sentiment—though the careful student might see in this not a profound shift in public opinion but an act of atonement, or a continuing paternalistic concern for the Negroes on the part of New York's upper classes that survived from the turn of the century.

The Negro population in the North was rather small, and if any substantial Negro recruitment for the Union forces were to take place, it would have to be among the Southern freedmen. At the end of March, 1863, Adjutant General Lorenzo Thomas was assigned the task of enlisting Negro troops in the Mississippi Valley. Thomas, in speaking to white Union troops in the course of his travels, made the project palatable to them by offering numerous commissions in the Negro regiments. Thus the creation of these new regiments offered enticing prospects for ambitious white soldiers of all ranks. Thomas' work was a distinct success: in March of 1865, nearly two thirds of the Union troops in the Mississippi Valley were Negroes. Altogether about 180,000 Negroes served in the Union Army, where they comprised about 9 or 10 percent of the total enlistment. Nearly 50,000 were in the Navy, amounting to about one quarter of the total naval forces.

Negro servicemen faced hardships unknown to the white soldiers and sailors. One very serious problem was the Southern policy of either killing Negro soldiers and their white officers, even those who surrendered, or returning the captured Negroes into slavery. The most notorious instance followed the battle of Fort Pillow, on the Mississippi above Memphis, in April, 1864. A rebel force captured the fort, and of the 262 Negroes stationed there, scores were massacred after surrendering. Lincoln warned of retaliation on Confederate prisoners, though the effectiveness of this threat was debatable. The conclusion of Dudley Cornish, the leading scholar on Negro soldiers in the Civil War, is that the main result of the barbarous Confederate policy was to make the Negro troops fight harder, more ruthlessly, and with more determination, since they could expect no mercy.

A Negro serviceman had to contend with other difficulties. Having come reluctantly to the conclusion that Negroes might serve in the armed forces, the Union military leaders saw no reason to consider Negro soldiers the equals of whites. In fact one of the arguments against the use of Negro soldiers had been skepticism about their courage in battle, despite the evidence that Negroes had served effectively in the American Revolution and the War of 1812. Consequently, abolitionists circulated pamphlets to make this information available to the public. At the bloody battles of Port Hudson on the Mississippi below Vicksburg in May, 1863, at the battle of Milliken's Bend on the Mississippi a few weeks later, and at Fort Wagner in South Carolina in July, 1863, Negro troops once again proved their valor. Even though the assault on Port Hudson and the attempt to take Fort Wagner were Union defeats, the steadfastness of the Negroes and the high death rate sustained by them impressed many whites. Yet for the rest of the war, Negro soldiers had to prove themselves over and over again—always there was the lingering suspicion that they were not the equals of whites. Even some generals, like William T. Sherman, refused to the very end of the war to use Negroes in combat.

A disproportionate number of Negro troops were thus relegated to laboring rather than combat duties, and there were other evidences of discrimination as well. Negroes were resentful that few colored men were ever commissioned, and there was even reluctance to promote Negro soldiers to the grade of sergeant. The highest-ranking Negro officers were eight majors in the medical corps, one of whom became a lieutenant colonel, and Martin R. Delany, who was commissioned a major of infantry at the very end of the war. Aside from chaplains, the number of Negro commissioned officers did not exceed one hundred. Most of them served in the Louisiana Native Guards, and even there, when Negro officers died in battle, they were usually replaced with whites.

The pay provisions were also discriminatory. The War Department paid Negro privates ten dollars instead of the thirteen dollars a month received by whites, and of the ten dollars, three was withheld for clothing, rather than permitting the Negro soldiers to purchase it as white soldiers did. Even the few Negro commissioned officers were drawing only ten dollars a month.

The Massachusetts governor proposed that the state pay the difference for the Negro troops of the state, but the 54th and 55th Massachusetts regiments rejected this compromise because on principle they believed that the federal government should end the wage discrimination. Finally, in July, 1864, Congress passed a bill granting equal pay to those Negro soldiers who were free when the war began in 1861, but it was not until March, 1865, that it passed an act providing for full payment for all Negro soldiers retroactive to the date of enlistment.

The efforts of the black and white abolitionists combined with the exigencies of war had led the Union government to free the slaves and enlist Negroes as soldiers. Thus the first steps toward freedom and toward recognition of the Negro as a human being had been taken.

2

Nevertheless there were other problems clamoring for attention—economic conditions, education, civil rights, and the franchise. These were the big issues of the Reconstruction period, as far as Negroes were concerned, and they were also raised during the war. The basic questions at stake were: What would be the future of Negroes in the United States? Would they be full-fledged citizens? Or would the pattern of the Revolutionary era be repeated, and would the promise of American life prove elusive once again?

Just as the Negro leaders had protested discrimination against free Negroes as well as the institution of slavery during the ante-bellum period, so during the war they held that the emancipation of bondsmen would leave the task of the Negroes and their friends only half done. Articulate Negroes expressed a vision of a land of equality, and they realized that freeing the slaves would be but the beginning of their work. In this they were far ahead of most white abolitionists. Frederick Douglass set forth the situation clearly enough in addressing the Third Decade Anniversary Celebration of the American Anti-Slavery Society in December, 1863:

> I am . . . of those who believe that the work of the American Anti-Slavery Society will not have been completed until the black men of the South, and the black men of the North, shall have

been admitted, fully and completely, into the body politic of America. . . . A mightier work than the abolition of slavery now looms up before the Abolitionist. This society was organized, if I remember rightly, for two distinct objects: one was the emancipation of the slave, and the other the elevation of the colored people. When we have taken the chains off the slave, as I believe we shall do, we shall find a harder resistance to the second purpose of this great association than we have found even upon slavery itself.

The views of many Northern Negroes on the future of the race were exemplified by the proceedings of the National Convention of Colored Men, held at Syracuse, New York, in October, 1864. With Frederick Douglass in the chair, about 150 leading colored men formulated a program of action for the months that lay ahead and organized a National Equal Rights League, selecting J. Mercer Langston for president. They were cognizant of the fact that the majority of Northern states still failed to grant Negroes the ballot, and they entertained no illusions that either party—even the Republican—was unprejudiced toward Negroes. Their two chief demands were abolition and political equality. To those, including some abolitionists, who thought Negroes should be satisfied with "personal freedom"—the right to testify in courts of law, the right to own, buy, and sell real estate, the right to sue and be sued—they countered that without the right to vote, "personal freedom" was meaningless. Though Henry Highland Garnet expressed continuing support for colonization, in the light of the changed situation since 1860 most of the delegates were prepared to stake all on their American nationality. While addressing the nation on matters of abolition and citizenship, the convention exhorted the freedmen to moral, educational, and economic elevation. However, at a time when ex-slaves in the South were clamoring for land through expropriation of the plantations, this convention of Northern colored men sidestepped that basic issue and confined itself to a resolution recommending that Negroes from all parts of the country settle "as far as they can, on public lands."

Subsequent conventions, both in the North and South, down to the end of the Reconstruction period, played variations upon these same themes. As in the ante-bellum period some leaders were disturbed by the idea of meeting in segregated "caste" conventions—and indeed with the passage of the Fourteenth Amendment and the Reconstruction Acts, the frequency of state conventions declined noticeably, and national conventions tended to be devoted to efforts to secure specific achievements, such as the national convention of 1873, called for the purpose of rallying support behind Sumner's Supplementary Civil Rights Bill. During the period of Presidential Reconstruction (1865–66), when the Southern states passed the highly discriminatory Black Codes that attempted to remand Negroes almost to a state of servitude, the Negro state conventions in the South took a remarkably sycophantic tone—stressing the importance of behaving well and of acquiring education and property instead of rights, even abjuring at certain conclaves any interest in the ballot. In general, however, the Southern elite Negroes, who met in state conventions from New Orleans to Richmond, expressed the same ideologies as the national conventions. For example, the colored citizens of Norfolk exhibited a typical range of interests when in an "Address . . . to the People of the United States," they urged Negroes to form associations for the agitation of political rights and equality before the law, labor associations to protect colored farm workers, and land associations to aid the freedmen in buying farms.

3

The elite Negroes tended to place primary emphasis on civil and political rights, but what the ex-slaves wanted most of all was land of their own to cultivate and the opportunity to secure an education. Their interest in political activity was somewhat less intense. The freedmen's desire for land mirrored the American faith in property and landownership, in middle-class virtues and pioneer independence. As was true of peasants the world over, their whole lives had been bound up with the soil and its cultivation; to them freedom, respectability, and getting ahead were inextricably associated with farming their own land. Southern planters, on the other hand, wanted to depart as little from ante-bellum conditions as possible, and Northern politicians and philanthropists were divided on the propriety of confiscating Southern plantations and carving homesteads out of them for the freedmen. Consequently the plantation system survived, though organized along new lines, and the sharecropping and crop-lien systems developed as a replacement for the slave labor system.

The evolution of the sharecropping and crop-lien systems began during the Civil War itself. In 1861–62, as the Union armies entrenched themselves on the South Carolina Sea Islands and in the Mississippi Valley, the government was confronted with the problem of providing for the physical needs of the Negroes. There was also the problem of cultivating and harvesting the cotton wanted by Northern textile mills and a potential source of revenue for the Treasury. In the ensuing years the freedmen suffered from the lack of forethought on the part of government officials and power rivalries between the Treasury and Army departments, both of whom were given imprecise control over the affairs of freedmen and plantations. They suffered also from differences of opinion among the missionaries and philanthropists who were sincerely trying to assist the Negroes. Not until the creation of the Freedmen's Bureau in March, 1865, was it definitely settled that the War Department would have the responsibility of protecting and providing for the welfare of the freedmen; and at no time was congressional approval obtained by the advocates of land expropriation and subdivision for the sake of the freedmen. The result was confusion in freedmen's affairs, gross exploitation of the Negroes by unscrupulous entrepreneurs and, in some cases, by dishonest missionaries and army officers, and frustration for the freedmen who had anticipated, with good reason, receiving land of their own. The disillusionment that many abolitionists, missionaries, and Radical Republicans felt with the state of Negro progress by the 1870's was mainly a consequence of this extraordinary mismanagement of freedmen's affairs.

After the Federal authorities first occupied the Sea Islands in November, 1861, the Treasury Department paid the freedmen low wages to work on confiscated cotton plantations, supervised by agents from the private freedmen's aid societies of the North. The missionaries disagreed among themselves: one segment favored land redistribution, while the rest, fearful that such a policy would encourage laziness, preferred the wage system, which they hoped would stimulate thrifty freedmen to purchase their own land. After the administration of freedmen's affairs on the islands was transferred from the Treasury Department to the War Department in July, 1862, General Rufus Saxton encouraged economic independence among the Negroes by dividing plantations into small family units. The Treasury Department, however, decided to sell most of these plantations for unpaid taxes. Although a few Negroes were able to buy some of this land, most of it fell into the hands of white entrepreneurs. The most noted of these was Edward Philbrick, who organized a company among his Boston friends with the intention of uplifting the freedmen and proving their superiority over slave labor, while personally making a financial profit. After operating a highly lucrative venture for a few years, he sold his properties. Meanwhile, when General William T. Sherman came to the Beaufort area on his sweep across the Southeastern states, he issued his famous Order No. 15 of January, 1865, which definitely appeared again to guarantee Negroes the right of pre-emption on the plantation lands. After the war, when President Andrew Johnson restored most of the plantations to their former owners, Negroes who had bought some of Philbrick's land were able to retain title, but thousands of others who had purchased directly from the government lost their holdings. Similarly, in Mississippi, the Army made another unsuccessful attempt to provide Negroes with the opportunity to obtain homesteads. On the plantations of Jefferson Davis and his brother, Negroes were encouraged to run their own affairs under the leadership of Benjamin Montgomery, a freedman who had formerly been a slave overseer on one of these plantations. But this promising community disbanded when some of the land reverted to its former owners and the rest of it was sold to other whites.

Elsewhere, practically no effort was made to encourage Negro landownership. In the Mississippi Valley, Virginia, and North Carolina it was Federal policy to permit the original owners to run their plantations, or if they had fled with the retreating Confederate forces, to lease the land to Northern entrepreneurs. Neither group had any philanthropic concern for the Negro. In Louisiana, where many planters had taken an oath of loyalty to the government, General Nathaniel P. Banks issued regulations in 1863 and 1864 requiring the freedmen to return to the plantations and work for extremely low wages. Under Banks's orders, the Negroes were forbidden to leave the plantation without a pass, and "insolence" or the absence of "perfect subordination" could result in freedmen losing pay or food rations. Negro and white abolitionists condemned the Banks program of servitude; Frederick Douglass charged that "it practically enslaves the Negro and makes the Proclamation of 1863 a mockery and delusion." The New Orleans *Tribune,* a Negro-Creole publication, found little difference between the serfdom imposed by Banks and the old Louisiana slave code:

> If we except the lash, which is not mentioned in these communications, one is unable to perceive any material difference between the two sets of regulations. All the important prohibitions imposed upon the slaves, are also enforced against the freedman. The free laborer, as well as the slave, has to retire into his cabin at a fixed hour in the evening; he cannot leave on Sunday, even to visit friends or simply to take a walk in the neighborhood, unless he be provided with a written authorization. . . . It is true that the law calls him a freeman; but any white man, subjected to such restrictive and humiliating prohibitions, will certainly call himself a slave. . . .

The only aspect of the Banks program which Negroes applauded was the provision establishing a common school system.

Those who hoped that the government would later divide the plantations and distribute the parcels among the freedmen were disappointed. The editors of the New Orleans *Tribune* in 1864— like many of the Negro delegates to the South Carolina constitutional convention in 1868—regarded the tillers of the land as rightfully entitled to the possession of the soil, and urged the creation of a new class of small landholders as the foundation of a truly republican form of government. Washington paid no attention. The *Tribune* might optimistically assert that "revolutions never go backward," but the fact of the matter was that the policy of leasing the plantations to former Southern planters and Northern adventurers remained the general practice in Louisiana and along the Mississippi Valley from Memphis to Vicksburg and Natchez as Federal forces moved South. Lessees interested in making a fast dollar could rent the plantations for ridiculously low sums, paying the Negro laborers very little in wages. In some arrangements, Negroes were paid partly in food, clothing, and medical care, but lessees had endless opportunities to fleece the Negroes of what little they had, and medical care was practically never provided. Government agents interested in the Negroes' welfare, attempted to draw up regulations to mitigate the problems, but at best these were compromises with the demands of the plantation owners and the lessees, and at worst were flagrantly ignored.

Despite the government's failure, and despite the unwillingness of whites to sell land to Negroes, during Reconstruction a significant number of ex-slaves bought farms. Northern observers, Freedmen's Bureau agents, and missionaries enthused over the evidence of such progress. Examples were cited of Negroes who had pooled their resources to buy plantations, which they then divided among themselves. A Boston planter-philanthropist on the Sea Islands reported "a black Yankee," whose industry and sharp dealing had put him ahead of the others on his plantation:

> Limus in his half-acre has quite a little farmyard besides. With poultry-houses, pig-pens, and corn-houses, the array is very imposing. He has even a stable, for he made out some title to a horse, which was allowed; and then he begged a pair of wheels and makes a cart for his work; and not to leave the luxuries behind, he next rigs up a kind of sulky and bows to the white men from his carriage. As he keeps his table in corresponding style . . . the establishment is rather expensive. So, to provide the means, he has three permanent irons in the fire, his cotton, his Hilton Head express, and his seines. . . . While other families "carry" from three to six or seven acres of cotton, Limus says he must have fourteen. . . . With a large boat which he owns, he usually makes weekly trips to Hilton Head, twenty miles distant, carrying passengers, produce and fish. . . . He is all ready to buy land, and I expect to see him in ten years a tolerable rich man.

If Northern authorities were indecisive and confused on the question of Negro landownership, Southern lawmakers were not. During 1865 and 1866 they enacted the Black Codes as a system of social control that would be a substitute for slavery, fix the Negro in a subordinate place in the social order, and provide a manageable and inexpensive labor force. Negroes who were unemployed or without a permanent residence were declared vagrants. They could be arrested and fined, and, if unable to pay, be bound out for terms of labor. States enacted careful provisions governing contracts between employer and laborer—in several states the words "master" and "servant" were freely used—and particularly in South Carolina the terms of the contract were minutely defined. Stiff penalties were provided for those who did not fulfill these contracts or who encouraged Negroes to evade them. These statutes generally guaranteed Negroes the right to sue and be sued and to own property, but they ordinarily could not bear firearms, could testify only in cases involving Negroes, and in Mississippi could own only certain types of property. South Carolina went so far as to exclude Negroes from skilled trades and some types of businesses. Mississippi, Florida, and Texas even enacted Jim Crow transportation laws.

In the face of the Black Codes of 1865–66 and the intransigence of the planters on the one hand, and of President Andrew Johnson's pro-Southern attitude on the other, the Freedmen's Bureau found it difficult to do much for the elevation of the Negro. Its efforts to distribute among the freedmen the abandoned lands which Congress placed under its jurisdiction were thwarted by Johnson's decision to return these properties to pardoned Confederates. Its desire to protect the freedmen with labor contracts was frustrated by the enormity of the task and by the resistance of the planters. The Bureau drew up its own contract forms, but these bore a striking similarity to the unsatisfactory regulations arranged by the Army during the war. The planters received considerable disciplinary authority over their employees, who were forbidden to break the contracts. Through special courts created by the Freedmen's Bureau, the Negroes enjoyed some protection from abuse by their employers. Planters resented the Bureau's interference in their affairs, its attempt to provide protections for Negroes, and the powers of its courts. Yet from the point of view of the freedmen, the Bureau's contracts often seemed like coercive instruments substituting federal force for the ante-bellum slave codes, and many Bureau officials— often paternalistic if not actually prejudiced against Negroes— indeed viewed their basic duty as compelling Negroes to work. In Mississippi, in fact, the Bureau's courts did not function and the contracts provided by state law were allowed to remain in effect. Like the Bureau's contemporaries, historians have disagreed over the way in which the Bureau actually operated, though recent research suggests that it was a far less radical, pro-Negro agency than traditionally believed.

Even more uncertainty surrounds the process by which the

system of farm tenancy known as sharecropping emerged from the labor contract system that prevailed during the Civil War and early Reconstruction years. Under a sharecropping arrangement the freedman, instead of working for a wage, rented a plot of land and paid to the plantation owner a certain proportion of the cotton crop. The origins of this system are extremely obscure. There is at least occasional evidence that some wartime, Army-supervised contracts provided for sharecropping as an alternative to the wage system. Planters generally would have preferred a system whereby Negroes contracted by the year to work for speci-fied wages, but the shortage of available cash right after the war encouraged them to adopt a plan whereby they shared the crop with the Negro workers. A number of scholars hold that the freedmen themselves were largely responsible for the develop-ment of sharecropping, because they regarded the contract labor system, under which they worked in labor gangs, as too reminis-cent of slavery times. Where they were unable to purchase their own land, as was usually the case, the Negroes preferred to be renters rather than hired laborers. Renting was desirable, even under a sharecropping rather than a cash arrangement, because a tenant could organize his own time and be more independent than a hired laborer. Moreover he could raise his own food. Planters, however, also found advantages in the sharecropping system. A hired laborer would work no harder than forced to and, despite the law, might break his contract. But a share-cropper had a vested interest in the crop which he could not afford to leave standing in the field, so that originally the arrangement was one that probably motivated him to work hard for his own advancement. Moreover, the evolution of the system was complicated by the fact that it was not uncommon at first for hired laborers to be paid in whole or in part with a share of the crop at the end of the year. For some years in fact, until the courts straightened the matter out, the two types of sharecrop-ping were not clearly distinguishable.

Whether the chief original impetus came from the planters or from the black peasants, the Freedmen's Bureau officials often either encouraged or permitted the sharecropping contract, and the practice seems to have been stimulated by the shortage of cash resulting from poor crops in 1866 and 1867. Before the end of Reconstruction the sharecropping system appears to have been quite generally adopted. As late as the 1880's, however, the specific terms varied from place to place, and there were still plantations with mixed systems of cultivation, encompassing hired laborers, cash renters, and sharecroppers. Indeed cash renting and hired-laborer work remained significant aspects of the Southern agricultural labor system.

Typically the cropper kept one quarter to one half of the crop, depending on what he supplied in the way of mules, tools, and seed. Planters' evaluations of the system varied. Complaints were made against the inefficiency of the unsupervised tenant farmers, who lacked initiative to improve their plots and maintain the capital improvements on the plantations. Yet the system had its profitable aspects for the planter, and especially for those who, commonly enough, were not overly scrupulous. It was the planter who weighed the cotton and kept the accounts. Due to the inadequate schools the croppers were only semiliterate, and in view of the locus of power in the rural South, even if they knew what was going on, they were unable to assert their rights. This system reached its depths in the crop lien. The croppers paid heavily for the purchases they were compelled to make at the plantation store. Buying food and clothing on credit with the crop as lien, they were charged high prices, outrageous interest rates, and were forced to depend upon the planter's rendition of accounts. After the crop was sold, they were likely to end up in debt to the planter, particularly in a poor year. Out of this arose the system of debt peonage, whereby insolvent croppers, unable to repay debts from one year to another, were required by law to work indefinitely for the same unscrupulous planter.

4

If land ownership was central to the lower-class freedmen's wishes, close to it in importance was the desire for education. Identifying it with the superior status of white men, the freedmen naturally shared the American passion for common school instruction. Old and young flocked to the schools opened by the missionaries as the Federal armies moved southward.

The freedmen's aid societies that sprang up in the North in 1861–62 among both whites and Negroes, aimed to provide the contrabands with food, clothing, medicine, and the rudiments of an education. The activities of the white societies are better known, both because of white tendencies to ignore what Negroes were doing and because the work of the white groups had greater financial resources and was therefore more extensive. Northern Negroes were active as well, under both religious and secular auspices. Among the outstanding Negro freedmen's aid societies were the Contraband Relief Association and the Union Relief Association of Israel Bethel Church (AME), in Washington; the Contraband Committee of Mother Bethel Church, in Philadelphia; and the Freedmen's Friend Society of Brooklyn. The African Civilization Society switched its activities from colonization to establishing schools among the contrabands in Washington. Between 1862 and 1868 the African Methodist Episcopal Church contributed nearly $167,000 toward freedmen's aid.

The white nonsectarian benevolent associations that dominated the work among the freedmen during the war underwent kaleidoscopic reorganization between 1862 and 1866. Sectarian missionary societies entered the field in 1864, and after the war they displaced the secular groups. Even the most important of the organizations assisting the freedmen, the American Missionary Association, which had been founded by leaders of the American and Foreign Anti-Slavery Society in 1846 as a nonsectarian antislavery missionary organization, ultimately became an arm of the Congregational Church.

While the freedmen's aid societies performed a valuable service in providing various forms of relief for the contrabands, their most permanent contribution was in education. Apparently the earliest school for contrabands was opened by Mary Chase, a free Negro of Alexandria, Virginia, on September 1, 1861. Two weeks later, Mrs. Mary Peake, a colored woman, opened the first of the freedmen's aid societies' schools, under the auspices of the American Missionary Association, near Fortress Monroe in Virginia. Early in the following year Northern abolitionists energetically took up the task of education among the freedmen. As the Union armies advanced, increasing opportunities for "good work" led to a proliferation of freedmen's aid societies. The overwhelming majority of workers sent South by the white benevolent societies were Caucasians, but there were some Negroes among them. Charlotte Forten, granddaughter of James Forten, joined the teachers at Port Royal, South Carolina, in the summer of

1862. Francis L. Cardozo, a free-born Charlestonian educated at the University of Glasgow, was the first principal of the American Missionary Association's Avery Institute in his native city.

The mushrooming activities of the freedmen's aid societies would not have been possible without the endorsement of the federal government and the active co-operation of the military authorities, whatever the strains and stresses that the co-operation between these two very different groups entailed. In fact, in 1863–64 in Louisiana, it was the military authorities who created the first system of public schools for freedmen in New Orleans and its environs. This pattern of joint participation between the missionaries and the War Department was expanded under the Freedmen's Bureau, which gave hundreds of thousands of dollars to Negro education between 1866 and 1870. Under the terms of the law, the Bureau supplied the buildings while the freedmen's aid societies paid the salaries of the teachers. Since in many cases the Northern philanthropic groups had difficulty in raising enough money, the Bureau often rented buildings owned by the freedmen's aid societies, and with this money the latter paid their teachers.

With the financial resources at its disposal, the Bureau was especially helpful in establishing some of the stronger schools that included college departments. In part because of the close relationships General O. O. Howard, Commissioner of the Bureau, enjoyed with his fellow Congregationalists of the American Missionary Association, and in part because of the superiority of the leadership and administration of the AMA schools, that organization benefited more than any of the others from Howard's funds. The Bureau financed only one collegiate institution of its own, Howard University in Washington, but the roster of American Missionary Association schools included most of the finest institutions of Negro higher education: Atlanta University, Fisk University in Nashville, Talladega College in Alabama and Tougaloo in Mississippi, and the fountainhead of industrial education in Negro schools, Hampton Institute in Virginia.

The response of the freedmen to instruction was enthusiastic. Missionary teachers were uniformly impressed by the ex-slaves' passion for learning. A teacher at Port Royal, South Carolina, recorded how families moved across the river so that their children could attend school; one woman "came to school daily with a baby in her arms and two boys by her side. They all stood up to read together." In 1866 the Freedmen's Bureau superintendent of education not only found that Negroes of all ages were attending school, but that black children attended more regularly than white ones. Especially impressive were the numerous efforts of Negroes to develop their own schools, hiring the teachers and even erecting buildings. In December, 1866, South Carolina Negroes raised $1,000 for their schools; in Georgia at that time there were ninety-six schools supported in whole or in part by the freedmen, who owned fifty-seven of the buildings. Such efforts ranged from the newly taught and barely educated, who were engaged in teaching those unable to read at all, to more elaborate efforts under adequately equipped teachers. At Goldsboro, North Carolina, in 1865, for example, the Freedmen's Bureau superintendent of education found that "two colored young men, who but a little time before commenced to learn themselves, had gathered one hundred and fifty pupils, all quite orderly and hard at study. A small tuition was charged, and they needed books. These teachers told me that no white man, before me, had ever come near them."

As a result of congressional action in 1867, Southern Negroes were enfranchised and new constitutions written in each of the ex-Confederate states. The new regimes, adopting a reform instituted in the North a generation earlier, provided for universal common school education. In the constitutional conventions held in South Carolina, Louisiana, and Virginia, there was considerable debate over the question of school segregation, and South Carolina and Louisiana provided for legally unsegregated schools. In South Carolina the Negro members of the convention insisted that the state constitution explicitly make schools open to all, though they predicted that the two races would of their own accord tend to go to separate educational institutions. In the end only New Orleans instituted a system of mixed elementary and high schools. South Carolina leaders made no effort to compel acceptance of Negro youth in white schools, and the university was the only integrated school in that state. Virginia, which very shortly passed under the control of the whites, or "Redeemers,"* quickly enacted a law requiring school segregation. Everywhere

---

* "Redeemers" is a term used to refer to the men under whose leadership the South was restored to white domination.

in the South separation was the administrative policy of school boards where it was not specifically demanded by legislation. Without exception the segregated schools were inferior and failed to give Negroes even the rudiments of an adequate education.

Consequently, the real burden of training a Negro professional elite and an educated leadership fell upon the missionary schools. The Northern teachers conceived of their task in broad terms. They aimed to give the rudiments of learning necessary for the ex-slaves to function as free men even in a rural environment; to inculcate habits of thrift, industry, and Christian character, which would enable their students to rise to middle-class status (hence the homilies on middle-class ethics, and the interest in "industrial" classes for sewing and various trades, and in manual labor schools like Hampton); to train teachers for the public schools (hence the prevalence of normal schools on the secondary level); and to provide a college education for those intending to enter other professions. There was much condescension and paternalism among the white missionaries, particularly among those advocates of industrial education who thought higher education unsuitable for the freedmen, at least for the present; but there was also much serious interest in proving Negroes capable of the highest intellectual endeavor and in encouraging the full participation of the ex-slaves in American society.

In the early years the missionary schools concentrated on elementary and normal training, because in the short run this was the most essential, and also because the public schools were so inadequate. In fact, until the twentieth century, private secondary institutions were the chief source of competent Negro public school teachers in the South. Moreover, the missionary societies discovered that in order to obtain qualified college students, they needed to maintain their own elementary and secondary departments. For years the college departments were small. Even the very best Negro colleges maintained elementary and secondary school programs until well into the twentieth century. Leading liberal arts institutions like Tougaloo College in Mississippi and Spelman College (founded in 1881 as Atlanta Baptist Female Seminary) were originally superior normal and industrial schools and did not offer liberal arts college programs until around 1900.

The development of private schools on all levels, especially those aspiring to offer collegiate work, was in part a philan-

thropic mission and in part the result of denominational ambitions. Ordinarily each of the private colleges was connected, at
least informally, with a church established to proselytize among
the Southern Negroes. This was particularly true of the Methodist
Episcopal Church, North, which developed a sizable Southern
Negro membership and opened schools in most of the Southern
states. Among the more important Methodist institutions whose
origins go back to this period were New Orleans University (later
merged with Congregationalist Straight University to form Dil-
lard University), Clark College in Atlanta, and Claflin University
in Orangeburg, South Carolina. The Episcopalians and Presbyterians established only a few schools, but the Baptists did
extensive work, though only a few of their numerous institutions
became really outstanding. Among the most successful ones were
Shaw University in Raleigh, North Carolina, Virginia Union
University in Richmond, and Morehouse College (originally
Atlanta Baptist College). The Baptists and Methodists were the
only denominations that founded medical schools in connection
with their colleges: Leonard Medical School at Raleigh, Meharry in Nashville, and Flint in New Orleans.

Of these Northern-based, predominantly white denominations,
only the Baptists worked out co-operative arrangements whereby
the independent Negro connnections (or organizations) of the
same faith contributed to the support of these missionary schools
and colleges. On the other hand, the various Negro Methodist
denominations established their own elementary, secondary, and
collegiate institutions in the South. With the advance of the
Union Army, Negro Baptist churches had sprung up everywhere
and the AME Church had spread rapidly throughout the South.
The AME Zion Church was especially successful in North Carolina under the zealous missionary work of Rev. J. W. Hood, who
took an active part in freedmen's educational and political affairs
and made North Carolina the new center for his denomination.
After the Civil War the Negro members of several Southern white
churches established their own denominations. With the religious
expansion went an interest in the education of the freedmen,
though meager financial resources limited activity in this field.
Both Methodist and Baptist white churches founded a number of
elementary and secondary institutions. Then in 1878 the Colored
Methodist Episcopal Church (established in 1870 as the result of

a friendly withdrawal from the Methodist Episcopal Church, South) opened Lane College in Jackson, Tennessee. The AME Zion Church founded its only college, Livingstone, in North Carolina, in 1879 under the leadership of J. C. Price. Price when he died in 1894 was an accommodationist leader of such prominence that had he lived he might have occupied the place later held by Booker T. Washington. Finally in 1881 and 1885, the AME Church established its first two Southern colleges: Allen University in Columbia, South Carolina (an outgrowth of Payne Institute, established at Cokesbury in 1871) and Morris Brown College in Atlanta.

In the South during the three quarters of a century following Reconstruction, most of the leading professional men and many prominent businessmen were the products of the church-related colleges, although above the Mason-Dixon line leading physicians, lawyers, and teachers were more likely to have graduated from the best Northern colleges and universities. The Southern church colleges also served as transmitters of Northern polite culture to the children of the modestly educated artisan elite of the postwar years, and as a route of upward mobility for men of humbler status. However, in regard to these matters, there was a hierarchy among the colleges in each of the states and major cities. Generally the Congregationalist schools were the best and therefore the most prestigious, while the Negro-owned institutions were the least highly regarded. This was chiefly a reflection of the fact that the relative financial strength of their backers determined the quality of instruction offered by the schools of these various denominations. Congregationalist Atlanta and Fisk universities were the fashionable institutions in their respective cities, though both Atlanta and Nashville had several Negro colleges, and in Nashville the Methodist Meharry Medical College attracted many upward-mobile young men. In fact Fisk and Atlanta became the most highly regarded Negro schools in the entire South, and along with Howard and Lincoln universities produced the largest number of distinguished alumni. On the other hand, in Virginia where the Congregationalists sponsored Hampton Normal and Agricultural Institute, Virginia Union University (Baptist) was the leading liberal arts college. And in South Carolina where upper-class and aspiring Charleston children attended the American Missionary Association's secondary school, Avery Institute, there was no Congregationalist college and a high proportion of the state's leaders were therefore graduates of the Methodist Church's Claflin University.

The contribution of the private colleges was made against enormous odds. Even prior to the cessation of Freedmen's Bureau assistance in 1870, Northern philanthropy had declined precipitately. A few years later the panic of 1873 curtailed the income and operations of the schools even further. Meanwhile, beginning in the late 1860's, the violence, including murder and arson, perpetrated by Southern whites against the Northern schoolteachers and their institutions, had forced a number to close their doors. Moreover, it became less fashionable for whites to work among the freedmen, and mediocrity increased in the ranks of the white instructors. Nevertheless, despite the intimidation, despite the difficulties in obtaining financial support and qualified teachers, the schools struggled on. In the 1880's and 1890's the millionaire philanthropists began to turn their attention to Negro schools, but even then the assistance was directed more toward providing industrial training than college education.

5

Negroes, in addition to recognizing that education and the opportunity for economic advancement were essential for full participation in American society, or in the "body politic," as the phrase of the time went, also focused their attention on the full attainment of constitutional rights, full equality before the law.

During the war Negroes and white abolitionists continued their campaign of ante-bellum days against discrimination in the North. By 1865 Congress had repealed the 1825 act prohibiting Negroes from being mail carriers and had provided that Negro witnesses were not to be excluded from federal courts. In a number of states Negroes took the initiative in fighting oppressive legislation. As a result of this pressure, in 1863 California repealed its anti-Negro testimony law, and in 1865 and 1866 Illinois and Indiana repealed their anti-Negro testimony and anti-Negro immigration legislation, more widely known as the Black Laws. In Illinois the agitation was conducted by a Repeal Association, organized by Chicago Negroes under the leadership of the prosperous merchant-tailor, John Jones.

The situation in the 1860's is thus comparable to that in the 1960's: changes in white sentiment connected with the Civil War made it possible for Negroes to achieve their successes, but it seemed that Negroes still had to battle every step of the way for the recognition of their citizenship rights. Even where legal impediments to civil rights were removed or did not exist, patterns of segregation retained much vitality. Under the leadership of the noted caterer and protest leader, George Thomas Downing, of New York and Newport, Negroes fought against segregated schools in Rhode Island and in 1866 succeeded with a campaign that had begun in 1857. They also protested against the continuing use of segregated streetcars. In Washington incidents occurred when streetcars refused to pick up colored people. Negroes protested and Senator Charles Sumner obtained a law prohibiting such discrimination in 1865. The practice continued, however, and not until Sojourner Truth secured the arrest and dismissal of a streetcar conductor who had assaulted her was the matter settled. Even more celebrated was the agitation against discrimination on horsecars in Philadelphia. Under the leadership of William Still, Negroes intensified their fight on this issue during the Civil War. Securing the support of an impressive array of white citizens, they nevertheless failed with appeals to the streetcar company and the city authorities. Finally, in 1867, the state legislature passed a law prohibiting segregation in public transportation. Only Massachusetts, however, actually outlawed discrimination in hotels, restaurants, theatres, and other amusement places.

In the South, segregation was extended as a tool of racial domination in place of slavery. Most of the segregation, however, was still licensed by custom rather than law, and considerable historical research is needed to determine its exact extent. Also deserving of careful inquiry is the extent to which Negroes protested against the discrimination. The New Orleans Negro press denounced the "star" streetcars intended for Negroes, and in 1866 groups of Negroes blocked their passage in the streets. Consequently, the military authorities required the provisional governor to outlaw the separate streetcars. In both Charleston and Richmond in 1867, Negroes decided to defy streetcar segregation. In Richmond violence resulted, but in Charleston the military commander ordered an end to the discrimination. During

the period when Negroes were holding elective office in South
Carolina, legislation was passed penalizing discrimination in
places of public accommodation, and Negroes freely used the
theatres and hotels in the leading cities and the first-class railway
cars. In Louisville, in 1871, Negroes protesting against transportation segregation entered the horsecars reserved for whites until
they wrested the right to ride in them without discrimination.

Meanwhile Congress had turned its attention to civil rights. In
1866 it passed over President Johnson's veto the Civil Rights
Act, which defined American-born Negroes as citizens and enumerated certain rights to which they were entitled: to sue and be
sued; to give evidence; and to buy, sell, and inherit property. It
also provided vaguely that Negroes had the right to the full and
equal benefit of all laws. The Fourteenth Amendment, proposed
by Congress in June, 1866, and ratified July, 1868, added a
similarly vaguely worded constitutional guarantee against discrimination by the states. Continuing segregation indicated that
the amendment did not include sufficient sanctions, and Negroes
accordingly threw their vigorous support behind Senator Sumner's
Supplementary Civil Rights Bill, which specifically offered protection against segregation in transportation, schools, and public
accommodation. The largest of the Negro national conventions,
held in Washington in 1873, was devoted entirely to propagandizing for this bill, which, with the clause regarding mixed
schools deleted, was finally passed in 1875. When Negroes tested
the law in Northern and Southern cities, they discovered that
there were many evasions and violations. Moreover, they soon
found the machinery of enforcement so cumbersome, and relief
so uncertain, that they ceased trying to secure the rights which it
aimed to guarantee. Eventually, in 1883, the Supreme Court declared the law unconstitutional.

6

The history of the Negro's political rights followed a course
roughly parallel with that of civil rights. Negro leaders considered
the right to vote as central to all others. They viewed it as the
means to gain and protect their other rights in American society.
At the same time, extending the franchise to Negroes would
vindicate American institutions before the world. Time and time

again during the war Negro leaders agitated on the question, and it became a major theme in the postwar Negro conventions. A convention of Pennsylvania leaders declared in 1868:

> The vote of one black man now—today—right here in his native land, is worth to the nation, to liberty, to the securing of our rights as citizens, and the establishing of the Republic on the eternal foundations of truth and justice, more than is involved in the theory of civilization of all other parts of the world. It is America that you have to civilize, to Christianize, and compel to accept and practically apply to all men, without distinction of color or race, the glorious principles and precepts laid down in her immortal Declaration of Independence. To build up a nation here, sacred in freedom, as an example to the world, every man equal in the law and equally exercising all rights, political and civil . . . is the surest way to civilize humanity.

Southern Negroes were also evincing interest in the franchise. In November, 1863, a mass meeting of New Orleans colored men petitioned the state's military governor, requesting the right to vote in the election for delegates to the forthcoming state constitutional convention; and in January, 1864, they petitioned President Lincoln on the same matter. Lincoln wrote to the provisional governor, suggesting privately that the constitutional convention consider granting the ballot to at least some of the ante-bellum free Negroes. Nothing was done about this proposal, and continued efforts to secure the vote failed until Congress acted in 1867.

The Reconstruction Act of 1867 provided that each of the Southern states was to be placed under a military governor until a convention, chosen on the basis of universal manhood suffrage, wrote a constitution that would meet the requirements set by Congress. The constitutions thus adopted did extend the suffrage to all adult male citizens. The Fifteenth Amendment, proposed by Congress in 1869 and ratified the following year, reinforced the Reconstruction Act and the new Southern state constitutions. It also secured the vote for Negroes in those Northern states where they were disfranchised. Because these states in the North failed to ratify the amendment, its ratification by the reconstructed Southern states actually enabled Negroes in many parts of the North to exercise the franchise.

The constitutional conventions called in accordance with the

Reconstruction Act of 1867 all contained Negro members. Only in South Carolina, however, were they in the majority in the convention, and Louisiana was the only other state where they comprised as many as half of the delegates. Nor can it be said that Negroes and their white carpetbagger allies together controlled all of the conventions. In Georgia, for example, the influence of native whites was so strong that the legislative seats were apportioned to the advantage of the predominantly white counties. The first legislature elected after the constitution had been adopted even ousted its Negro members. Before departing, Representative Henry M. Turner, an AME minister, delivered a sarcastic denunciation from the floor of the House. But Negroes were not readmitted until the state supreme court ruled in their favor in 1869.

As a result of the new constitutions Negroes were elected to public office in all the Southern states. The highest position held was that of United States Senator. Two men, Hiram Revels and Blanche K. Bruce, represented Mississippi in the United States Senate, the former for a two-year unexpired term, the latter for a full term that commenced after Reconstruction had been overthrown in the state. Fourteen Negroes sat in the House of Representatives between 1869 and the end of Reconstruction in 1877. The highest state office attained was lieutenant governor. Two men held this office in South Carolina, one in Mississippi, and three in Louisiana. P. B. S. Pinchback served as acting governor of Louisiana for over a month when the carpetbagger chief executive was on trial for corruption. Negroes served as secretaries of state in Florida, Louisiana, Mississippi, and South Carolina; as superintendents of education in Arkansas, Florida, Louisiana, and Mississippi; and as state treasurers in Florida and South Carolina. Jonathan C. Gibbs was first secretary of state and then superintendent of public instruction in Florida; Francis Cardozo acted first as secretary of state and then as state treasurer in South Carolina. J. J. Wright, who had been the first Negro lawyer in Philadelphia, was an associate justice of the South Carolina Supreme Court. John R. Lynch, who was later a congressman, served as speaker of the Mississippi House of Representatives.

An adequate analysis of Negro leaders at all political levels in this period remains to be made. Most of them seem to have been either ex-slaves or from the North. It would appear that the ante-bellum free Negro artisan class was too closely identified with upper-class whites to be trusted by the freedmen. Some, like Francis Cardozo and South Carolina's Congressman Robert Brown Elliott, both of whom graduated from college in Great Britain, were well-educated men, whose training was far superior to practically all of the white officeholders during Reconstruction or after. A high proportion of the Negro political leaders were ministers and teachers.

The white Southerners who overthrew Reconstruction, and their apologists ever since, have charged Negro domination and corruption as justification for their acts. Actually, at no time can Negroes be said to have been in control of any Southern state. None was ever elected or nominated for governor. Only in the lower house of the South Carolina legislature were colored men ever in a majority. South Carolina was the only state with a Negro serving as supreme court justice, Mississippi the only one that sent Negroes to the United States Senate. Obviously, even in these two states, where Negroes were over half the population, they never really controlled the governments since the highest state office eluded them and the majority of important offices were always in white hands. And for a state like Georgia, where there was only one Negro congressman and no Negroes at all in high executive or judicial office, the charge of Negro domination is clearly without substance.

Nor can it be said that Negroes were consistently identified with the corrupt elements among the carpetbaggers and scalawags. Actually, the highest costs of state government arose out of the corruption associated with railroad construction and railroad subsidies, and in these Democrats participated as much as Republicans, and the post-Reconstruction regimes as much as or more than the Radical Republican regimes. Mississippi, with more Negro officials than most Southern states, had no graft on the state level, and very little lower down in the political hierarchy, during Reconstruction, but a considerable amount of it under the Redeemers afterward. In Louisiana and South Carolina, where corruption seemed especially flamboyant, certain prominent Negro politicians supported conservative coalitions that attacked the corrupt elements in the Republican Party. In Louisiana, while Pinchback appears to have been an opportunist, Lieutenant Governor Oscar J. Dunn fought the corrupt group. In

South Carolina Martin R. Delany and R. H. Cain, a two-term congressman and later bishop in the AME Church, for a while at least supported the Democrats in preference to the graft-ridden elements in their own party.

Most historians have concluded that as a group Negro politicians accomplished little. The exact way in which Negro politicians functioned during Reconstruction, however, has never been analyzed. In view of their range of abilities and talents, it seems likely that just as the white Republicans prevented Negroes from receiving even a proportionate share of high offices and legislative seats, in the decision-making process they mostly ignored those few Negroes who did achieve high position. The two Senators from Mississippi, for example, were rather conservative Negroes, who were useful as symbols to the Negro voters. Neither these men nor the more militant political leaders seem to have been consulted much in matters of importance. After all, if white abolitionists practically ignored Negroes in the counsels of their movement, it was unlikely that an assortment of idealists, Southern whites, and opportunists would do more.

In any event, whether black politicians were powerless or influential, corrupt or incorruptible, Southern whites resented them. In the 1860's, as in the 1960's, the Southern white man perceived the black man as a threat to his security, his status, his dominance. During the 1870's white Southerners used a variety of methods to reassert their control. In states where Negroes were in a minority, or where, as in Georgia and Florida, the apportionment of legislative seats favored the whites, it was a relatively simple matter to overturn the radical regimes. In some cases, notably Virginia, Negroes for many reasons sided with the upper-class white conservatives. Even in South Carolina many Negroes believed Wade Hampton's promises when he ran as the Democratic candidate for governor in 1876; and he in turn kept his word to the extent that for years those Negroes who had voted for him remained on the suffrage rolls. White Southerners also terrorized Negroes and their white sympathizers from the North. Techniques of intimidation included economic pressures against recalcitrant Negroes and violence in the form of beatings, murders, and even race riots.

Southern whites were not entirely responsible for the success of their methods. The fact was that the North had changed its mind. Most Northerners had never been racial egalitarians, and they had had to be pushed and shoved to accord equal constitutional rights to Negroes. When it came to essential economic reform in the South, the North failed entirely. The economic interests which had looked to the Republican Party and its continued hegemony as the basis for advancing their own interests eventually formed an alliance with substantial Southern business elements which had complementary needs. They arranged for the Compromise of 1877 whereby Southern Democrats acquiesced in the elevation of the Republican Rutherford B. Hayes to the Presidency in the disputed election with the Democrat Samuel J. Tilden. Even those individuals who had been most sincerely interested in the Negro became tired, disillusioned with the freedmen, and enamored of the idea of sectional reconciliation. They had anticipated great things of the black man. When, very largely because of the confusion and halfheartedness of the policies of their supposed benefactors, the freedmen did not live up to these high expectations, those very benefactors concluded that the ex-slaves were not ready for self-government. Corruption in high circles did not disqualify whites for self-government, but somehow it did seem to disqualify the Negroes, who had been notably less corrupt. Thus, even the Northern humanitarians deserted the freedmen and left them under the control of their former masters and the even more hostile working-class whites.

All in all, the Northern whites—including many former abolitionists—found it relatively easy to pay the price of sectional reconciliation. That price was the rejection of the idea of a racially egalitarian society—and even the desertion of the Negro's fundamental constitutional rights. The Negroes' vision of a just and democratic society seemed doomed to frustration. A hundred years after Emancipation Martin Luther King could still best express the extent of Negro participation in American society by saying, "I have a dream. . . ."

V

"UP FROM SLAVERY": THE AGE OF ACCOMMODATION

1

DURING THE GENERATION following the Compromise of 1877 Negroes throughout the country found themselves increasingly the victims of discrimination, proscription, and mob violence. This was particularly true in the South, where the withdrawal of federal military support from the last of the "radical" governments and the acceptance of white and Democratic hegemony in the South by the officials at Washington left Southern Negroes without any effective defense, permitting the unimpeded development of a race system that supplanted the old institution of slavery as a mechanism of social control.

Negro voting fell off precipitately with the restoration of the Southern state governments to the control of the Redeemers. First by violence primarily, and then by ballot-box stuffing, false returns, and complicated registration and voting procedures, Negro political influence was effectively curtailed. It was not at once completely eliminated, however. Democratic votes were cast by some Southern Negroes, who were mainly of the old servant class, or successful, conservative farmers and businessmen, with close ties to the ante-bellum Southern white aristocracy. A Mississippi Negro owner of five or six hundred acres of land and more than a hundred head of cattle, all acquired since the war, told a Senate committee in 1879 he voted Democratic "because I sympathize with my own self, knowing that I expected to stay with them [the Southern white Democrats] to make property if I could, and the South has always been kind to me. My master that I lived with I nursed him and slept at his mother's feet and nursed at her breast, so I thought my interest was to stay with the majority of the country who I expected to prosper with." Moreover, in the predominantly Negro counties of both Mississippi and South Carolina during the 1880's and early 1890's, there appeared the practice known as "fusion"—dividing up the offices between Negro Republicans and white Democrats so that the former held a seat or so in the legislature and a share of the less important local positions.

Indeed, there was something of a revival of Negro voting as alliances with independent parties like the Virginia Readjusters, the Greenbackers, and the Populists helped to stave off complete political effacement for a while; but this trend only culminated in the final wave of race riots and constitutional disfranchisement. Mississippi in 1890 and South Carolina in 1895 were the first states to amend their constitutions effectively to disfranchise practically all Negroes; between 1898 and 1903 Louisiana, North Carolina, Alabama, and Virginia imitated them, followed by Oklahoma and Georgia in 1907 and 1908. Generally these revised constitutions required poll taxes and literacy and/or property qualifications, which could be applied discriminatorily by voting registrars, especially in the case of literacy qualifications. Some constitutions provided an obvious escape hatch for Southern whites by the device of a "grandfather clause," which waived these requirements for those whose ancestors had voted in 1860. Florida, Arkansas, Tennessee, and Texas employed poll taxes and other devices short of constitutional change.

Between 1896 and 1915 all Southern states passed legislation that permitted the Democratic Party, nomination by which was nearly always tantamount to election, to declare only whites eligible for voting in primary elections. The United States Supreme Court consistently refused to intervene in these disfranchisement regulations, until in 1915 it declared the Oklahoma grandfather clause unconstitutional. In view of these facts, and in the face of the riots in Wilmington, North Carolina, in 1898, and Atlanta, Georgia, in 1906, which capped the disfranchisement campaigns in those states, Southern Negroes became increasingly disillusioned with political activity.

The wave of disfranchisement legislation after 1890 was contemporaneous with the Populist movement and the rise of the so-called "poor whites" to political consciousness and power. The agrarian protest of the Populist Party was rooted in the work of the Northern and Southern Farmers' Alliances that developed during the 1880's. Allied with the Southern Farmers' Alliance was the Colored Alliance, formed in Texas in 1886 by a white Baptist preacher. The Colored Farmers' Alliance and Co-operative Union spread over the South and at its peak claimed a membership of over a million members. Unfortunately little is known about the organization, but evidently, like the white Alliance, it sponsored farmers' co-operatives. By and large the platform of the Colored Alliance resembed that of the white Southern Alliance. Yet there were differences. The Colored Alliance favored the Lodge Federal Elections Bill, designed to guarantee the voting rights of Negroes in the South in national elections through the use of federal troops; the Southern Alliance opposed it. Disagreement also arose over the question of a cotton pickers' strike fostered by the Colored Alliance in 1891 but opposed by the Southern Alliance, many of whose members employed Negro cotton pickers. Two years before the strike, a group of North Carolina Negroes accused the Southern Alliance of setting low wages and influencing the legislature to pass discriminatory laws. The Colored Alliance appears to have collapsed about the end of 1891, shortly after the cotton pickers were defeated.

The alleged membership figures of the Colored Alliance probably makes it the largest Negro organization in American history. It is all the more amazing therefore that it has left so little evidence of its existence. The paucity of data merely leaves a number of intriguing questions: Under what circumstances did Negroes join and to what extent, if any, was participation encouraged (or even demanded) by white employers who were members of the Southern Alliance? (In this connection it is noteworthy that the organization's founder and president was a white Texas preacher.) Why did it collapse so quickly after the cotton pickers' strike, and was the strike really at fault? Is it possible that the Colored Alliance was something like a company union, disintegrating only when it became evident that the Negro tenant farmers refused to follow the dictates of their white employers? To what extent did the Colored Alliance engage in large-scale co-operative enterprise? And to what extent did its members share in a conscious feeling of class solidarity against the Redeemers and capitalists? If, as claimed by romantic writers seeking to establish a historical base for united action of poor whites and Negroes, genuine solidarity along class lines was evident in the Alliance, why were Negroes organized into a separate Alliance? And how was it that the Alliance men and Populists were later so easily led into extreme anti-Negro actions? In spite of various gestures to obtain Negro support, attitudes such as those exhibited in North Carolina and on the Lodge Bill would argue that whatever interracial solidarity existed was not firmly rooted.

Confusing and paradoxical are the only terms to describe the radical agrarian movement when it entered politics in the 1890's. In South Carolina, Benjamin Tillman captured the Democratic Party in the name of the radical agrarians, partly by appealing to race prejudice; under his leadership South Carolina became the second state to enact constitutional disfranchisement. Yet in other situations, the agrarians did make substantial efforts to obtain the support of Negroes, who responded to a considerable degree. Even though the back-country whites were traditionally hostile to Negroes, and even though the Lodge Federal Elections Bill alarmed Southern white farmers and played into the hands of the Democrats, part of the Populist political strategy was a coalition with Negro farmers. A few Negroes were delegates to the St. Louis conference of Farmers' Alliances and other organizations in 1892, which in effect launched the Populist Party in national politics. One Negro served as assistant secretary at the conference. His election was made all but unanimous on the motion of a white Georgian, who said, "We can stand that down in Georgia." A Negro's name appeared on a call for the national nominating convention held at Omaha by the Populist Party in July, 1892.

In some states at least, Negro participation in the Populist Party was significant. As early as 1890 the Kansas Alliance Party had nominated a Negro for state auditor, and at least a sizable minority of Negro voters supported Populists in that state in 1892. In the same year, the Arkansas Populist platform contained a resolution proposed by a Negro delegate, "that it is the object of the People's Party to elevate the downtrodden, irrespective of race or color." In Louisiana among the delegates to the first convention of the party in that state were twenty-four Negroes, one of whom was nominated for state treasurer but withdrew. In Texas two Negroes were named to the party's executive committee in 1891, and there were always colored members of that body until 1900. In Georgia occurred perhaps the most spectacular effort to enlist Negro support, with Tom Watson, the white Populist leader, openly espousing the cause of Negroes and defending his Negro backers against violence. Generally, Populist platforms in the Southern states denounced the convict lease system* and lynching, and supported political rights for Negroes.

The evidence concerning political coalitions between Republicans and Populists on state and local candidates is difficult to evaluate. In a number of states in 1892, 1894, and 1896, fusion was attempted—sometimes formally, sometimes informally. But Populist fusion with Republicans did not necessarily mean with Negroes. In Georgia, for example, in 1896, the white Republican leaders, whom Negroes accused of racism, supported the Populists. On the other hand, prominent Negro members of the state Republican executive committee maintained close connections with upper-class white Democrats and urged colored men not to back the Populists. It was generally agreed by Negroes in a position to know that in Alabama and Georgia colored men supported the Democrats rather than the Populists on the whole, though of course this was accomplished largely by intimidation, fraud, and other pressures. Broadly speaking, fusion tended to be between the Populists and the Lily-white Republican faction rather than between Populists and the Black-and-Tan faction of the party.† On the other hand, the election of 1896 in North Carolina was a notably successful example of fusion between Populists and Negro Republicans.

* Under the convict lease system, state and county governments leased prisoners to plantation owners and industrialists for a small fee. An incredibly brutal system of labor exploitation developed on plantations, in mines, turpentine camps, and railroad construction. Negroes who had been convicted of committing petty crimes were the chief victims of this system.

† In the Southern states the Lily-whites were the white Republican faction that sought to purge Negroes from leadership positions in the

Of all Southern states North Carolina was the least discriminatory in its racial practices. For example, it sent a Negro to Congress during most of the 1880's and 1890's. In 1894 fusion was not officially adopted, but Republicans nominated the same slate of state officials as the Populists. Populists failed to endorse the Negro candidates of the Republicans, but remained silent rather than attacking them, and as a result the two parties together acquired a majority in the legislature and elected other state officials. Although certain eminent Negro Republicans had been active in the arrangements, six of the black counties were found in the Democratic column. In 1896 the Republicans fused successfully with the Populists on most state and congressional offices, electing white Republicans to the offices of governor and senator and one Negro, George H. White, to the U.S. House of Representatives. The campaign of 1898, however, was marked by a vituperative and successful use of the race issue on the part of the Democrats, resulting in the defeat of the fusionists, with its dreadful aftermath, the Wilmington, North Carolina, race riot. Disfranchisement followed as a matter of course. The charge of Negro domination used by Democrats to wean upland whites from the policy of fusion was, of course, a myth. But it would appear that the fusion arrangements here—and in other states— were chiefly a marriage of political convenience rather than a coalition signifying any genuine consciousness of common class interest between Negroes and lower-class whites.

All in all, it would be hard to say just how many Negroes espoused the Populist cause. Democrats were usually able to secure Negroes to speak and organize clubs against the Populists. Furthermore, as in North Carolina, those Negroes who did support the Populists usually remained Republicans, and frequently they were registering a negative vote against the Democrats rather than for any positive policy. The election returns showing heavy Negro support for the Democrats in the Black Belt are, of course, open to question. Many planters saw to it that their Negro tenants voted for the Democrats, and the party also used intimidation and fraud to obtain large majorities for its candidates. It was this situation which caused Populists like Watson to turn against Negroes and become extreme purveyors

---

party. The Black-and-Tan Republican faction was the one that included Negroes and their white allies.

of racial hatred. In general, Southerners' deeply held prejudices could not be easily eradicated, and most rank-and-file Populists never had any real conviction of racial equality. The tendency to segregate Negroes in Populist Party units and at Populist rallies bears eloquent testimony to this fact. The Democrats found it all too easy to destroy the party on the basis of an appeal to white supremacy.

The net result of the Populist movement, then, seemed to be increased racial hatred and the embitterment of race relations. In the disfranchisement campaigns at the turn of the century, the conservative Democrats and the radical agrarians each variously favored and opposed Negro suffrage according to what seemed politically advantageous. In Alabama, for example, it was the conservative elements who exhibited whatever sentiment there was for permitting Negroes to vote. In view of the shifting positions which both white factions took on the issue, the most valid conclusion seems to be that each faction was motivated less by ideological considerations than by the fluctuating tactical considerations of practical politics.

Like disfranchisement, the great wave of segregation laws came with the entrance of the agrarians into politics. The occasional laws and customary *de facto* segregation of the antebellum period and Reconstruction received new impetus after Redemption. Statutes requiring segregation appeared first in the field of education. By 1878 the majority of the Southern and Border states had placed legal sanction behind what was already universal practice, and the rest of the states followed in the 1880's and 1890's. There was also growing discrimination in the appropriation of school monies. By the end of the century funds for Negro schools were in many localities actually being reduced; and, over all, while the average per capita expenditure for Negro children rose slightly, the divergence in per capita appropriations for the two races widened rapidly. One observer reported in 1910 that in most of the Southern states at least twice as much was spent per pupil on whites as on Negroes. The consequences in regard to attendance, length of school terms, quality of buildings, and teacher pay and qualifications were all too evident. Conservatives acceded to the desirability of industrial education for the uplift of a "backward race," but extremists like Governor

J. K. Vardaman of Mississippi, who voiced the hatreds of the lower classes, objected to any sort of education for Negroes.

During the post-Reconstruction years segregation in transportation was less uniformly practiced, and laws on the subject came later than in the case of school segregation. The earliest Jim Crow railroad car law was enacted by Tennessee in 1881. There were increasing incidents involving Negroes with first-class tickets who were ejected from first-class or "ladies" coaches and Pullman cars, though for financial reasons most Negroes of both sexes ordinarily bought second-class tickets and rode in the smoking car. As late as 1887, W. H. Councill, president of a Negro state college in Alabama, who customarily purchased a first-class ticket, was surprised to find himself directed to the smoking or Jim Crow coach. He filed suit with the newly established Interstate Commerce Commission, charging discrimination in railroad rates since his ticket had not been honored in the first-class coaches. Ruling on his and other similar complaints, the Commission held that equal facilities must be provided for members of both races. This decision prompted a rush of "separate-but-equal" railroad legislation in the Southern states, all but three of which passed such laws between 1887 and 1891. In practice, first-class accommodations were not made available even to the most refined Negro ladies, who were relegated to the coarse and dirty environment of the smoking cars, used also by white male passengers with their cigars and profanity. The Supreme Court nevertheless upheld the validity of the separate-but-equal transportation laws in the famous *Plessy v. Ferguson* case of 1896. On the other hand, transportation segregation was not yet uniformly applied throughout the South. Negroes could still ride with whites in the first-class coaches in Virginia and the Carolinas until those states passed Jim Crow car laws at the very end of the century. Legislation requiring separate Pullman cars and waiting rooms did not come in most states until after 1900, though custom often supplied what the law left unsaid.

Thereafter the Jim Crow principle was applied with inexorable logic. For years, streetcar segregation had been practiced unevenly by Southern traction companies. Georgia had enacted a law on the matter in 1891, and after 1900 nearly all of the Southern states passed such legislation. Segregation had prevailed at an early date in state penal and welfare institutions, and now became the universal practice in parks and other recreational facilities. As the textile industry moved into the piedmont, certain states protected the underpaid white workers against Negro competition by requiring segregation in the factories. In 1913 there was even agitation in North Carolina for restricting Negro farm ownership to certain areas. Beginning in 1910 a number of cities, including Baltimore, New Orleans, Louisville, Atlanta, Augusta, and Richmond, passed residential segregation ordinances, a practice that was declared unconstitutional by the Supreme Court in 1917.

The Southern race system also involved inequities in the administration of justice. Although the Supreme Court insisted that Negroes had the right to sit on juries, they were, in fact, almost completely excluded. The convict lease system, with its many abuses, had been instituted in Louisiana before the Civil War and elsewhere in the South during Reconstruction, but under the Redeemers it expanded rapidly, to the profit of planters and industrialists and the misery of the prisoners. Lynching was another important instrument for maintaining the racial system. The number of persons lynched, most of them in the South, reached its height in the 1880's and early 1890's, averaging about 150 a year during the two decades and climbing to a peak of 235 in 1892. Thereafter lynchings declined somewhat to an average of between 60 and 70 a year after 1905, though they grew in barbarity as the number of those burned at the stake increased. Lynching was mainly a rural phenomenon; in the growing Southern cities mob violence became more common, exploding in the race riots at Wilmington, North Carolina, in 1898 and Atlanta in 1906. Popular opinion held that Negroes were lynched for raping white women, and the hysteria arising from newspaper propaganda about such attacks precipitated the Atlanta race riot. Actually, in less than a third of the lynchings was the crime of rape even alleged, much less proved. Underlying both the Wilmington and Atlanta outbreaks was the hatred whipped up during the disfranchisement campaigns in North Carolina and Georgia.

Thus, piece by piece the patterns of disfranchisement, segregation, and racial subordination were brought to completion during the early part of the twentieth century. It is important to emphasize that this racial system evolved over a long period of years.

On the one hand, its roots went back to the ante-bellum period; much *de facto* segregation existed during the height of Reconstruction; and mob violence was an essential element in the strategy of the Redeemers who overthrew the radical state governments in the 1870's. On the other hand, as late as the 1880's distinguished Southerners were accepting Negro voting as an accomplished fact, and in certain places Negroes were still being called "mister," being buried in the same cemeteries as whites, and being served in white restaurants. Negro expectations revealed the extent to which nonsegregated patterns persisted. W. H. Councill, even though dependent on the favor of state officials, did not become an "Uncle Tom" until after the railroad car incident mentioned earlier. In 1894 even the accommodator Booker T. Washington noted with approval that by boycotting the Atlanta streetcars Negroes had recently secured the abrogation of a newly instituted segregation policy. As late as the period between 1898 and 1906 Negroes in a dozen Southern cities unsuccessfully employed the same technique when Jim Crow trolley cars were introduced in their communities. In Houston, Austin, Nashville, and Savannah Negroes even organized their own short-lived transportation companies. In 1905 Jacksonville, Florida, residents temporarily held the line by securing a court decision declaring the city's segregation ordinance unconstitutional. In the end all of the efforts proved unavailing, and the wave of segregation swept relentlessly on.

Southern Negroes might have continued the battle for their constitutional rights, but by the opening of the century it was clear that even the Supreme Court would permit only a very narrow definition of those rights. In 1883 the Court voided the Civil Rights Act of 1875 on the grounds that discrimination by individual citizens was not prohibited by the Fourteenth Amendment. The Court in 1896 went further and sanctioned segregation laws, enforced by the police power of the states, on the basis of the separate-but-equal doctrine. Then in 1898 it upheld literacy and poll-tax qualifications for voting. Five years later it refused to interfere with franchise restrictions that did not explicitly disqualify people because of race, color, or previous condition of servitude. Thus, the effect of the Court's actions were to emasculate the Fourteenth and Fifteenth amendments and to cloak with respectability the subterfuges enacted by the Southern states.

One reason for the South's ability to flout the Constitution was that by the end of the century Northerners were becoming more hostile toward Negroes. This is revealed by the actions of the state governments, the attitudes of trade unions, and the policies of the national administrations in Washington. Protective state legislation, Negro officeholding, and the racially egalitarian policies of the Knights of Labor marked the 1880's as a period of rising status for Northern Negroes. But evasion of state civil rights laws was easy, the progress in politics and labor proved temporary, and in retrospect it is clear that by the 1890's the Republican presidents had all but deserted the Negro's cause.

During the 1880's Negroes came to occupy positions in the legislatures and city councils and in a few cases on the bench in several areas of the North. Officeholding, which reached a high point around 1890, thereafter declined. True, in Illinois there continued to be one or two Negroes in the legislature, but in Massachusetts, for example, though Negroes still received appointive offices, the lawyer W. H. Lewis was the last one to sit in the legislature (1902), and in Boston, where there had been three Negroes on the Common Council in 1894–95, only one served in 1909.

As for civil rights, Northern states generally gave legislative support to the Fourteenth Amendment. In 1874 Kansas and New York followed Massachusetts' earlier example in prohibiting segregation in places of public accommodation, and by 1880 Negroes in the North had secured recognition of their right to an education, albeit usually a segregated one. After the Supreme Court had declared the federal Civil Rights Act unconstitutional in 1883, Negroes and their friends agitated for state guarantees against discrimination. California and almost all of the Northern states east of the Mississippi River passed public accommodation laws. The typical statute forbade discrimination in restaurants, hotels, barbershops, theatres, public conveyances, and places of amusement. California and the majority of Northeastern states also abolished their separate schools.

Such laws, however, were of little value in the face of hostile public opinion. Relatively few cases came to the attention of the courts, the fines meted out to guilty parties were small, and local custom, particularly in areas contiguous to the South, often acted as an effective deterrent to the exercise of rights protected by legislation. Moreover, school integration was commonly accomplished at the expense of colored teachers who were excluded from jobs in the mixed systems. A student of conditions in southern Ohio in 1913 found that despite strong civil rights legislation Negroes were excluded from restaurants, hotels, and some stores, and were educated in separate schools. About the same time another investigator reported that in Pennsylvania "this disposition to discriminate against Negroes has greatly increased within the past decade." In Cleveland and Boston, where abolitionist traditions lingered longest, where schools were still integrated, and where a few Negroes achieved significant successes in the white business and professional world, even the old humanitarian supporters of the race were becoming indifferent. Nothing illustrated the trend of the times more dramatically than race riots which occurred in New York City in 1900 and in Springfield, Illinois, in 1908. In fact, the New York riot was the first major racial clash in a Northern city since the draft riots of 1863.

Two thirds of the Northern Negroes at the turn of the century were city-dwellers, and like the 20 percent of Southern Negroes who also lived in cities, most of them still had to work at menial occupations and at unskilled labor in heavy industry. In the North employers continued to find Negroes useful as strike-breakers. It was mainly discrimination on the part of organized labor that led Negroes to play this role in industrial conflict, a situation which in turn further exacerbated the antipathy between black and white workers.

Before the Civil War the weak trade-union movement had been highly discriminatory, and during Reconstruction the efforts of the leaders in the National Labor Union to include Negroes foundered on the hostility of the skilled white workers who composed the membership of the organizations affiliated with it. In the 1880's, however, the Knights of Labor seriously sought to recruit Negro members, even in the South, and for a brief period a genuinely interracial trade-union movement seemed possible. In 1886 it was estimated that the Knights had 60,000 Negroes in a total membership of 700,000. In all sections of the country they formed both mixed and all-Negro assemblies. A few of the latter admitted white members and became interracial. In the Southern cities craft unions had Negro locals; in Savannah, New Orleans, and Galveston Negroes were integrated in longshoremen's units; and in New Orleans organized labor called a sympathy strike in support of a union of Negro draymen, who thereby won their demands. The Knights even organized Southern Negro farmers. Among the cotton pickers in Pulaski County, Arkansas, a group of perhaps a hundred Negro Knights unsuccessfully struck for twelve days in 1886. In the fall of 1887 nine thousand Negroes and a thousand whites, in a mixed union, struck against the Louisiana sugar planters for higher wages. Except on a few plantations, the effort failed after a long and bitter conflict.

By the end of the decade, the American Federation of Labor, established in 1881, was superseding the declining Knights. At first the AFL took a stand against discriminatory practices on the part of its affiliated unions. In 1888 the International Association of Machinists, a largely Southern organization, applied for membership but was rejected because its constitution excluded Negroes. In 1890 the Federation went on record as opposing unions which barred colored men and urged the Machinists to remove their restriction. Finally in 1895 the union dropped the color provisions in its constitution and was accepted by the Federation. But the Machinists had eliminated the color line in name only, as they maintained exclusion in the initiation ritual. Similarly, the International Brotherhood of Blacksmiths was barred from the Federation in 1893 but admitted in 1897 after removing the offending clause from its constitution only. By the end of the century the AFL was even admitting unions with exclusion clauses in their constitutions. Federation leadership, although fearing the use of Negroes as strikebreakers, had been brought to accept, even condone, the practice of barring Negroes from a union or organizing them into powerless Jim Crow locals. A few AFL unions—the cigarmakers, the coal miners, the garment workers, and the longshoremen—did accept Negroes without discrimination. Some others, fearful of Negro competition in the skilled trades, admitted them with varying restrictions. Thus several building-trades unions barred Negroes in the North but admitted them in the South, where there were still substantial numbers of colored craftsmen. In Nashville, where Negroes outnumbered whites as artisans in 1880, whites joined the unions, often learned the skills from the Negro members, and then, having achieved a commanding majority, voted to eliminate the Negroes from membership as rapidly as possible. By 1910 control of the crafts in the city had passed to the whites.

By the turn of the century most unions excluded Negroes to a greater or lesser extent—a dozen openly, the majority by subterfuges. Some unions, most notably perhaps the railroad brotherhoods, eliminated Negroes from certain types of work by striking against their employers. Yet on the railroads and elsewhere there were occasional strikes notable for their expression of interracial labor solidarity, as in the case of the Alabama coal mine strike of 1908. Of the labor federations, however, only the syndicalist Industrial Workers of the World (organized in 1905) had an explicit philosophy of interracial unity, which it applied even in the Deep South.

The policies of the Republican Party mirrored the changing attitudes of its Northern constituents. From championing tne Negro cause it shifted first to compromise and then to acceptance of the Southern race system. The Compromise of 1877 revealed that the Republicans were unwilling to enforce the Reconstruction legislation in the South. During the 1880's President Chester A. Arthur courted anti-Negro "independent" political organizations in the South in an effort to increase Republican strength. Not only did the party fail to halt mob violence and disfranchisement, but it was a Republican Supreme Court that found the Civil Rights Act unconstitutional; and it was a Republican Congress that in 1890 repudiated campaign pledges by failing to pass the Lodge Federal Elections Bill. Then, during the 1890's, the Lily-white faction made its appearance, while Republican presidents grew increasingly silent on the question of Negro rights.

The impetuous Theodore Roosevelt alternately pleased and angered Negroes by his actions. He won their approval by inviting Booker T. Washington to dinner at the White House, by closing the Indianola, Mississippi, post office rather than acceding to white demands that he dismiss the Negro postmistress there, and by insisting on appointing a Negro as collector of the Port of Charleston despite powerful Southern and senatorial opposition. At the same time, he was playing a shifty game with the anti-Negro Lily-white Republicans. He spoke favorably of Southern traditions and falsely asserted that most lynchings were caused by sexual assaults on white women. In 1906 he summarily discharged three companies of the Negro 25th Regiment on unproved charges of rioting in Brownsville, Texas. No action of the President hurt and angered Negroes more than this one. William Howard Taft's pronouncements, while he was still Secretary of War under Roosevelt, were also unacceptable to Negroes, for he endorsed ballot restrictions and criticized higher education for Negroes. The race had been pleased by Roosevelt's well-publicized appointments (though his policy was to put fewer colored men in office than his predecessors), but Negroes deplored President Taft's open policy of not appointing Southern Negroes to office where whites objected. The Lily-whites made even more progress under Taft than they had under Roosevelt; and he permitted segregation to be introduced in a few of the federal office buildings. By the election of 1912 Negroes faced a choice among the Democratic candidate, Wilson, born in the South, who would make only the vaguest promises to Negroes; the Republican candidate, Taft, who had completely alienated the race; and the Progressive Party candidate, Roosevelt, who appealed to Negro voters in the North but refused to seat Negro delegates from the South at the Progressive Party convention. Under the circumstances most probably voted for Roosevelt. Those who supported Wilson soon discovered that he ignored Negroes when it came to making appointments and that he permitted even greater segregation in the federal office buildings.

By the opening of the twentieth century Southern extremists were influencing public opinion in the North and West more than before. A spate of ultra-racist books appeared with such titles as *The Negro a Beast* and *The Negro: A Menace to Civilization.* Southern polemicists held not only that Negroes were an innately inferior, immoral, and criminal race that could never catch up with the whites in civilization, but that in fact freedom had caused a reversion to barbarism. Many of the Southern propagandists believed colonization the only alternative to violent extermination. There were differences in degree, but scarcely in basic outlook, between conservatives like Thomas Nelson Page, who glorified the aristocratic plantation tradition, and extremists like Governors Vardaman of Mississippi and Hoke Smith of Georgia, who voiced the hatreds of the lower classes. In the North weighty scholarly opinion in the biological and social sciences supported Southern racist doctrines. Distinguished anthropologists and anatomists regarded Negroes as a separate species next to the ape, and eminent historians and political scientists reinterpreted Reconstruction in a manner favorable to the white South. Almost alone among the prominent social scientists, the anthropologist Franz Boas maintained that innate racial differences were inconsequential. Like the Southerners, Northerners widely believed that Negroes were less industrious, less thrifty, less trustworthy, and less self-controlled than their ancestors. These views were reinforced by the justification of American overseas imperialism on the basis of white racial superiority and the notion of the "White Man's Burden." Probably nothing symbolized so clearly the thinking of the American public about Negroes at the eve of the First World War as the enormously popular racist melodrama, the movie *Birth of a Nation.*

2

In the face of the deteriorating conditions of the late nineteenth century, the dominant trends in Negro thinking shifted gradually from protest to accommodation, especially in the South. There was first of all a growing tendency to minimize the value of political participation. A few leaders, especially during the 1880's, openly advocated supporting the Democratic Party. More widespread was the belief that the race should accept the disfranchisement constitutions. When Isaiah Montgomery, the lone Negro member of the Mississippi constitutional convention of 1890, advocated this, his remarks were greeted with shock and dismay. "Judas" and "traitor" were words commonly used to describe him. Yet five years later, when the Negro delegates to the South Carolina constitutional convention proposed the acceptance of literacy and/or property qualifications, as long as they were equitably applied to both races, it did not seem so extraordinary. This formula was acceptable to the more conservative Negroes. Even if honestly applied, it would have disfranchised a greater proportion of Negroes than whites. In actual practice, of course, these qualifications were administered dishonestly, drastically reducing the remaining number of Negro voters. Nevertheless, the ideas provided a face-saving device for Negroes by holding out the hope that as they acquired property and education they could gain the franchise.

If politics was closing as an avenue of racial advancement, if segregation was growing apace, and if whites were becoming more inimical, what route lay open for the ambitious Negroes who were striving to rise up from slavery? Most Southern and many Northern leaders felt it lay in the economic realm, and most articulate Negroes throughout the country stressed the ideals of self-help and racial solidarity.

Protest organizations like the Afro-American Council, founded in 1890, acted on the principle that since whites had lost interest in Negroes, colored men would have to stick together and help themselves. In extreme form the ideologies of withdrawal were manifested in the continuing interest in African colonization on the part of a few of the articulate and in efforts to establish all-Negro communities.

Usually, however, self-help and racial solidarity were still combined with an economic ideology that preached the acquisition of middle-class virtues and Negro support of Negro business. Advocates of this economic philosophy looked in two directions. They insisted upon the necessity of Negroes "buying black" if Negro business was to develop in the face of declining white support for Negro barbers, artisans, and retail merchants. They also held that if Negroes acquired wealth and middle-class respectability the race would thus earn acceptance from whites and the walls of prejudice would crumble. On the one hand, this cluster of ideologies functioned as an accommodation to the system of segregation and discrimination; in fact, in contrast with the 1850's when this viewpoint was held by militant protest leaders like Frederick Douglass, in the expression of Southern leaders it became explicitly identified with a program of conciliation and accommodation. On the other hand, this way of thinking also functioned as a means of inculcating group pride and self-respect.

The ascendancy of this cluster of ideologies was caused not only by the declining status of Negroes in American society; it was also related to a fundamental shift in the character of Negro business and the Negro class structure. During the last third of the nineteenth century, the entrepreneurial class in the Negro community continued to depend in considerable part upon the support of white customers. As before the Civil War, this group was composed primarily of barbers, skilled artisans, hackmen and draymen, grocers, and caterers. In certain Southern cities the more prominent carpenters and masons had become contractors who built residences for whites. The more successful among these entrepreneurs, along with the better-educated ministers, still formed an important part of the Negro upper class, but the inclusion of civil servants, postal workers, college-trained teachers, Pullman porters of good family background, the growing number of physicians, and an occasional lawyer reflected the occupational diversification that had taken place. Accordingly, by the end of the century the domestic servants in wealthy families, the headwaiters and bell captains in fashionable restaurants and hotels, and the stewards at exclusive country clubs were beginning to decline in social status.

By about 1900 these economic and social changes were well under way. A growing antipathy on the part of whites toward trading with Negro businessmen and changes in technology and business organization forced many of the small entrepreneurs out of business. At the same time the urbanization of Negroes and the increasing tendency to live in ghetto neighborhoods supplied a base for professional and business men dependent on the Negro market. Of course certain businesses, such as newspapers, undertakers, some barbers, and storekeepers, had always relied on the Negro market, and these now grew in number; but the most important new enterprises catering to Negroes were banks (the first two founded in 1888), cemetery and realty associations, and insurance companies.

Examples of what contemporaries referred to as "co-operative" businesses were not lacking in previous years, but their number rose sharply in the last decade of the nineteenth and early years of the twentieth century. The most celebrated of the earlier enterprises had been the Chesapeake and Marine Railroad and Dry Dock Company, formed by the Baltimore ship calkers after a strike against colored mechanics and longshoremen resulted in the dismissal of a thousand Negroes from the city's shipyards in 1863. The company operated successfully for eighteen years. During the 1880's and 1890's exclusion from white cemeteries and difficulties in borrowing money from white lending agencies played an important role in the creation of cemetery and building and loan associations. In Philadelphia, for example, the first building and loan association was founded in 1886;

twenty years later the number in that city had reached ten. Successful realty companies also appeared, like one in New York which, employing over two hundred persons, was the largest Negro enterprise in the city before the company collapsed around 1910.

Especially significant was the growth of Negro insurance, today the most important of Negro business enterprises. This development was closely related to the mutual benefit fraternal organizations, which enjoyed a great boom beginning in the 1890's. The 1880's had been the heyday of the local, usually church-oriented mutual benefit and burial societies. Though such organizations are to be found in the rural South to this day, and though a few of them, like the Afro-American Industrial Insurance Society of Jacksonville, developed into full-fledged insurance companies, by the end of the century they had been eclipsed by the fraternal orders. Among the secret orders the Odd Fellows forged into the lead, growing from eighty-nine lodges to a thousand lodges in the eighteen years between 1868 and 1886, and then more than quadrupling the number of its lodges in the next eighteen years, 1886–1904. By 1906 the organization had investments of $3,000,000. The Masons and the Negro Knights of Pythias (formed in 1880) also experienced significant expansion. Among the nonsecret, quasi-religious fraternal orders, the Galilean Fishermen, and the Independent Order of St. Luke (founded in Richmond in 1865) were among those enjoying phenomenal growth, but the most celebrated was the Grand Fountain of the United Order of True Reformers founded in Virginia in 1881. Before it failed in 1911 it had become a mutual benefit stock company with a membership of 100,000, operating a bank, five department stores, and a weekly newspaper in addition to its insurance department. Inspired by the success of these associations, the secret orders improved their insurance features. Meanwhile, regularly chartered mutual aid and beneficial societies, specializing in weekly sickness and health insurance, had appeared (the first one in Baltimore in 1885). The final step in the evolution of Negro insurance was the appearance of the regularly chartered legal reserve company, the first one being organized in Mississippi in 1909.

In the life of John Merrick, the man chiefly responsible for North Carolina Mutual, one of the two largest Negro life insurance companies, one observes the evolution of Negro insurance from the quasi-religious fraternal society through the chartered mutual aid organization to the legal reserve company. Merrick was a Durham barber who catered to upper-class whites. In 1883 he and some friends obtained control of a quasi-religious fraternal order, the Royal Knights of King David. Then in 1898 the business was twice reorganized, first as the North Carolina Mutual and Provident Association, and then as an insurance company. Alonzo Herndon, who in 1905 founded the Atlanta Life Insurance Company, today the chief rival of North Carolina Mutual, had a similar personal career, though his company began as a frankly commercial venture rather than as a mutual benefit society.

Related also to the fraternal organizations was the development of Negro banking. After the failure of the federally owned Freedmen's Bank following the panic of 1873, the first two Negro banks were the True Reformers' Bank in Richmond and the Capital Savings Bank of Washington, both founded in 1888. By 1900 there were four Negro banks. Thereafter the number increased rapidly, reaching fifty-six by 1911. Most of these, however, went under in subsequent financial depressions. The great majority of the banks originated as depositories for the fraternal orders. The importance of the fraternities in the development of Negro banking is suggested by the fact that in 1907 the first and third largest in capitalization and deposits were the True Reformers' Bank and the Mechanics Savings Bank, the latter established in Richmond by the grand chancellor of the Virginia Knights of Pythias.

It is also noteworthy that although the secret fraternal organizations like the Masons and the Odd Fellows had lost the close connections with the churches which had existed before the Civil War, the relationships between the ministers and the mutual benefit societies survived to a considerable extent in the prominent role clergymen played in organizing the insurance societies and banking enterprises. The True Reformers' Bank, the Galilean Fishermen's Bank, and the St. Luke's Bank were all either founded by ministers or closely connected with the churches. Again, in Philadelphia the pastor of the Berean Presbyterian Church organized the largest building and loan association in the state as a service provided by his "institutional" church. By the end of the century, however, this ministerial influence was declining, and it waned even more during the twentieth century as the Negro community leadership and class structure became more highly differentiated.

The impact of the newer type of business enterprise and the expansion of the Negro entrepreneurial and professional group were evident in the changing nature of the Negro class structure. In general, between about 1890 and the 1920's the forces of segregation and discrimination were instrumental in creating a *petite bourgeoisie* of professional and business men almost completely dependent for their livelihood on the Negro masses. The majority were self-made men, of humble origin, on the whole a darker-skinned group than the older upper class, less likely to be descended from ante-bellum house slaves or from free people of color. They formed an ambitious, striving middle class, and the more successful among them were achieving upper-class status before the First World War. The process occurred at different rates and times in different cities, most markedly in those communities where the largest in-migration and residential segregation were taking place.

It was chiefly from the members of this rising middle class, and from men of the older upper class who, like Merrick and Herndon, turned from serving white customers to serving the Negro community, that the chief impetus for the philosophy of Negro support for Negro business emanated. The whole process is dramatically symbolized by a comparison of the sources of two of the largest fortunes made by Negroes before the First World War. R. R. Church of Memphis, the son of a wealthy white man, was reputed to have amassed over a million dollars out of speculation and investment in white real estate between Reconstruction and the time of his death in 1912. A few hundred miles north on the Mississippi River, with a business started in the 1890's, a St. Louis laundress, Madam C. J. Walker, reportedly made a million dollars as a result of her invention of the first commercially successful hair-straightening process. Madam Walker was never accepted by "the cream of colored society," but in the 1920's her daughter became a noted social leader among the literary and artistic elite in Harlem.

3

Interwoven with these changes in economic life and outlook and in the class structure was the educational system. The public schools remained inferior. Even after the revised land-grant college act of 1890 compelled each of the Southern states to establish a Negro land-grant college, the only adequate higher education was to be obtained in the private schools. These institutions, especially the better ones, continued to be identified with middle- and upper-class Negroes, and were the source of the great majority of Negro leaders, particularly in Southern communities. This was especially true of the Congregationalist colleges in the South and the Presbyterian Church's Lincoln University in Pennsylvania, in spite of their paternalistic reluctance to employ Negroes as teachers and administrators. (The Methodists and Baptists, on the other hand, were more sensitive to Negro opinion on this matter, for the Methodists had many Southern Negro members and the Baptist schools were aided financially by the Negro Baptist conventions. Both denominations were using Negroes to staff their schools well before the end of the nineteenth century.)

In the 1890's the liberal arts colleges were being temporarily eclipsed in popular esteem and financial resources by the rise of industrial education. "Industrial education" was a catchall term that included manual training, home economics, and preparation for farming and for trades such as shoemaking, printing, carpentry, and bricklaying. As already indicated, a number of abolitionists and ante-bellum Negro conventions had been interested in manual labor schools. During Reconstruction many of the freedmen's schools boasted of "industrial work," which usually consisted merely of home economics and odd jobs for the men. At several places, however, most notably Hampton Institute in Virginia, successful manual labor and vocational institutes were established.

In the 1880's industrial education was widely adopted in the curricula of white high schools, and, under the aegis of the John F. Slater Fund, industrial and agricultural education on the secondary level became popular among a large number of Negro institutions, even among many known for their college departments. Both Hampton Institute's founder, Samuel Chapman Armstrong, and the Slater Fund trustees viewed industrial education as particularly adapted to fitting Negroes for the environment in which they were to live. At the same time it would uplift them by creating a class of self-sufficient artisan-entrepreneurs in farming and the skilled trades. Throughout the writings of the advocates of industrial education was a stress upon the moral virtues which it allegedly implanted, and which were regarded as essential to the Negro's progress as a man and a citizen. But in the view of these educators and philanthropists it would be years—even centuries—before Negroes would be prepared to enjoy the rights of citizenship equally with whites.

Industrial education was widely adopted because philanthropists encouraged it and because Southern whites saw it as keeping Negroes in the subordinate position of working with their hands rather than preparing them for professional careers. Industrial training was a particularly expensive form of education. Therefore, in view of the inadequate funds received by Negro schools, they had inferior, inadequate programs, except for a few like Tougaloo and Spelman, Tuskegee and Hampton. Ironically, the vogue of industrial education came when white artisans were forcing Negroes out of the skilled trades. For both these reasons the Negro graduates of industrial schools were usually unable to practice their skills, and most of them became teachers of the trades rather than the independent artisans the propagandists for industrial education dreamed of creating. Nevertheless many Negro leaders found industrial education appealing, partly because philanthropy subsidized it, and even more because it fitted the moral-economic ideology of advancement that was in the ascendancy. And though clothed in a philosophy of racial advancement, its advocates—from Samuel Chapman Armstrong to Booker T. Washington—saw it as a platform of compromise and accommodation between the North, the South, and the Negro. It satisfied those philanthropists and leading Southerners who opposed race equality yet liked to think that they were in favor of Negro uplift. Finally it enabled many Negroes to convince themselves that it was a way not only of obtaining money for Negro schools but also of indirectly and ultimately elevating the race to the point where it would be accorded its citizenship rights.

Although the major thrust of educational philanthropy in the

Southern states at the turn of the century was to improve the quality of white public schools, Negro institutions received some assistance in addition to that accorded to industrial education. The Rockefeller interests, working through the General Education Board (founded in 1902), made some contributions to Negro institutions and began the financial aid that was to make Spelman College one of the two best-endowed colleges for women in the South. Andrew Carnegie contributed libraries to a number of Negro institutions, ranging from Booker T. Washington's Tuskegee Normal and Industrial Institute to Fisk University. During the early years of the twentieth century other funds of importance to Negro education were established, most notably the Anna T. Jeanes Fund (1905), which paid the salaries of supervising teachers in order to raise standards in rural schools, and the Julius Rosenwald Fund (1913) which contributed money for the erection of school buildings.

4

Epitomizing these varied strands—accommodation, self-help, racial solidarity, acceptance of disfranchisement, economic accumulation and middle-class virtues, and industrial education—and doing more than anyone else to popularize this particular complex of ideas, was Hampton Institute's most distinguished alumnus, Booker T. Washington, who was catapulted into world fame in 1895 by a speech he made at the Cotton States and International Exposition in Atlanta.

Washington's address made evident his belief that the solution of the race problem would come through an application of the gospel of wealth. He urged Negroes to stay in the South, since it was in the South that the Negro was given a man's chance in business. Whites were urged to help uplift Negroes and thereby further the prosperity and well-being of the region. Coupled with this appeal to the white South's self-interest was conciliatory phraseology and a criticism of Negroes. Washington deprecated politics and the Reconstruction experience. He criticized Negroes for forgetting that the masses of the race were to live by working with their hands and for permitting their grievances to overshadow their opportunities. He reminded whites of the loyalty and fidelity of Negroes "the most patient, faithful, law-abiding, and unresentful people that the world has seen." He denied any interest in social intermingling when he said, "In all things that are purely social we can be as separate as the fingers, yet one as the hand in all matters essential to mutual progress." He asked only for "justice" and an end to sectional differences and racial animosities. These, combined with material prosperity, would usher in a new era for "our beloved South."

Thus Washington was advocating a conciliatory and gradualist philosophy. He minimized the extent of race prejudice or discrimination and referred to Southern whites as the Negro's best friends. He held that discrimination and prejudice were basically the Negroes' own fault. Poor and ignorant as most of them were, Negroes naturally alienated white people. They must therefore take the chief responsibility for their own advancement. Whites could help, but basically Negroes would have to come up from slavery by themselves. Accordingly, Washington accepted segregation and criticized political activity. He believed that economic accumulation and the cultivation of morality were the methods best calculated to raise the Negro's status in American society. Agricultural and industrial training was far more appropriate for the mass of Negroes, just then, than education for the professions.

Not perceiving the inexorable trends toward urbanization and technological change, his program stressed farming and animal husbandry and training in the hand crafts. He constantly deplored the tendency of Negro farmers to move to the cities, and though his message was most successfully communicated to the Negro urban businessmen, Washington's vision was fundamentally of virtuous, landowning peasants proving their worth in their native Southland. He even approved literacy and property qualifications for voting; they would stimulate Negroes to obtain education and wealth. Yet, while stressing the need for Negro self-improvement, Washington insisted that Negroes should be proud of their race and should loyally support it. Especially should Negroes support Negro businessmen, in order to advance the race economically. With such solid economic foundations, Negroes would receive their constitutional rights and the respect of whites. But Washington was basically tactful, vague, and even ambiguous, so that most whites confused his means for his ends and assumed that for an indefinite period at least he anticipated that

Negroes would continue to occupy a subordinate place in American society.

Booker T. Washington's public image as an accommodator was one thing; his covert behind-the-scenes activity was another. Privately he appeared to contradict his public stance. He might denounce higher education as a "bacillus," but his own children received not only training in the trades but a thorough grounding in the liberal arts. Overtly he might urge Negroes to acquiesce in the separate-but-equal doctrine; privately he had entrée to white social circles in the North and abroad that few Southern whites could enter, and secretly he aided the fight against railroad segregation. On one occasion, working through intermediaries, he hired a lobbyist to defeat legislation that, if passed, would have encouraged segregation on interstate trains in the North. Overtly he denied any interest in politics and urged Negroes to soft-pedal the desire for the franchise; behind the scenes he was the most influential politician in the history of American Negroes, and surreptitiously fought the disfranchisement laws. He served as political adviser on Negro affairs to Presidents Roosevelt and Taft. All colored men who were appointed to office by Roosevelt, and most appointed by Taft, were recommended by Booker T. Washington. Among his most notable recommendations were: Robert H. Terrell, who served as judge of the municipal court in Washington, 1901–21; Charles W. Anderson, collector of internal revenue in New York, 1905–15; and William H. Lewis, assistant attorney general, 1911–13. These were the highest federal judicial and executive appointments of Negroes thus far made; and they were not to be equaled or surpassed until after the Second World War. Even more revealing of Washington's private ideological ambivalences was the way in which he clandestinely spent thousands of dollars financing the fruitless test cases taken to the Supreme Court against the Southern disfranchisement amendments.

Washington wielded more power within the Negro community than anyone else had ever done. This authority derived from his political influence and from his popularity with the philanthropists. No Negro schools received contributions from Carnegie, Rockefeller, and lesser donors without Washington's approval. In short, ambitious men and institutions found it difficult to get ahead without the Tuskegean's support. Washington also assiduously cultivated influential leaders in the Negro community; for over a decade it was impossible to achieve a major position in the Negro churches if one attacked him, and judicious advertisements and contributions kept the Negro press in line.

Booker T. Washington's career was truly a remarkable one. Born an obscure slave in western Virginia, he had risen to a pinnacle of international fame. He appropriately entitled his autobiography *Up From Slavery,* and indeed his life epitomized what thrift and industry—and diplomacy—might accomplish in an age of accommodation.

5

Despite Washington's prominence, Negro protest never entirely disappeared. The Afro-American Council, which lasted, with periods of inactivity, from 1890 to 1908, had been founded as a militant protest organization and always retained something of a protest outlook. Its sessions at the close of the century were enlivened in fact by attacks on Washington by such people as the noted antilynching crusader Ida Wells-Barnett. By then, however, the Council was coming under Washington's influence, and after 1900 its annual conventions expressed a rather mild point of view until Washington's critics obtained control in 1906–7. Even in the South, as our previous discussion of streetcar boycotts illustrates, protest activity had not completely vanished, but the chief opposition to accommodation came from a small group of Northern intellectuals. For the most part they were an upper-class elite of editors, lawyers, ministers, and teachers. The majority of them had attended prestigious Northern universities. From Harvard came the two best-known critics of Washington's policies: William Monroe Trotter and W. E. B. Du Bois.

Trotter in 1901 founded the militant Boston *Guardian,* the most caustic of the handful of newspapers that opposed Washington. It epitomized the anti-Bookerite sentiment of "Radical"* New England Negroes. In July, 1903, Trotter and his associates unsuccessfully challenged the Tuskegeean for control of the Afro-American Council. The following month the embittered Radicals precipitated disorder and pandemonium when they heckled Washington at a public meeting in Boston. This "Boston Riot"

* "Radical" Negroes in this period were anti-Washington advocates of militant protest.

widened the cleavage between the two groups, especially after Trotter was jailed and his antagonists financed a libel suit against the *Guardian.*

A few months prior to this event, W. E. B. Du Bois had published a volume of essays, *The Souls of Black Folk,* which contained an incisive and critical analysis of Washington's leadership. James Weldon Johnson, the noted author and later executive secretary of the National Association for the Advancement of Colored People (NAACP), credited Du Bois' analysis of racial leadership with effecting "a coalescence of the more radical elements . . . thereby creating a split of the race into two contending camps." During the 1890's Du Bois, who held a doctorate from Harvard and was a professor at Atlanta University, had supported most of Booker T. Washington's program. He had been a strong advocate of self-help and of Negro support of Negro business, and in 1890 had even opposed the Lodge Federal Elections Bill on the grounds that many Negroes were "not fit for the responsibility of republican government. When you have the right sort of black voters you will need no election laws." The chief differences between the two men had been that Du Bois never flattered the white South as Washington did and that Du Bois saw a place for higher education as well as industrial training. Now, in 1903, in *Souls of Black Folk,* Du Bois, though he continued to share Washington's interest in racial solidarity and self-help, denounced the Tuskegeean for condoning the caste system and for shifting to Negroes the major responsibility for their elevation. Du Bois held that Washington's accommodating ideology had brought together the South, the North, and the Negro in a monumental compromise that "practically accepted the alleged inferiority of the Negro." He observed that in the period of Washington's ascendancy segregation and disfranchisement laws had risen in number, while philanthropic support for higher education had declined, and he held Washington accountable for the acceleration of these trends. Because Washinton's popularity with whites had led Negroes to accept his leadership, criticism of him had virtually disappeared. Du Bois hoped, however, that prominent Negroes would now speak out, for it had become obvious that justice could not be achieved through "indiscriminate flattery"; that Negroes could not gain their rights by voluntarily throwing them away, or obtain respect by constantly belittling themselves; that, on the contrary, Negroes must speak out constantly against oppression and discrimination.

In Du Bois' view, the Negro race could be saved only by the "Talented Tenth"—i.e., the minority who had received a liberal arts education and thus were in a position to elevate Negroes both culturally and economically. As he said, "Progress in human affairs is more often a pull than a push, a surging forward of the exceptional man, and the lifting of his duller brethren." Du Bois was disturbed by Washington's exclusive preoccupation with industrial education and the financial support whites gave it at the expense of Negro colleges. Du Bois did not deprecate industrial education and in fact agreed that it made a significant contribution in teaching the masses of the race to work, but he reminded Washington that many of the teachers of the industrial and elementary schools had attended liberal arts institutions, and that until many more did so, Negro leadership and the Negro race would be seriously retarded.

In order to inaugurate an organized program of public agitation for the Negro's constitutional rights, Du Bois in 1905 founded the Niagara Movement. In sharp vigorous language the Niagara declarations placed the responsibility for the race problem squarely on the shoulders of whites. White America was crisply told that Negroes were dissatisfied and would continue to be until they had obtained voting rights and "the abolition of all caste distinctions based simply on race and color." In Philadelphia and Chicago its members actively opposed school segregation. The movement's legal redress committee won a railroad segregation suit, receiving a judgment of one penny in damages. Although the concrete achievements of the Niagara Movement were indeed few, it clearly articulated the Negro protest, contrasting the Washingtonian assertions that Negroes were content to make the climb from slavery by "natural and gradual processes." The Niagara men told whites that they should not be lulled into thinking that "the Negro-American assents to inferiority, is submissive under oppression and apologetic before insult. . . . We do not hesitate to complain, and to complain loudly and insistently."

Washington used all reservoirs of power at his disposal to silence his critics. He placed spies in radical organizations, attempted to deprive opponents of their government jobs, subsidized the Negro press to ignore or attack "the opposition," successfully exerted pressure to prevent the election of radicals to high office in the Negro churches, and used his enormous influence with the philanthropists to divert funds away from educators who were inimical to him. Washington's control over the advancement of Negroes in government, education, and the church probably discouraged many ambitious men from affiliating with the Niagara Movement.

The Niagara Movement was thus no match for Washington. It was further weakened by a rupture between Du Bois and Trotter in 1907. After that the organization merely limped along. Nevertheless, particularly in view of the Tuskegeean's opposition, it was significant because, as the journalist Ray Stannard Baker reported, "It represents, genuinely, a more or less prevalent point of view among many coloured people."

While the Niagara Movement was losing its momentum, liberal whites who had previously supported Washington were becoming increasingly impatient with his tactics and with his efforts to monopolize Negro leadership. Outstanding among this group was Oswald Garrison Villard, the grandson of William Lloyd Garrison and publisher of the New York *Evening Post*. The tide of segregation, disfranchisement, and racial violence seemed irresistible and in 1908, in a letter to Washington, Villard concluded that only "a strong central defense committee" could effectively advance Negro interests. In 1909, in response to a call issued by Villard, a National Negro Conference was held in New York which led to the formation of the National Association for the Advancement of Colored People. Those present included prominent members of the Niagara Movement and eminent white Progressives and Christian Socialists. A number of the Negro Radicals who attended, most notably Du Bois, also considered themselves Socialists. It should be emphasized, however, that only a small minority of white Progressives were supporters of the NAACP. Most were either supporters of Washington, like Roosevelt, or were, like Wilson, quite indifferent to the Negro. In fact Washington's *petit bourgeois* philosophy of thrift and industry and self-help reflected the basic values of most American leaders at that period, whether conservative or progressive.

In their speeches at the conference Radical leaders like Ida Wells-Barnett and Du Bois stressed the importance of the ballot.

The conferees denounced mob violence and segregation, demanded academic training for the gifted, and above all insisted on the right to vote. The NAACP did not actually unite with the Niagara Movement, but most of its members joined the new organization. The interracial character of the NAACP was essential to the success of its early work. The prestige of the names of well-known white Progressives like Villard, Lillian Wald, Jane Addams, John Haynes Holmes, Moorfield Storey, and Clarence Darrow gave the agitation for Negro rights better financial support and, more important, a wider audience. Except for Du Bois, who became director of publicity and editor of the Association's organ, the *Crisis,* all of the chief officials were at first white. Several of these white leaders seemed paternalistic and condescending in their dealings with Negro associates in the NAACP. Nevertheless, as Du Bois observed, the interracial tensions during the early days of the organization were mild when compared to those in the abolitionist movement. In any case, from the first the real backbone of the Association consisted of an elite, college-educated Negro membership. By 1914 the Association had 6,000 members in fifty branches. Mainly a legal action organization from the very beginning, the NAACP achieved its first important victory just a few months before Washington's death in 1915 when the United States Supreme Court declared the Oklahoma grandfather clause unconstitutional.

Beginning in 1909 Booker T. Washington took steps to limit the effectiveness of the new organization, and the old pattern of various forms of pressure was repeated. For their part Du Bois and his Negro associates openly attacked Washington, though Villard insisted that this was not the official policy of the NAACP and encouraged the efforts of R. R. Moton of Hampton Institute, Washington's successor at Tuskegee, to effect an understanding between the two groups.

For the first decade of the century at least, the majority of articulate Negroes had supported Washington. This was even true of many of the Northern intellectuals, for originally only a small minority of them had deemed it desirable to battle the Tuskegeean. Many of them, it is true, did not endorse his entire program wholeheartedly, and others changed their attitudes toward Washington over the years. Yet he enjoyed enormous support in the Negro community. What were the reasons for this?

First, there was the discouraging trend of the times. Protest, agitation, political action had failed. There had been a definite trend in the direction of accommodation in the 1880's and 1890's, and at the turn of the century certain prominent protest leaders, who would later be among Washington's most prominent critics, in their despair hoped that his method might be of some help. Even Du Bois had expressed an ideology remarkably similar to Washington's. Only when it became evident that the worsening situation persisted in the face of Washington's program did many who had supported him change their minds.

Second, Washington's emphasis upon economic development and Negro support of Negro business undoubtedly attracted the majority of the rising bourgeoisie, whose income was based on the Negro market. And in the South those who still depended on white customers were drawn to that side of his philosophy which insisted upon the value of conciliating Southern whites, whose respect for business acumen would, Washington believed, lead them to patronize energetic Negro entrepreneurs.

Nor can one neglect Washington's power over political appointments and philanthropy as a third factor in shaping ideological expression during his ascendancy, making the combination of ideas he represented more palatable than they otherwise would have been. School officials, finding Washington's blessing essential for securing the funds from the philanthropists, cultivated Washington and endorsed his leadership and ideology. With ample backing from Andrew Carnegie, Washington in 1900 founded the National Negro Business League, which provided him with an influential platform for propagandizing the values of thrift, industry, self-help, and Negro support of Negro business, and for downgrading the values of agitation and the franchise. Washington's income from speaking and philanthropy enabled him to use advertisements and, in half a dozen cases, actual subsidies to encourage newspaper editors to support him and his program. There is a fascinating irony in noting, for example, that the *sine qua non* in receiving Washington's endorsement for political office was to declare constantly that, for Negroes, office-holding was unwise or unimportant.

Finally, Washington's very prominence in the eyes of white America drew Negro support for his program, his fame making the complex of ideas that he represented far more fashionable than it otherwise would have been. Beyond this, his achievement made him the very image of success for countless thousands in the Negro community, a model to be not only admired but emulated as well.

Space here will not allow exploration of the complexities of thought in the Age of Booker T. Washington. A number of men shifted from one point of view to another. Some, especially in the North, saw no contradiction in endorsing Washington's leadership while engaging in protest themselves; an overwhelming majority of articulate Northerners supported both protest and economic accumulation, both citizenship rights and racial solidarity, and many tried to maintain friendship with both the Bookerites and the Radicals during the bitter struggle. Du Bois himself consistently encouraged the building of Negro enterprise and enthused over Negro support of Negro business, or what he described as a "group economy," which he viewed as the only way to advance the race economically, given the circumstances under which Negroes lived.

Though the Niagara Movement was disappearing by 1909, Negro protest grew stronger with the founding of the NAACP. At the very time that the NAACP, with its prominent backers, was making Negro protest more respectable, Washington's power was declining. He had less political influence with Taft than with Roosevelt and none at all with Wilson. Meanwhile, it was clear that even if, as has been claimed, his conciliatory program had perhaps slowed down the pace of deterioration in the Negro's status, it certainly had not halted the process. Given this combination of circumstances, a revival of Negro protest was almost inevitable. By the time Washington died, even some of his closest friends found it wise to identify themselves with the NAACP. And a year after his death, the NAACP played an ironic master stroke by inviting James Weldon Johnson, one of the most versatile figures in the Washington camp, to join its staff as national organizer.

VI

NEGROES IN THE URBAN AGE:
THE RISE OF THE GHETTO

AFTER THE CIVIL WAR and Emancipation, the major watershed in American Negro history was the Great Migration to Northern cities that began during the First World War. According to the census of 1910, Negroes were overwhelmingly rural and Southern; approximately three out of four lived in rural areas and nine out of ten lived in the South. Today Negroes are mainly an urban population, almost three fourths of the 20,491,000 nonwhites being city-dwellers, according to the 1960 census. About half live outside of the old slave states. The changes in the texture of Negro life that have resulted are enormous, though unfortunately the subject is one that has yet to be systematically studied.

1

Migration of Southern Negroes searching for better conditions was not new. In the years since the Civil War there had been a steady drift of Negroes to Southern urban centers, along with a trickle to the North. Negroes left the land at about the same rate as Southern whites, and for the same economic reasons. Moreover, there was a considerable interstate and intrastate movement of Negro farmers into newly developed agricultural lands, particularly in Florida, parts of Georgia and Alabama, the Yazoo-Mississippi Delta of northwestern Mississippi, and Arkansas and

Texas, resulting in a net southwestward movement of the center of Negro population. At certain dramatic times, such as during the Kansas Exodus of 1879, Negro migrants, and more especially their supporters among the better-educated classes, expressed an ideology that protested against all aspects of race discrimination. But the main push seems to have been economic. Negroes left worn-out land and moved toward more fertile fields in an effort to raise themselves from day laborers or sharecroppers to cash renters and even farm owners. In fact, as the sociologist Charles S. Johnson has demonstrated, often the largest Negro migration was into counties with the highest incidences of mob violence and lynchings. Though the evidence is sketchy, it would appear that the peaks of Negro movement were during periods of acute economic crisis—toward the close of the depression of the 1870's; at the height of the Populist-agrarian agitation around 1890; and perhaps again during the minor depression that hit the United States on the eve of the First World War.

In 1912 the year-old National Urban League, the major social welfare agency working among Negroes, reported that "the migration of Negroes to the cities, as a part of the general movement . . . to the cities, is a fact of common observation." Between 1890 and 1910 the proportion of Negroes classified as urban by the United States census had risen from about 20 to 27 percent. In the latter year there were a dozen cities which had over 40,000 Negroes. Between 1900 and 1910 large percentage increases in the Negro population occurred in New South cities like Birmingham (215 percent) and Atlanta (45 percent). New York City had a gain of 51 percent, while Philadelphia and Chicago each reported increases of more than 30 percent. The growing northward movement was noted by Du Bois as early as 1903 when he asserted that "the most significant economic change among Negroes in the last ten or twenty years had been their influx into northern cities." About that time New York had three fourths as many Negroes as New Orleans, Philadelphia had almost twice as many as Atlanta, and Chicago had more than Savannah. During the next years the population movement produced even more striking consequences. According to the census of 1910, two cities, Washington and New York, had over 90,000 Negroes; and three others, New Orleans, Baltimore, and Philadelphia, over 80,000. Of these five cities, only one was in the Deep South.

Those Negroes who moved to the cities in the decades preceding the First World War entered an environment in which racial lines were being more and more tightly drawn. One manifestation of this trend was the expansion of residential segregation. The pattern of Negroes living in scattered enclaves about the town, with some individuals here and there living in white neighborhoods, was giving way to larger concentrations of Negro population limited to one or two sections of a city. Mixed neighborhoods survived in the older sections of Southern seaports like Charleston and New Orleans, but the New South mercantile and industrial centers like Atlanta and Birmingham had known only residential segregation, while in the major cities of the Border and Northern states the growth of ghettos was greatly accentuated. As the Fisk University sociologist and National Urban League official George Edmund Haynes said in 1913, "New York has its 'San Juan Hill' in the West Sixties, and its Harlem district of over 35,000 [concentrated] within about eighteen city blocks; Philadelphia has its Seventh Ward; Chicago has its State Street, Washington its Northwest Neighborhood, and Baltimore its Druid Hill Avenue. Louisville has its Chestnut Street and its Smoketown; Atlanta its West End and Auburn Avenue."

The Great Migration of the World War I era stimulated trends already under way. While Negroes were clearly dissatisfied with the whole pattern of race relations in the South, it was an economic crisis arising from several converging factors that precipitated the population movement. Cotton agriculture was suffering from the ravages of the boll weevil, which had entered the United States from Mexico and gradually moved eastward through Texas. Then in 1915 disastrous floods in Alabama and Mississippi increased the misery of hundreds of thousands of rural Negroes. At the same time, Northern industry, fed by demands from the Allies in Europe, felt a great need for unskilled and semiskilled labor. Since the World War cut off immigration from Europe, some Northern manufacturers encouraged the poverty-stricken Negroes to leave the South. Their efforts were greatly aided by several Northern Negro newspapers, particularly the Chicago *Defender,* which painted a glowing picture of Northern living conditions and denounced Southern racism. Indeed, as in earlier periods, much of the explanation given by contemporaries emphasized disfranchisement, Jim Crow, and mob violence.

The result of all these forces was a clear-cut reversal of the main tendencies in the Negro population movement since Emancipation. The principal direction of Negro migration shifted away from the undeveloped Southern rural areas toward the cities particularly of the North. Contemporaries found the effects startling. There were accounts of towns practically depopulated of Negro residents, of Negro preachers, physicians, and morticians moving North because of the departure of the people whom they served. Southern states and communities, alarmed by the loss of cheap labor, blamed Northern labor agents for enticing unwilling Negroes to make secret nighttime departures. Certainly the movement was considerable, far greater than ever before, yet only a few hundred thousand probably migrated. Still, this was enough to intensify the gradual changes in the pattern of life of Northern urban Negroes, and to set in motion a population stream that was to continue, in war and peace, prosperity and depression, until the present day.

2

What were the conditions that the migrants met in the "promised land"? There was the animosity of white workers, even though Negroes mostly received the heavy, laborious, unskilled jobs. In 1917 the fears and suspicions of whites erupted into race riots in Philadelphia and Chester, Pennsylvania, and at East St. Louis, Illinois, where the most serious racial outbreak in the twentieth century cost the lives of at least thirty-nine Negroes. Friction also resulted from the competition between Negroes and whites for limited housing. Yet despite resistance, both during and after the war, the ghettos expanded irrepressibly, block by block. Discrimination was increasing in other aspects of everyday life. Even in cities like Chicago or Boston, hotels and restaurants which had previously served Negroes now barred them. As conditions worsened, earlier Negro settlers blamed the mass of Southern newcomers, with their awkward and unrefined ways, for the more intense prejudice which all Negroes in the North now faced.

During the war this pervasive pattern of discrimination extended even to the treatment of Negroes as members of the armed forces. Negroes were allowed to serve in the Navy only as messboys and barred entirely from the Marines. The Army accepted enlisted men, but planned originally not to commission Negroes. The highest-ranking Negro officer, Colonel Charles Young, was retired, allegedly on grounds of ill health. Only after agitation by Negro college students, NAACP officials, and a committee of prominent white citizens, did the War Department finally establish a Negro officers' training camp at Des Moines, Iowa. Many criticized the NAACP leaders for endorsing a segregated camp, but their position was that without accepting such arrangements no Negroes would have been trained as officers. In October, 1917, 639 men were commissioned with the ranks of captain and first and second lieutenants; later other Negroes became officers at unsegregated officer-training camps and in the field.

YMCA recreation units at army camps made no provisions for Negroes. Conditions in the South were especially difficult because of the actions of white civilians. At Houston in late summer of 1917 Negro soldiers who had been insulted and beaten by whites broke into an army ammunition storage room and marched on the city's police station. There followed a riot that cost many lives. After a perfunctory trial, thirteen soldiers were hanged on charges of murder and mutiny, and forty-one others received life sentences. A similar occurrence at Spartanburg, South Carolina, in October was only narrowly averted by hastily sending the Negro regiment overseas. The Army in these situations did nothing to protect its men against civilian attack; it either disarmed the Negroes or shipped them to Europe. The War Department, however, did appoint Emmett J. Scott as a special assistant to the Secretary of War on matters affecting Negroes. Scott attempted to deal with Negro complaints, but it would appear that he functioned principally as a device that the War Department used to divert dissatisfaction, at least temporarily, away from the responsible authorities. It was a symbolic role that Emmett Scott, Booker T. Washington's former private secretary, must have understood very well.

Despite discrimination at home and attempts by American troops—even high army authorities—to inculcate race prejudice among the French abroad, Negro soldiers performed honorably and courageously in battle. Most Negro newspapers supported the war effort, and even the militant Du Bois wrote a famous editorial in the *Crisis* urging Negroes to "close ranks" with white Americans in defeating the nation's enemies. "If this is our country, then this is our war," he declared. He hoped that by proving their patriotism, Negroes would receive greater recognition of their manhood and their citizenship rights in the postwar era. Some Negro editors, however, were critical of Du Bois' stand, believing that he had conceded too much in asking Negroes "to forget our present grievances" until war's end.

Du Bois' hopes for the postwar reconstruction were completely frustrated. Returning soldiers in 1919 found themselves in a situation that if anything was worse than the one before they left: a revived Ku Klux Klan, loss of job opportunities due to demobilization, and an extraordinary outbreak of race riots—over twenty in that "Red Summer" of 1919. They ranged from Washington, D.C., to Elaine, Arkansas, from Longview, Texas, to Chicago. The basic cause of most of these riots lay in white fears of economic competition and the voting power of urban Negro migrants. The mobs harassed and murdered Negro victims without hindrance because of police prejudice and ineptitude. In some communities state militia reinforcements were called in too late, and even when deployed they often proved no better than the police. Generally all that Negroes could do was attempt to flee.

Yet there was unmistakable evidence of increasing Negro militancy, and it is likely that the riots reflected to some degree white fear of this militancy. In 1919 the NAACP was disturbed by carefully verified reports from many places, even in Mississippi—where one would have thought that the oppressive race system had snuffed out all significant protest—of Negroes planning to meet fire with fire, to fight back. Moreover, acts of retaliatory violence on the part of Negroes actually triggered some of the major race riots of the war and postwar years.

In these cases Negroes, goaded and angered by increasing numbers of white assaults during the months of rising racial tension that always precede a riot, struck back. The East St. Louis race riot of 1917 was precipitated when Negroes, having been beatened repeatedly by white gangs, shot into a police car. In the dusk they mistook it for another Ford automobile containing white joy-riders who had shot up Negro homes earlier in the evening. Two detectives were killed and white reaction led to the bloodiest race riot of the twentieth century. A similar sequence of events occurred at the Houston riot a few weeks later, and in Chicago in 1919. In the same year the Longview, Texas, riot occurred after Negroes shot whites who entered the ghetto seeking a teacher who had reported a recent lynching to the Chicago *Defender*. The event that triggered the Elaine, Arkansas, riot of 1919 was the shooting into a Negro church by two white law-enforcement officers. The Negroes returned the fire, causing one death. The white planters in the area, already angered because Negro cotton pickers had banded together to compel fairer treatment from the landlords, embarked upon a massive Negro hunt to put the black men "in their place." Two years later, in 1921, a riot in Tulsa, Oklahoma, originated when a crowd of armed Negroes assembled before the courthouse to prevent the possibility of a lynching of a Negro arrested for allegedly attacking a white girl. The Negroes shot at the white police and civilians who attempted to disperse them.

In each of these conflagrations, the typical pattern was Negro retaliation to white acts of persecution and violence, and white perception of this resistance as an organized, premeditated conspiracy to "take over," which unleashed the armed power of white mobs and police. In the face of overwhelming white numerical superiority, Negro resistance ordinarily collapsed fairly early during the riots, especially in the South. Generally white mobs would attack individual Negroes who happened to be passing through white areas, and those whose homes were on the borders of white neighborhoods or in small enclaves surrounded by white residences or businesses. Often armed, but terrified, Negroes fled their homes, leaving guns and ammunition behind. Occasionally, however, Negro retaliation occurred toward the close rather than at the start of a riot. Such was the case in the unusual, if not unique, Washington riot of 1919, when Negroes attacked white passengers on trolley cars passing through Negro areas.* Nevertheless, Negroes were generally defenseless in the face of superior numbers and force and police support for the rioters. While some whites were killed in the riots by Negroes who did retaliate, by far the greater number of victims were

* The Atlanta riot of 1906 was another example where Negro retaliatory violence occurred toward the end of the riot. There white mobs and police were shot at when they invaded the heart of a Negro ghetto, rather than remaining at the periphery

black men, unable to do anything effective to protect themselves or their families.

The idea of retaliatory violence was occasionally reflected in the utterances of leading intellectuals during the war and post-war years. In 1916, inspired by the Irish rebellion, Du Bois had admonished Negro youth to stop spouting platitudes of accommodation and remember that no people ever achieved their liberation without armed struggle. In 1920, embittered at the wave of racial proscription that followed the war, and reiterating a thought he had expressed as early as 1905, the year in which he founded the Niagara Movement, Du Bois predicted a race war in which Negroes, allied with Asians, would overwhelm the white race. In 1919, A. Philip Randolph, editor of the militant Socialist monthly, the *Messenger,* advocated physical resistance to white mobs. He observed that Anglo-Saxon jurisprudence recognized the law of self-defense, and that Negroes should use armed force against their attackers. Half a dozen years later, in the noted Sweet Case of 1925,* the NAACP also espoused the idea of the legality of retaliatory violence in self-defense and won. The open expression of such doctrines was thus a significant, though rare, theme in the statements of Negro leaders and intellectuals.

3

What programs did the established leadership organizations have to offer in the face of these trying conditions? Actually they could do little for the masses of people; middle class in their orientation, they had little to offer the urban slum-dweller. The National Urban League, founded in 1911 by a group of conservative Negroes and white philanthropists and social workers, all allied with Booker Washington, took as its special province improving the employment opportunities of urban Negroes. Basically, the League approach was a gradualist and conciliatory one of attempting to convince employers of the moral righteousness and economic value of hiring Negroes—to persuade them that Negroes were efficient workers. Attempts at negotiation with the discriminatory AFL unions got nowhere, and, indeed, if concessions were to be gained, it was certainly to come from philanthropic, if paternalistic, businessmen rather than from workers

* For Sweet Case, see p. 198.

who regarded Negroes as economic rivals. The unionization of industrial plants often led to the expulsion of Negro employees. On the other hand, many employers wanted to use Negroes to destroy or suppress union activity, which of course only antagonized white workers even more.

In the wave of labor difficulties and mass unemployment of the first postwar years, the Urban League wrestled with this predicament. At a Detroit conference of Urban League officials in 1919, a resolution was passed which declared that directors of local leagues should be guided by their particular situations. If the opportunity existed, Negro workers should be urged to join labor unions, but where there were barriers, it might be appropriate to supply strikebreakers to employers during labor disputes. Some local leagues did indeed send Negro strikebreakers, but the results seldom if ever led to any permanent rise in Negro employment. Jobs or promotions obtained during strikes usually proved only temporary; once the labor disputes ended, no matter which side won, white workers generally took the jobs. The antiunion attitudes of many Urban League officials have been attributed to their middle-class background and outlook, and this is in part undoubtedly the case. In the context of trade-union discrimination, however, it is hard to see how Urban League executives could have acted much differently. Yet even their appeal to businessmen in economic and moral terms gained little. League reports magnified minor accomplishments into major achievements. The Atlanta League even boasted about training Negroes to be better janitors. Whatever gains the League did make during the prosperous 1920's were wiped out by the Depression. The League was honestly trying to improve Negro employment opportunities, and in view of trade-union attitudes it is difficult to see that any approach would have been more successful. It is only a sign of the bitter context in which it operated that the League's efforts were futile.

The NAACP concerned itself only slightly with discrimination in employment, leaving the job situation chiefly with the Urban League in a division of function that was not really disturbed until the rise of the NAACP's labor department around the middle of the century. It did extraordinary service, however, in legal defense of victims of race riots and unjust judicial proceedings. It secured the release of the imprisoned Houston soldiers; it successfully defended the Negroes charged with insurrection in the Elaine riot; and in numerous cases it worked to prevent miscarriages of justice against innocent Negroes. One of the most celebrated cases was its defense of Dr. Ossian Sweet and his family. The Sweets had moved into a white neighborhood in Detroit, and in self-defense shot at a mob that came to attack the home, killing one man. The NAACP employed Clarence Darrow to defend the Sweets, who were eventually acquitted. A major effort of the NAACP during the 1920's was to secure passage of an antilynching bill. Though the law was not enacted the NAACP rallied a great deal of public support, and the number of lynchings gradually declined in the nation.

In the long run the most important of the NAACP's activities was the litigation designed to secure the enforcement of the Fourteenth and Fifteenth amendments. In two landmark cases almost at the outset of its career, the NAACP began the long uphill fight against disfranchisement and segregation. In 1915 the Supreme Court declared grandfather clauses to be unconstitutional limitations on the right to vote. Two years later it outlawed municipal residential segregation ordinances. White property-owners and realtors then retreated behind other subterfuges, particularly restrictive covenants, under which homeowners' associations excluded Negroes through agreements among themselves. The decade of the 1920's saw the beginning of the lengthy legal battle against this form of Jim Crow. At the same time the NAACP embarked upon the almost endless fight against the white primaries. The Association, despite its immediatist philosophy, was compelled to use an essentially gradualist approach, attacking one small aspect of discrimination at a time, hacking away piece by piece at the structure of discrimination. Though recognition of the Negroes' constitutional rights was still a long way off, the NAACP could at least point to a corpus of definite accomplishment. Less successful, however, were the attempts to prevent the development of school segregation in Northern cities. Gerrymanders of school boundaries and other devices initiated by boards of education were fought with written petitions, verbal protests to school officials, legal suits, and in several cities school boycotts, but in the end all proved to be of no avail.

The NAACP appealed to the "New Negro," to the business and professional people of the ghettos—North and even South.

The Association in part depended on the new militance of the postwar years and in part was responsible for it. For the Negro upper and middle classes, Du Bois, as editor of the *Crisis,* symbolized that militance and exerted an enormous influence on their thinking. When R. R. Moton, principal of Tuskegee Institute, though still a conciliator and gradualist, spoke out in unmistakable terms against racial injustice in *What the Negro Thinks* (1929), it was clear that the protest ideology represented by the NAACP had been generally accepted.

The Association, considering itself heir to the abolitionist tradition, and regarded as radical during the ascendancy of Booker T. Washington, now found itself in the curious position of being lumped together with Tuskegee, Hampton, and the Urban League as a conservative institution. Or so it was regarded by that economic and social radical, the *enfant terrible* of Negro journalism, A. Philip Randolph. His editorials in the *Messenger* even roasted and satirized Du Bois as a renegade Socialist, a political opportunist, and a "handkerchief head . . . hat-in-hand" Negro. The *Messenger's* point of view was that the NAACP was basically a middle-class organization unconcerned about the pressing economic problems of the masses. The *Messenger* took an outright Marxist position regarding the causes of prejudice and discrimination. It attributed these to capitalism, which kept white and black workers apart and exploited both by an appeal to race hatred. To Randolph and his colleagues the postwar era called for a New Negro, a radical Negro demanding the Negro's rights, concerned with the problems of the working class, and dedicated to the theory that only by united action of white and black workers against the capitalist class would social justice be achieved. Randolph appealed to Negroes to join trade unions, and he called upon trade unions to admit them. In practice his theory worked no better than the strategy of the Urban League in solving the economic problems of the race. One accomplishment Randolph did chalk up: the organization of the Brotherhood of Sleeping Car Porters in the mid-1920's. This was achieved against the determined opposition not only of the Pullman Company but also of much of the Negro leadership class—ranging from the conservative Chicago Urban League to the militant Chicago *Defender.*

Although Randolph addressed himself to the urban working

masses, few of them knew or understood the intellectual theories of the *Messenger*. The magazine circulated chiefly among elite Negroes; its scintillating wit and mordant satire made it a conversation piece in middle-class homes; and for several years in the early 1920's its pages were devoted very largely to singing the praises of Negro business enterprise. The one man who really reached the frustrated and disillusioned masses in the ghettos was a Jamaican citizen, Marcus Garvey.

Garvey, founder in 1914 of the Universal Negro Improvement Association (UNIA), which after the war had branches in many cities in the United States and in several foreign countries, aimed to liberate both Africans and American Negroes from their oppressors. His utopian means of accomplishing both goals was the wholesale migration of American Negroes to Africa. He contended that whites would always be racist and insisted that the Negro must develop "a distinct racial type of civilization of his own and . . . work out his salvation in his motherland, all to be accomplished under the stimulus and influence of the slogan, 'Africa for the Africans, at home and abroad.'" On a more practical level he urged Negroes to support Negro businesses, and the UNIA itself organized a chain of groceries, restaurants, laundries, a hotel, a doll factory, and a printing plant. Thousands bought stock in the UNIA's Black Star Steamship Line, which proposed to establish a commercial link between the United States, the West Indies, and Africa. Tens of thousands of Negroes swelled with pride at the parades of massed units of the African Legion in blue-and-red uniforms and the white-attired contingents of the Black Cross Nurses. Garvey's followers proudly waved the Association's flag (black for Negro skin, green for Negro hopes, and red for Negro blood), and sang the UNIA anthem, "Ethiopia, Thou Land of Our Fathers." Stressing race pride, Garvey gloried in the African past and taught that God and Christ were black.

He denounced the light-skinned, integrationist, upper-class Negroes active in the NAACP for being ashamed of their black ancestry and desiring to amalgamate with the white race. Garvey insisted that the UNIA was the only agency able to protect the darker-skinned Negro masses against the Du Bois-led "caste aristocracy" of college graduates. Thus while the *Messenger* denounced Du Bois as a cowardly renegade Socialist, Garvey

charged him with preferring white men to black.* In turn both
the *Messenger* and the *Crisis* joined in condemning Garvey. The
established Negro leaders resented and feared the "Provisional
President of the African Republic" and several of them called the
attention of the United States government to irregularities in the
management of the Black Star Line. Once Garvey had been jailed
and then deported on charges of using the mails to defraud, the
movement collapsed. But Garvey dramatized as no one before
had done the bitterness and alienation of the Negro masses.

Thus the Garvey Movement provided a compensatory escape
for Negroes to whom the urban promised land had turned out to
be a hopeless ghetto. It is significant, however, that the relationship between Negro migration and nationalist ideologies was not
a new one. The peaks of interest in African colonization among
Negroes since the Civil War coincided with the peaks of domestic
migration—in the late 1870's, around 1890, and again on the
eve of the First World War. In many cases, in fact, spokesmen
for the migrants regarded African colonization as an alternative
to seeking better opportunities elsewhere in the United States.
Ordinarily, colonization attempts had a strong nationalist emphasis, even though economic misery seems to have been the chief
stimulus. Moreover, some of the migration movements within the
United States were associated with strongly ethnocentric ideologies. Thus there were a number of attempts to establish all-
Negro towns, especially within the South and in the Far West.
The best known of these was Mound Bayou, Mississippi, founded

* Ironically, at this very time Du Bois was busily engaged in projecting
his own program for African and Afro-American unity—the anti-imperial-
ist Pan-African congresses of 1919–27. As early as the 1890's Du Bois
embraced "Pan-Negroism" and hoped to create among Negroes everywhere an emotional commitment to one another. He believed that regardless of where Negroes lived, they owed a special attachment to Africa as
the race's "greater fatherland." Upon the initiative of a group of West
Indian intellectuals the first Pan-African Conference was held in London
in 1900. Du Bois wrote the "Address to the Nations of the World," urging
self-government for Africans and West Indians and the creation in Africa
of "a great central Negro State of the world." Although he envisioned no
Back-to-Africa Movement, Du Bois believed that the formation and
growth of such an African state would raise the status of Negroes in all
countries. Between 1919 and 1927 Du Bois convened four Pan-African
congresses in Europe and the United States. Like the original London
conference, these conclaves were dominated by the personality of Du Bois
and ceaselessly condemned both beliefs in racial inequality and the imperialist exploitation of Africa.

in 1887 by Isaiah Montgomery, whose father had been the leader of the Davis Bend agricultural community during the Civil War. Mound Bayou expressed a chauvinistic ideology of Negroes working out their own destiny without white assistance. More significant for our discussion at this point was the attempt to erect an all-Negro state in Oklahoma, an effort initiated by E. P. McCabe, formerly state auditor of Kansas. Disillusioned when the Republicans failed to renominate him, McCabe urged Negroes to migrate to the Oklahoma Territory when it was opened for settlement. He painted a vision of a Negro-governed commonwealth, sending Representatives and Senators to the United States Congress. Between 1891 and 1910 about twenty-five towns were established. The migration aroused fears in the whites and eventuated not in political power but in disfranchisement. Then the economic dreams of the all-Negro towns in Oklahoma completely collapsed during the cotton depression of 1913–14. As a result, many Negroes of Oklahoma and surrounding states became intensely interested in the prospects of large-scale African migration. Tremendous excitement was generated in 1914–15 by an apparently fraudulent venture whose promoter, "Chief Sam," an alleged Ashanti chieftain, claimed that he had land in Africa on which American Negroes could settle. A few hundred actually sailed on an ill-fated expedition for the African homeland.

Thus, though it existed in a ghetto setting, the Garvey ideology and movement were part of a larger pattern associated with migration tendencies among Southern Negroes. Except for a few prominent leaders like Bishop Henry M. Turner, who for half a century after the close of Reconstruction, denounced American hypocrisy and advocated migration to Africa, colonization at this time was almost entirely an ideology of the lower classes. This fact is in marked contrast to the ante-bellum period, when many prominent, articulate Negroes were its advocates at one time or another.

That these colonization efforts manifested themselves as nationalist movements does not contradict the thesis that their motivation was largely economic. Mob rule and other forms of oppression played their roles, but just as the highly nationalistic Fascist organizations of Italy and Germany did not become mass movements until a period of acute depression, so ideologies of the sort represented by "Chief Sam" and Garvey flowered at times of intense economic discontent.

4

The patterns of adjustment of the rural Southern Negro to the urban environment and the institutional adaptations made by the Negro community have not been studied. The paucity of data may make it difficult, if not impossible, ever to analyze the process adequately. Yet a few observations can be made. In the first place the migrants brought with them two institutions—the church and the matrifocal family—which, in modified form, functioned to adjust Negroes to the dismal realities of urban life.

The rural Negro Baptist church became transformed in the cities into the store-front evangelical churches and sects, and the religious frenzy of Sunday worship allowed communicants to forget briefly the realities of daily life. These numerous churches were forums for ambitious men of humble origins wishing to develop their leadership talents. They were also the root from which the larger-scale sects, which flowered during the 1930's and 1940's, grew—those led by Father Divine, Daddy Grace, and Elder Lightfoot Micheaux. These organizations also gave their members a sense of self-esteem. Daddy Grace's "House of Prayer for All People," for example, by its very title indicated that everyone was welcome and important. To the poor his sermons held out the possibility of self-improvement, upward social mobility, and respectability. The sect's organizational structure created offices for about 25 percent of its followers, thus giving them a feeling of importance and identity. Emotional release was provided through brass bands, syncopated music, ecstatic dancing, seizures and swoonings, and "speaking with tongues." In Daddy Grace members perceived a charismatic figure who offered security, "sweet Daddy Grace," healer and miracle worker, and to many, even God Incarnate, the second Christ. The dollars which Grace received from the poor who flocked to his services, and which made him a wealthy man, were for the people themselves a small price to pay for the void he filled in their lives.

These store-front churches and cult groups, creating a life meaning out of meaninglessness, self-respect out of poverty, functioned for the slum-shocked urban Negroes in much the same way that Garvey did. The promise of self-esteem, rather than nationalism, was the significant ingredient of the Garvey Movement. This is demonstrated by the fact that many followers of the nationalist Garvey ended up in the ostentatiously interracial cult of Father Divine, whose "Heavens" did not really multiply until the economic Depression of the 1930's. Undoubtedly these religious cults provided an alternative for what might otherwise have been a highly explosive nationalist movement. The more recent, and overly publicized, Black Muslims have combined the nationalistic and religious escape ideologies.

The high incidence of matrifocal families, whether or not the pattern had African roots, was a legacy of the plantation. Its persistence was encouraged, however, by conditions of urban life. When the migrants moved into the cities, they found that women could obtain and hold jobs more easily than men; women became domestic servants and their work was steadier and commonly more remunerative than that of men. In a society where the man is regarded as responsible for the support of his family, Negro men often felt inadequate. The results were frequent separations and many households where the mother or grandmother was the central figure. While it is customary to look upon the high incidence of such households as a sign of social disorganization among lower-class Negroes, viewed from this context the matrifocal family pattern can be regarded as a stabilizing influence in the lives of its members, as a creative response to the circumstances under which Negroes found themselves, first on the plantation and then in the urban ghetto. Economic factors are not wholly responsible for the matrifocal family, for, once established, such forms of institutional life tend to perpetuate themselves.*

Along with the lower-class migrants from Southern towns came a professional and business elite, whose numbers were increased by aspiring members from the lower classes. Bred in the ideology of self-help and racial solidarity and Negro support of Negro business, which had become current during the Age of Booker T. Washington, this group, as the saying of the time put it, clearly took "advantage of the disadvantages" inherent in segregation and achieved economic success in the rapidly expanding

---

* In view of current misconceptions about Negro family life, it should be emphasized that matrifocal families, while common among lower-class Negroes, are not in the majority.

urban ghettos. In some cities, as in Atlanta, the upward-mobile men of wealth merged with members of the older pre-World War I upper class. In others, as in Chicago, they largely displaced the "old settlers" as the top stratum in Negro society.

Such men came to have a vested interest in the ghetto, for it was the source of their wealth, power, and social prestige. In the North this was also true of aspiring politicians. The "Dream of Black Metropolis," as St. Clair Drake and Horace Cayton termed it, was most forcefully advanced in Chicago, and there more than anywhere else the political aspect of the dream found fulfillment. In 1928 Chicago elected the first Negro to sit in Congress since the turn of the century. Chicago also boasted the biggest aggregation of Negro banks and insurance companies north of the Mason-Dixon line. The Black Metropolis ideal also had its development in the South, especially in Atlanta and Durham, where the three largest Negro insurance companies were located. In fact, E. Franklin Frazier in 1925 called Durham the "capital of the Black Middle Class."

To many, this vision of creating a business, professional, and political elite on the basis of a concentrated Negro market and on Negro votes was viewed as a temporary expedient, at best only an indirect way of achieving full participation in American life. To them it was clearly no solution to the problems of the race because the political and economic dominance still remained in white hands. Yet to some Negroes the dream was inspiring in and of itself, and they believed that a well-organized community supporting black "captains of industry," professional men, financiers, and politicians was a satisfactory alternative to the destruction of segregation. As Gunnar Myrdal was to observe, the Negro middle class was in a cruel and tragic dilemma: earning their bread from at least an implicit appeal to race loyalty and segregation, they were also the backbone of organizations like the NAACP, dedicated to moving Negroes into the mainstream of American life. Thus, in contrast to the turn of the century, the Black Metropolis ideal was now usually coupled, not with a philosophy of accommodation, but with one of protest. Then the dream, however psychologically satisfying, however materially advantageous to a few, collapsed in the face of the Depression of the 1930's when the flimsy foundation of the Negro business world became evident. Nevertheless, Negro business and professional men still appealed for support on the basis of race pride. They did so, however, not with the vision of creating a self-sufficient black community, but as a device to insure their own economic survival.

5

The sense of community and racial solidarity characteristic of the Garvey Movement and the Dream of a Black Metropolis had its intellectual counterpart in the "Harlem Renaissance," the literary and artistic movement summed up by the term, the "New Negro." In 1925 when *Survey Graphic* published its special Harlem issue edited by Alain Locke, a Harvard Ph.D. and the first Negro Rhodes scholar, it suddenly became apparent to the educated public that a cultural renaissance was under way. The New Negro was militant and proud of his race, desired to perpetuate the group identity and yet participate fully in American society. The New Negro protested and demanded his rights of citizenship and insisted upon the value of a Negro subculture. Intellectually and artistically, he believed that Negroes should have pride in their past and their traditions; and by using the themes from Negro life and Negro history as an inspiration for his literary work, the New Negro intended to enrich the culture of America.

The ethnic dualism and cultural pluralism of the New Negro movement or Harlem Renaissance had diverse origins. Interest in the race's past had been rapidly growing since the beginning of the century. The first courses in Negro history were introduced in a few Negro colleges about the time of the First World War. The Association for the Study of Negro Life and History, founded in 1915 by Carter G. Woodson, placed on scholarly foundations the investigation of both the African and American past.

At about the same time, many white authors were exploring in their novels the rich regional diversity of American culture. During the 1920's DuBose Heyward enlarged this interest to include Negro life. His novel *Porgy,* the inspiration for George Gershwin's famous musical *Porgy and Bess,* was set in the coastal area of South Carolina, where African survivals were strong. Many white literati who, during the heyday of Greenwich Village, made a cult of primitivism regarded the Negro and Africa as possessing intriguing qualities of savagery, occultism, and uninhibited sexuality. Indeed, the 1920's was the period, as Langston Hughes has said, when "Harlem was in vogue." Whites, attracted by jazz and the alleged exotic way of life among Harlem's citizens, flocked to the Harlem speak-easies, and to such spots as the Cotton Club, where entertainment was supplied by a chorus line of light-skinned Negroes, but where Negroes themselves could enter only as performers and employees, not as paying guests. The result of these and other converging currents was a remarkable outpouring of literature, painting, and sculpture. It was a movement with many midwives, among whom were white sponsors such as author Carl Van Vechten, the aesthete and scholar Alain Locke, Charles S. Johnson, editor of the magazine *Opportunity,* and W. E. B. Du Bois. The *Crisis* and *Opportunity,* published by the National Urban League, printed much of the new writing and awarded prizes for the most creative work.

Some of the whites connected with the Urban League were originally responsible for the publication of the *Survey Graphic*'s Harlem number. The white reading public made it profitable for book firms to publish volumes written by Negroes. Whites, ranging from the equalitarian Amy and Joel Spingarn of the NAACP to the paternalistic Park Avenue matron who subsidized Langston Hughes's career for a time, encouraged the young Negro writers. They provided money for prizes, grants, and scholarships. Paradoxically, therefore, the race-proud Harlem Renaissance was largely made possible by white interest. Paradoxically also, the race-proud New Negro writers and artists, associating with white literati like Carl Van Vechten and the Greenwich Village aesthetes, and gathering at places like A'Leila Walker's Dark Towers on 136th Street, where celebrities of both races jammed the fabulous parties, were almost certainly the best-integrated group among American Negroes, and stylistically they were strongly influenced by current white literary vogues.

The white support and financing of the Renaissance created some serious problems. Themes which concerned the writers were often seen differently by their white patrons and the reading public. Tensions arising over the color line within Negro society and the problem of "passing" were genuine concerns for the middle-class and upper-class Negroes. Yet they were also subjects of incredible fascination for whites who thought in terms of stock characters such as the "tragic mulatto" and assumed that

Negroes really wanted to be white. So also the unique aspects of the life of the folk Negro was a genuine subject for artistic representation, but whites found the material interesting mostly if it was exotic and played up lower-class sexuality. Thus the conflict between artistic integrity and commercial success assumed a particularly aggravated form among the Negroes of the Renaissance. Langston Hughes, for example, recounts the painful experience he had when the woman who was financing his work, and whom he deeply admired, insisted that his writing was not "primitive" enough. Hughes had the integrity to break the tie, though it was economically difficult and psychologically traumatic to do it.

The artistic outpouring of the 1920's was, it should be pointed out, rooted in the past. Since the 1890's there had been an incipient interest in folk materials, in the richness of life on the Sea Islands, in the African background, in the mystique of cultural nationalism, and in the insistence on the racial experience as a source of artistic inspiration. Negro theatre had been flourishing on Broadway since the 1890's; the productions were mostly stereotyped musicals and included the dialect comedy team of Bert Williams and George Walker, who made the cakewalk fashionable. During the prewar years there had also been a rise in literary works by Negroes. Much of this literature had either tended to be imitations of conventional Victorian poetry and melodramatic novels or to be written in stereotyped dialect, such as many of the poems and short stories of Paul Laurence Dunbar. On the other hand, Charles Chesnutt in his short stories had started to explore folk culture in a serious way, while his novels were vigorous protests against American racism. And in 1912 appeared anonymously James Weldon Johnson's volume, *The Autobiography of an Ex-Coloured Man,* the first and most successful novel about passing, but more significant for its glorification of ragtime, a Negro folk-music idiom then considered unrespectable, and for its portrayal of the somewhat unconventional life among the the theatrical and sporting elements in Negro society.

During the the 1920's Negroes were allowed for the first time to pursue serious careers in the theatre and the concert hall. The great nineteenth-century American Negro Shakespearean actor Ira Aldridge forged his remarkable career in England and Europe, not in the United States. In the 1920's dramatic roles still tended to be somewhat stereotyped, it is true, but Paul Robeson first achieved fame not in some forgotten musical but in a serious play by one of the great writers for the American stage, Eugene O'Neill. The concert stage remained closed to Negro instrumentalists, and no recital by a Negro singer was considered complete without the rendition of a group of spirituals. But working against incredible odds, the tenor Roland Hayes became the first Negro to be accepted as a concert artist.

The writers of the Renaissance articulated the various ideologies of the 1920's. The interest in the race's past was reflected in such poems as Langston Hughes's "The Negro Speaks of Rivers"; in the rather ambivalent poem of Countee Cullen, "Heritage," which appears to accept white stereotypes about the sensuous, exotic, and primitive quality of African life and the difficulty of even educated Negroes assimilating Anglo-Saxon culture; and in novels such as Arna Bontemps' *Black Thunder,* based on Gabriel's Revolt. Overlapping this historical concern was the exploration of traditions in the Negro subculture. In *Cane,* a series of poems, short stories, and vignettes, Jean Toomer, the most sophisticated literary genius of the Renaissance, recaptured the life of the Negro folk who worked in the lumber camps of Georgia in the 1880's. James Weldon Johnson in *God's Trombones,* subtitled, *Some Negro Folk Sermons in Verse,* employed the cadence and imagery of the Negro rural preacher. Langston Hughes in numerous poems used the rhythms and moods of jazz and the blues as an inspiration for his poetry. Claude McKay in his novel *Home to Harlem,* Zora Neale Hurston in her renditions of Negro folk materials, and Sterling Brown in his poems about Slim Greer were among those who found in the common folk a subject for literary treatment. Thus, in "Memphis Blues," using the dialect of the Negro working class, Sterling Brown expresses the resignation of the poor. Langston Hughes combined the themes of working-class Negro life with an underlying spirit of protest in such poems as his "Brass Spittoons," an evocation of a hotel bellhop's daily life, and "To the Negro Washerwoman," whom he idealized for her self-sacrifice in supporting and educating her family.

Others portrayed Negro middle-class life, emphasizing its gentility and respectability, and often employing plots based on passing and on the color line within the Negro community—as in Walter White's *Flight* and the novels of Jessie Fauset. White, an NAACP staff member, who was to serve as its executive secretary during the New Deal and World War II years, also wrote a protest novel, *Fire in the Flint,* based upon his investigations of lynchings.

Protest was evident in some of the ironic poems of Countee Cullen; such as "Yet Do I Marvel," in which, after pondering on the ways of an inscrutable, omnipotent, but undoubtedly just God, Cullen concludes, "Yet do I marvel at this curious thing: / To make a poet black, and bid him sing!"; or in some of Claude McKay's poems like "The Lynching" and "If We Must Die": "If we must die—let it not be like hogs / Hunted and penned in an inglorious spot . . . If we must die—oh, let us nobly die . . . dying, but fighting back!" After the Renaissance, during the 1930's, protest was to replace folk culture as the dominant theme of Negro writing. In those years Langston Hughes penned his "Let America Be America Again," a protest against oppression of all the subordinated groups and a vision of an equalitarian society. The dominant literary figure of the 1930's and 1940's was Richard Wright, whose *Uncle Tom's Children* and *Native Son* portrayed with bitter sociological and psychological realism the plight of the oppressed working-class Negroes. Wright treated the same subject even more searingly in his autobiographical *Black Boy.* His achievement as one of the major writers of the twentieth century in the United States has been eclipsed among Negro authors only by the post-World War II novelist Ralph Ellison, whose heavily symbolic *Invisible Man* draws upon material of Negro life to pose the fundamental problem of freedom in modern impersonal society.

6

In *Native Son* Wright described the Negro of the Depression years, victimized and hardened by life in the urban ghetto. Despite the misery, squalor, and limited opportunity in the cities, the New Deal era witnessed a continued, though reduced, migration to urban centers. In effect, New Deal programs actually encouraged this population movement, both by the policies of the Agricultural Adjustment Administration as applied to the Southern plantations and by providing public aid to unemployed Negroes in the cities, particularly in the North.

The New Deal, though in certain particulars regressive for the status of Negroes, marked a real turning point in the trends of American race relations. Despite the work of the NAACP and the interest of philanthropic whites in the Urban League and the Harlem Renaissance, it was only during the 1930's that a clear-cut reversal in the attitudes of white Americans started to become evident. Of paramount importance was the genuine interest of prominent New Dealers in the status of American Negroes. Their concern was part of the larger humanitarian interest in the welfare of all the underprivileged in American society. At the same time, the Negro vote had reached sizable proportions in a number of Northern cities, creating an additional motivation for the attention to Negro welfare among New Deal politicians. Of top prominence among those promoting the Negro cause was the wife of the President, Eleanor Roosevelt, who more than any other person during this era symbolized genuine humanitarian concern in race relations. To the dismay and consternation of Southern supporters of the President, she was openly friendly with Negroes. The most dramatic incident illustrating her attitude came in 1939, when the Daughters of the American Revolution refused to permit Constitution Hall, Washington's only concert stage, to be used for a recital by the contralto Marian Anderson. Mrs. Roosevelt thereupon resigned from the DAR. Harold Ickes, Secretary of the Interior and a former president of the Chicago NAACP, arranged for Miss Anderson to give a concert from the steps of the Lincoln Memorial. On Easter Sunday, over seventy-five thousand people attended this memorable program.

Negro leaders wanted more than symbolism. They protested against the exclusion of Negroes from large federally financed construction projects. In 1933, under NAACP initiative, various race advancement organizations established the Joint Committee on National Recovery to fight discriminatory policies in the federal agencies. The JCNR was especially effective in exposing the unequal wage rates provided in the National Industrial Recovery Act codes. Meanwhile the Roosevelt Administration had decided to appoint race relations advisers in the major federal departments. At first Roosevelt appointed Southern whites, only some of whom were genuinely concerned about improving the Negro's status. Negroes protested, and soon the Administration began using highly talented and well-educated Negroes in these posts. Among the more noted of these were Mary McLeod Bethune, director of the Division of Negro Affairs of the National Youth Administration, and Robert C. Weaver, adviser to the Department of the Interior. These new positions were the highest held by Negroes in the federal government since Taft's Administration. Their importance was chiefly symbolic, however.

The New Deal's real impact upon Negroes came not from such well-publicized appointments but from more tangible benefits. Negroes were the ones hardest hit by the Depression, being the last hired and first fired. Compared with unemployed whites, a smaller percentage of the unemployed Negroes benefited from relief and public works programs. Despite this discrimination, a higher proportion of the Negro population than of the white population received government aid since Negro unemployment was so much greater. Thus Negroes felt singularly indebted to the New Deal and the Roosevelt Administration, and have felt so ever since (as testified to by John F. Kennedy's effective use of the Roosevelt mantle in Negro newspaper advertisements during the 1960 campaign). By 1936 the Negro vote had dramatically shifted from Republican to Democratic. The New Deal welfare programs, which were administered with less discrimination in the North than in the South, helped to accelerate Negro migration, and therefore increased the number of Negroes who would vote Democratic in subsequent elections.

Although the New Deal helped to create a new climate of opinion and supplied material benefits to the unemployed, in certain ways its policies were less helpful. In this connection, two areas are worthy of special mention: housing and agriculture. The federal housing agencies definitely supported and strengthened the trend toward residential segregation. In agreements with banks and other lending institutions, the Federal Housing Administration refused to guarantee mortgages on homes purchased by Negroes in white communities. The United States Housing Authority, while providing public housing for many Negro families, financed separate projects for the two races. In addition, the policies of the Agricultural Adjustment Administration were clearly discriminatory in their application. Cotton agriculture had been experiencing competition from synthetic fibers as far back as the 1920's. The Depression intensified the decrease in the demand for cotton and prices tumbled. The Southeastern states suffered the most, for they were faced with the continued ravages of the boll weevil at the same time that Texas and Oklahoma were recovering from the worst effects of the boll weevil infestation and therefore becoming more effective competitors to the older cotton states. As part of its general program for raising farm prices, the AAA paid farmers to restrict their acreage. Supposedly, tenant farmers were to receive a share of this money, but in practice they usually did not. In fact, because of acreage reduction plantation owners had less need for workers. Many sharecroppers were forced off the land and they moved to the urban ghettos. Later the final collapse of the cotton tenant-farm system in most of the Southeast occurred in the post-World War II years, due to the mechanization of cotton agriculture, the erosion and depletion of many older cotton lands, and the spread of cotton agriculture to mechanized plantations in the West, especially California.

During the New Deal period, the rise of industrial unionism and the formation of the Congress of Industrial Organizations, which broke with the AFL, proved of immense value to the urban Negro. Not only reflecting the idealism of the period, the CIO's policy, led by John L. Lewis of the racially integrated United Mine Workers, also recognized that in a time of labor surplus it was hardly possible to organize workers effectively by excluding Negroes and thereby forcing them into the ranks of strikebreakers. Of course, perfect racial egalitarianism did not ensue. In the South especially, the CIO felt it necessary to permit separate locals and the relegation of Negroes to inferior jobs. Not until the 1960's did even the very liberal United Automobile Workers elect a Negro to its international executive board, and even that development occurred only after a well-organized Negro caucus compelled it. Nevertheless the CIO's contribution to the changing patterns of race relations has been incalculable. It made interracial trade unionism truly respectable. It gave Negro and white workers a sense of common interest, of solidarity, that transcended racial lines. Although prejudice was not eliminated, it was certainly lessened among laborers who worked together in jobs of equal status and equal pay.

The interracial industrial trade unions had an important impact on the Negro protest movement. Negro labor leaders like Willard Townsend of the Red Caps and A. Philip Randolph, and Ralph Bunche and some of the other younger intellectuals, went so far as to predict that the solution to the whole problem of discrimination would be through an alliance of black and white workers in industrial unions that would fight to bring social justice for all. Many of the middle- and upper-class leaders in the established racial advancement organizations were initially skeptical, though the Urban League took concrete steps to educate Negro workers on the value of joining labor unions. NAACP leadership was divided for several years. The turning point came in 1941 when the United Automobile Workers requested NAACP assistance in getting Negro scabs out of the Ford automobile factories. After securing assurances that the union would cease discriminatory policies against Negro members, the NAACP executive secretary, Walter White, personally went to Detroit and circled the strikebound River Rouge plant in a car with a loud-speaker, urging Negro strikebreakers to leave. A large number did so. Negro-labor union solidarity was a cornerstone of NAACP policy for nearly twenty years thereafter, until disillusionment with the discrimination of many unions in the reunited AFL-CIO led to renewed criticism of the racial practices in organized labor.

Even before the CIO appeared, the economic catastrophe of the 1930's and the outlook and program of the New Deal had stimulated changes in the orientation of Negro protest thinking. Specific concern with economic problems became much more the order of the day. During the early 1930's this took a nationalist turn. In an effort to obtain retail sales positions for Negroes in white-owned stores, "Don't Buy Where You Can't Work" campaigns were conducted in a number of urban ghetto business districts.

The employment situation and the general radicalization of American thinking during the 1930's led to intensified criticism of the NAACP's program. Du Bois resigned as editor of the *Crisis* in 1934 largely because he was convinced that the NAACP emphasis on attacking disfranchisement and segregation without seriously pursuing an economic program proved its identification only with the bourgeoisie. Du Bois, furthermore, had never given up completely his belief in the value of collective racial economic endeavor. His ardent advocacy of a separate Negro co-operative economy as a solution to the problems posed by the Depression led to a clash with those who supported the NAACP's traditional position of opposing any form of segregation, and resulted not only in his withdrawal from his position with the NAACP but also, as a consequence, in his withdrawal from a position of effective leadership. Younger critics of the NAACP like Ralph Bunche, who was then a professor at Howard University, also attacked the Association for what they conceived to be its gradualist approach and its lack of attention to economic problems. From the beginning of the Roosevelt Administration, the NAACP as well as the Urban League protested against discrimination in the New Deal agencies, and, as we have seen, eventually the NAACP modified its platform and endorsed the new interracial, industrial unions.

The organization also broadened the scope of its legal work. It fought a vigorous, though unsuccessful, campaign for the abolition of the poll tax. It continued its attack on the white primaries, and eventually, in 1944, the Supreme Court handed down a decision ending Southern subterfuge on that particular issue. The heart of NAACP litigation in the 1930's was the beginning of a long-range battle against segregation. For tactical purposes, the main emphasis was placed on educational discrimination. The NAACP adopted the strategy of attacking the most obvious inequities in the Southern school systems: the lack of professional and graduate schools and the low salaries received by Negro teachers. The Association hoped that by this indirect method segregation would become so expensive that it would fall of its own weight. Not until about 1950 did the organization make a direct assault against school segregation on the legal grounds that separate facilities were inherently unequal.

7

A significant aspect in the history of the Negro protest movement during the New Deal was the role of the Communist Party. Because the great majority of Negroes belong to the working class, and because of the discrimination and oppression they have suffered, the Communists have considered American Negroes to be ideal material for a revolutionary movement. During the 1920's and early 1930's the Communists attempted to appeal directly to the Negro masses and attacked the Negro bourgeoisie, Negro advancement organizations, and Negro intellectuals. Though the Communists did much to publicize the injustices against Negroes and did significant organization work among Southern sharecroppers, Negroes at no time constituted more than about 10 percent of Communist Party membership. In other words, Negroes did not join the party any more readily than did whites.

Around 1935, with the rise of Hitler in Germany and the Nazi threat to Soviet Russia, Communist international policy shifted to courting Socialists, liberals, and even other middle-class groups in Europe and America, and to forming so-called popular fronts with them. A number of these groups eventually found themselves taken over and dominated by their Communist members. In the case of American Negroes, too, the Communists did an about-face and now wooed the NAACP, the Urban League, and the Negro middle-class in general. Walter White was no longer a lickspittle of the capitalists; Lester Granger of the Urban League was no longer a Judas of the race. Neither the League nor the NAACP, however, favored close co-operation with Communists, and generally the latter were obliged to look elsewhere to make significant gains among American Negroes.

Representative of the nature of Communist activity in the late 1930's was the career of the National Negro Congress. It was organized in 1936 under the auspices of a group of Negroes, chiefly younger intellectuals, who were critical of the conservatism of the NAACP and the Urban League, and especially of the reluctance of these two organizations to engage in a program that would be meaningful to the economically depressed Negro masses. Taking active parts were men like Ralph Bunche and A. Philip Randolph, the National Negro Congress' first president. A few Communists were also active; the executive secretary was sympathetic with the Communist point of view; and Communist co-operation seemed natural in the days of the popular front. The Congress was actually an organization of organizations; as such, its work was largely in the area of propaganda and publicity. Its program was similar to that of civil rights groups in that period, except for its strong prounion orientation. It received a great deal of publicity, and at the second conference in 1937 the National Negro Congress was addressed by a brilliant galaxy of Negro leaders, practically a Who's Who of the leadership elite among the Black Bourgeoisie.

In 1939, as a result of the Soviet-Nazi nonaggression pact, there was a reversal of Communist tactics. The popular-front strategy was shelved. Erstwhile friends now became enemies, tools of imperialist warmongers. Even A. Philip Randolph came under attack. The party packed the Congress' third convention in 1940. Speakers who did not agree with Communist-inspired resolutions were booed and hooted. Fully one fourth of the delegates were white representatives from pro-Communist trade unions, and when Randolph was delivering his speech, these delegates and a number of their sympathizers walked out. Disillusioned, Randolph, Bunche, and other prominent leaders withdrew their support from the organization, which declined rapidly into a small and impotent group consisting principally of Communists and their "fellow-travelers."

When Hitler attacked Russia, the Communists again reversed themselves. Now everything was to be sacrificed to winning the war and aiding Russia. The attack on discrimination in the armed forces and in the war industries was to be soft-pedaled because, the Communists held, such protests interfered with the effectiveness of the war effort. Randolph, the NAACP, and the Urban League replied that the full and unsegregated use of Negro manpower would actually bring victory closer.

8

The ambivalent legacy of the New Deal was very evident in the role that Negroes played during the war. On the one hand, conditions were markedly better than they had been in the First World War; on the other hand, the New Deal administration temporized, compromised, and moved only under pressure. As in the First World War, the major problems were: employment, racial tensions in the cities and at army camps, and the treatment of Negro soldiers. Although Negroes were sent to integrated army officers' training camps, in other respects they were segregated in the armed forces. There was segregation also in the blood banks, although, ironically, the process of storing blood plasma had been invented by a Negro physician, Dr. Charles Drew of Howard University Medical School. Precedents were shattered by the admission of Negroes into the Army Air Corps and the Marines, and for the first time since early in the century Negroes were accepted in naval grades above messmen. The first Negro naval officers and the first Negro brigadier general were commissioned. Yet at army posts Negroes were segregated in inadequate recreational facilities; there were reports from Italy of low morale because of prejudiced treatment by white army officers; in the South Negro soldiers were often insulted by white citizens; and William H. Hastie, supported by the NAACP, angrily resigned as civilian aide to the Secretary of War when, over his opposition, a segregated training base for Negro pilots was established at Tuskegee Institute. The fact that it was conservative Tuskegee which encouraged this offer, while the NAACP opposed it, is symbolic of the degree of improvement that had taken place since World War I, when the Association's leaders had welcomed a segregated officers' training camp. So also was the greater degree of freedom with which Negro leaders and editors criticized discriminatory policies on the part of industry and public officials.

As industry retooled for war production in 1940 and 1941 and absorbed many of the unemployed, Negroes at first found themselves without jobs or used only for menial employment. They protested vigorously, and after A. Philip Randolph had threatened a March on Washington of 50,000 to 100,000 black men, President Roosevelt issued his famous Executive Order 8802 establishing a Fair Employment Practices Committee. Although the Committee lacked enforcement powers and was stripped of any real influence when it became too controversial, it did perform some useful work in advancing the employment of Negroes in war industries; and the federal employment service in many communities encouraged the hiring of Negroes. In most cases they entered factories organized by CIO affiliates. The beneficial results of the racial policies of the industrial unions were thus further enhanced and carried over into the postwar era. Nevertheless, discrimination was still flagrant. Tensions among workers erupted into a series of race riots, most notably at Detroit, where in June, 1943, the most serious racial outbreak occurred. In contrast to the Red Summer of 1919, however, there was no postwar racial violence when the soldiers were demobilized.

Indeed, the Truman Administration in some ways opened a new era in the history of American race relations. The political impact of the heavy Negro migration to Northern and Western cities, and the shift in allegiance from the Republicans to the Democrats now became evident. As the number of migrants rose to new heights during the war, the West Coast for the first time attracting a substantial segment of them, the expansion of the urban ghettos accelerated. On the basis of these enlarged black ghettos the Negro politicians continued to augment their power. With the election of Adam Clayton Powell in 1944, New York became the second Northern city to send a Negro to Congress. Two decades later there were six Negroes in the House of Representatives, two from Detroit, and one each from Philadelphia, New York, Chicago, and Los Angeles.

In early 1948 the NAACP's public relations director, Henry Lee Moon, published the book *Balance of Power,* in which he held that the Negro vote in certain pivotal states was enough to swing close national elections. The presidential election of 1948 vindicated his thesis. President Truman, regarded as a certain loser by practically all observers, realized that to win he would need the Negro vote. It was the first election since Reconstruction in which the Negro's status was a major issue. Because the Democratic national convention adopted a strong civil rights plank, Southern elements walked out and backed their own "Dixiecrat" candidate, who captured four of the traditionally Democratic states in the election. The left-wing Progressive Party took a vigorous stand on Negro rights and siphoned off enough voters from the Democrats to throw New York into the Republican column. Nevertheless, Truman, with the overwhelming support of the Negro electorate, squeaked through to victory.

Though the Democratic Congress failed to enact a civil rights act as the party's platform had promised, the Truman Administration was marked by some advances. The President appointed William H. Hastie to the Third U.S. Circuit Court, making him the highest Negro judicial appointee up to then in American history. Truman issued the directive that ended segregation in the armed services, settling an issue about which Negroes had agitated constantly since Randolph listed it among his original demands when he proposed the March on Washington in 1941. This change of policy had an incalculable effect in changing white attitudes, for as a result of it millions of young men of both races lived and worked together, and fought together in Korea, and white men often served under Negro officers, especially noncommissioned ones. The President also ordered that firms doing business with the federal government should pursue a nondiscriminatory employment policy. The committee appointed by Truman and his successor, Dwight D. Eisenhower, was ineffectual in enforcing this directive, however. Truman also appointed a commission to study race relations in the United States. Its report, *To Secure These Rights,* called for the full integration of Negroes in all aspects of the society. The principal value of both these commissions, largely symbolic and educational, was their help in paving the way for new norms in American race relations. The shift in public opinion, abetted by the new power of Negro voters, was reflected in a trend toward enacting fair-employment-practice and public accommodations laws in Northern and Far Western states and municipalities.

Thus, at mid-century the Great Migration to the industrial centers since the First World War was about to usher in the most momentous changes in Negro-white relationships since the Civil War. The context and texture of Negro life had changed, and the process of future racial adjustment was to take place in a chiefly urban environment. The urban ghetto was at one and the same time the force which constricted Negro life and aspirations and yet formed the base for Negro political power and the activities of civil rights organizations. Because the Negro vote was often closely tied to Democratic city machines, it was not as effective a voice of protest as some believe it could have been; nevertheless by 1950 it had already determined a presidential election, elicited several important actions on the part of the Chief Executive, and secured the passage of some state and municipal antidiscrimination laws. Without the urban base, the Negro protest movement would have remained small, and without the political leverage the urban masses provided, it would have remained impotent. Though no one realized it at the time, and though other factors were also essential in bringing about the events that were to follow, by mid-century the vote of the black ghetto in the North had reached the proportions that made possible the civil rights revolution.

VII

THE CIVIL RIGHTS REVOLUTION:
"WE HAVE A DREAM..."

"THE NEGRO SCHOOLS OF THOUGHT," A. Philip Randolph, patriarch of the Negro protest movement said, "are torn with dissension, giving birth to many insurgent factions. . . . All are engaged in a war of bitter recriminations . . . while the long suffering masses . . . [are] victims of the vanities, foibles, indiscretions and vaulting ambitions . . . of various leaderships." This was written in 1923 when there was a conservative group best represented by Tuskegee Institute and the National Urban League, a radical left wing of Marxists connected with the *Messenger,* a radical nationalist Back-to-Africa movement, and, in the middle of the road, the NAACP. Randolph's words so aptly describe the situation throughout the twentieth century that they might just as easily have applied to the period a dozen years earlier when the conflict between "conservative" Booker T. Washington and the "radical" NAACP was raging, or to the recent period when the "conservative" NAACP has been criticized by the more "radical" activist civil rights organizations.

1

What has happened to the civil rights movement to produce a situation where a platform that nearly six decades ago was censured for its militancy is now being condemned for its gradualism? Externally there has been an impressive shift in white public opinion. Internally, what was once a liberal white and Negro upper-class movement, aimed at securing the colored man's constitutional rights through agitation, legislation, and court litigation, has become a completely Negro-led and largely working-class movement, emphasizing direct-action techniques and going beyond constitutional rights to demand special efforts to overcome the poverty of the black masses.

"Radical" is of course a relative term; and in a sense the central thrust of Negro protest, aiming at the inclusion of Negroes in American society on a basis of full equality, rather than at a fundamental transformation of its institutions, is not really radical at all. Negro protest has been for the most part firmly rooted in the basic values of American society, aiming not at their destruction but at their fulfillment. There have been, it is true, elements of extreme Marxist and nationalist thinking that call either for a revolutionary overthrow of the American social system, or for complete withdrawal from the society. But such solutions have been peripheral. Moreover, among the Marxists, only the Democratic Socialists have been a consistently important force in the civil rights movement, and their contribution has tended to go unrecognized because they have usually focused on immediate improvement in the Negro's position rather than on the larger Marxist goal of a fundamental root-and-branch reordering of American society. And it is difficult to know whether to classify nationalist groups like the Garveyites and Black Muslims as protest movements or not. Theoretically they protest against American racism, but by advocating separation or colonization they actually have functioned as an accommodating mechanism in the American social order.

The goals, tactics, and strategy of the mid-twentieth-century civil rights movement were clearly foreshadowed during the Second World War by Randolph's March on Washington Movement and the founding of the Congress of Racial Equality (CORE). Though its career was brief the former organization prefigured things to come in three ways: 1) it was an avowedly all-Negro movement; 2) it was deliberately based upon action on the part of the black masses; and 3) it concerned itself with the economic problems of the urban slum-dwellers. Moreover, the wartime Fair Employment Practices Committee that Roosevelt created in response to Randolph's threat was itself important, for it established a precedent suggesting that the right to fair employment might be regarded as a civil right.

The origins of CORE, responsible for projecting the use of nonviolent direct action as a civil rights strategy, lie in the activities of the Fellowship of Reconciliation, a Quaker social-action organization. Certain leaders of this group of religious pacifists, interested in applying nonviolent techniques to the solution of racial problems, and wishing to attract people whose interest lay in race relations rather than in pacifism, founded CORE in 1942. CORE combined lessons learned from Gandhi's use of *Satyagraha* in India with a new instrument of group action—the sit-in, apparently derived from the famous sit-down strikes in the Detroit automobile factories in the 1930's. CORE in its early years consisted principally of white liberals, Socialists, and pacifists. As late as 1961 two thirds of its membership and most of its national officers were white.

The drift in public opinion toward a more liberal racial attitude, which had begun during the New Deal, accelerated during the war and the postwar years. Thoughtful whites became painfully aware of the contradiction involved in fighting the Nazis with their racist philosophy while permitting race discrimination at home. After the war the revolution against Western imperialism, first in Asia and then in Africa, engendered a new respect for the nonwhite peoples of the world and a new importance for them in international councils. Ironically, nothing has been more helpful to the Negroes' cause than the Cold War, with the Communist powers holding American democratic pretensions up to ridicule before the uncommitted peoples of the world.

In this context of changing international trends and shifting American opinion the campaign for Negro rights broadened. The growing size of the Northern Negro vote had already made civil rights a major issue in national elections, and eventually, in 1957, led to the establishment of a federal Civil Rights Commission with the power to investigate discriminatory conditions throughout the country and to recommend corrective measures to the President. Under pressure from the NAACP and other organizations, both black and white, more and more Northern and Western states outlawed discrimination in employment, housing, and public accommodations. The NAACP, piling up victory upon victory in the courts, successfully attacked racially restrictive covenants in housing, segregation in interstate transportation, and discrimination in publicly owned recreational facilities. Finally, with the Supreme Court ruling of 1954 it brought its legal campaign against educational segregation in the South to a triumphant climax.

Over the years Negroes had gradually taken over most of the offices in the NAACP. In 1921 James Weldon Johnson became the Association's first Negro executive secretary. In 1935 the NAACP legal staff came under Negro direction when Charles Houston was hired as special counsel. In 1965 only two white people were on its national staff, and less than one fourth of the national board was white. During and after the Second World War the backbone of the NAACP's expanding membership came to rest among the working-class urban Negroes. In the postwar era, it continued to conduct voter-registration drives and established housing and labor departments to improve its program in these two areas. Thus, in the 1950's the NAACP was strengthening its work along the legal-legislative lines it had employed in earlier years.

CORE by mid-century was embarking upon demonstrations in the Border States. Public accommodations were still its major focus, but it also began experimenting with direct-action techniques to open employment opportunities. In 1947 CORE, in cooperation with the Fellowship of Reconciliation, conducted a "Journey of Reconciliation"—or what would later be called a "Freedom Ride"—in the states of the Upper South. Their purpose was to test compliance with the *Morgan v. Virginia* decision of the preceding year, in which the Supreme Court had declared that for states to require segregation on interstate buses was an undue burden on interstate commerce. The riders met resistance in some areas, and the pacifist Bayard Rustin, who was to become one of the prominent civil rights leaders of the 1960's, was one of those who was sentenced to a thirty-day jail term on a North Carolina road gang.

It was not CORE, however, but the Montgomery, Alabama, bus boycott of 1955–56 that captured the imagination of the nation and of the Negro community in particular, and was chiefly responsible for the rising use of direct action in the late 1950's.

In no small part this came about because the boycott, a local action, catapulted into national prominence the one person in the civil rights movement who has most nearly achieved charismatic leadership, Rev. Martin Luther King, Jr. Like the founders of CORE—but unlike the great majority of civil rights activists, who have regarded nonviolence as a convenient tactic—King professes a Gandhian belief in the principles of pacifism. In King's view, the civil rights demonstrators who are beaten and jailed by hostile whites educate and transform their oppressors through the redemptive character of their unmerited suffering.

Even before a court decision obtained by NAACP attorneys in November, 1956, had desegregated the Montgomery buses and spelled victory for the Montgomery Improvement Association, a similar movement had started in Tallahassee, Florida, and afterward one developed in Birmingham, Alabama. In June, 1957, the Tuskegee Civic Association undertook a three-year boycott of local merchants after the state legislature gerrymandered nearly all of the Negro voters outside of the town's boundaries. This campaign was crowned with success when, in response to a suit filed by the NAACP Legal Defense Fund, the Supreme Court ruled the gerrymander illegal. Today Negroes hold public office in the community where Booker T. Washington used to preach that Negroes had erred by starting in politics instead of at the plow. Events in Montgomery, Tallahassee, Birmingham, and Tuskegee were widely heralded as indicating the emergence of a "New Negro" in the South—militant, no longer fearful of white hoodlums, police, or jails, and ready to use his collective weight to achieve his ends. Seizing upon this new mood King in 1957 established the Southern Christian Leadership Conference (SCLC), designed to co-ordinate direct-action activities in Southern cities. Negro protest had now moved in a vigorous fashion into the South; like the Northern protest activities it was concentrated in the urban ghetto.

2

Nonviolent direct action attained popularity not only because of the effectiveness of King's leadership. The fact was that the older techniques of legal and legislative action had proved themselves limited instruments. Impressive as it was to cite the advances in the fifteen years after the end of World War II, in spite of state laws and Supreme Court decisions, something was clearly wrong. Though in the twelve years following the outlawing of the white primary in 1944 the NAACP and other groups had raised the total number of Negroes registered in Southern states from about 250,000 to nearly a million and a quarter, Negroes were still disfranchised in most of the South. Supreme Court decisions desegregating transportation facilities were still largely ignored there. Discrimination in employment and housing abounded, even in Northern states with model civil rights laws. Beginning in 1954 the Negro unemployment rate steadily moved upward. There was the Southern reaction following the Supreme Court's 1954 decision on school desegregation: attempts to outlaw the NAACP, intimidation of civil rights leaders, "massive resistance" to the Court's decision, the forcible curtailment of Negro voter registration, and the rise of the White Citizens' Councils.

At the very time that legalism was thus proving to be of limited usefulness, other events were bringing about a change in Negro attitudes: Negroes were gaining a new self-image as a result of the rise of the new African nations; King and others were demonstrating that nonviolent direct action could succeed in the South; and the new laws and court decisions, the international situation, and the evident drift of white public opinion had developed in American Negroes a new confidence in the future. In short, there had occurred what has appropriately been described as a "revolution in expectations." Negroes no longer felt that they had to accept the humiliations of second-class citizenship, and consequently these humiliations—somewhat fewer though they now were—appeared to be more intolerable than ever. Ironically, it was the NAACP's very successes in the legislatures and the courts that more than any other single factor led to this revolution in expectations and the resultant dissatisfaction with the limitations of the NAACP's program. This increasing impatience accounted for the rising tempo of nonviolent direct action in the late 1950's, culminating in the student sit-ins of 1960 and the inauguration of what is popularly known as the "Civil Rights Revolution," or the "Negro Revolt."

Many believe that the Montgomery boycott ushered in this

Negro Revolt, and the importance of that event in projecting the images of both King and nonviolent direct action cannot be overestimated. But the really decisive break with the pre-eminence of legalistic techniques came with the college student sit-ins that swept the South in the spring of 1960. In dozens of communities in the Upper South, the Atlantic coastal states, and Texas, student demonstrations secured the desegregation of lunch counters in drug and variety stores. Arrests were numbered in the thousands, and police brutality was only too evident in scores of communities. In the Deep South the campaign ended in failure, even in instances where hundreds had been arrested, as at Montgomery, Alabama; Orangeburg, South Carolina; and Baton Rouge, Louisiana. But the youths had captured the imagination of the Negro community and to a remarkable extent of the whole nation.

The civil rights movement would never be the same again. The Southern college student sit-ins set in motion waves of events that shook the power structure of the Negro community, made direct action temporarily pre-eminent as a civil rights technique, ended NAACP hegemony in the civil rights movement, speeded up incalculably the whole process of social change in race relations, all but destroyed the barriers standing against the recognition of the Negro's constitutional rights, and ultimately turned the Negro protest organizations toward a deep concern with the economic and social problems of the masses. Involved was a steady radicalization of tactics and goals: from legalism to direct action, from participation by the middle and upper classes to mass action by all classes, from guaranteeing the protection of the Negro's constitutional rights to securing economic policies that would insure the welfare of the culturally deprived in a technologically changing society, from appeal to the white Americans' sense of fair play to demands based upon the power in the black ghetto. Most of these things had been adumbrated by the March on Washington Movement of the early 1940's; but it was the train of events set in motion by the college generation of 1960 that made Randolph's vision of civil rights tactics and objectives a reality.

The election of John F. Kennedy in 1960 symbolized another set of factors that were to have importance for the course of the Negro Revolution. Kennedy campaigned vigorously for the Negro vote, and his narrow victory would not have been possible without it. At the same time he was heavily indebted to some segregationists who kept their states in the Democratic column, and he did not wish to jeopardize other parts of his legislative program by pushing for a civil rights bill to strengthen those passed in 1957 and 1960, which had provided mainly for a fact-finding but powerless Civil Rights Commission. He attempted therefore to placate Southern states by following their recommendations in making appointments to the federal district courts. This policy led to the selection of certain extremely segregationist judges and thus removed effective judicial assistance for Negroes in the Deep South to the more distant circuit and Supreme courts. On the other hand, Kennedy privately encouraged the Taconic and Field foundations to finance a voter-registration campaign among Southern Negroes being conducted by the various civil rights organizations. Despite resistance in many areas, particularly in the Deep South, Negro registration in the South as a whole roughly doubled to a total of about 2,000,000 between 1962 and 1964.

Basically Kennedy hoped to satisfy Negroes by relatively vigorous use of executive authority. After much delay Kennedy in 1962 ordered the federal housing authorities to cease discrimination connected with the financing of private homes. For the first time the presidential committee charged with securing fair-employment policies from firms with government contracts seriously attempted to put some pressure on the offending corporations. But the most effective vote-getting action he took was his appointments policy. For the first time Negroes received a significant number of positions at the middle and higher levels in the government departments, the most notable being the appointment in 1961 of Robert C. Weaver to head the Housing and Home Finance Agency. Although in retrospect Kennedy's program seems mild, one thing is clear: where President Eisenhower had proved vulnerable only to international pressures (as when he finally sent troops to Little Rock, Arkansas, to enforce the Supreme Court's decision integrating the white high school there), Kennedy was susceptible to pressures from Negro public opinion as well. He needed the Negro vote, and as subsequent events showed, both he and his successor could be pushed into progressively stronger action on behalf of the race.

3

The successes of the student movement threatened the existing leadership arrangements in the Negro community far more profoundly than had the Montgomery boycott and the rise of King and SCLC. What ensued was a spirited rivalry among all civil rights organizations. Both the NAACP and SCLC attempted to identify themselves with the student movement. The organizing meeting of the Student Nonviolent Coordinating Committee (SNCC) at Raleigh, North Carolina, in April, 1960, was called by Martin Luther King. The SNCC platform expressed the same ideas of religious pacifism as did King himself. But within a year the youth had come to consider King as too cautious, and not dedicated enough to the cause, and had broken with him and SCLC. The NAACP, which had previously engaged in demonstrations only in a peripheral way, now decided to make direct action a major part of its strategy. Its youth secretary organized and reactivated college and youth chapters in the Southern and Border states with the specific intention of promoting direct-action campaigns. Other staff members at regional conferences that spring urged the adult branches to support this kind of activity. In many cases eager youths pushed reluctant adults into backing direct action. Much as the latter might have initially opposed a demonstration, once dozens or hundreds of young people had been arrested, their elders could do nothing but rally to them. The young people, especially in NAACP branches, depended heavily on the legal and financial aid which adult citizens supplied. Yet the dynamics of the situation were summed up by a college student at the 1961 NAACP convention who remarked, "We don't need the adults, but they need us." CORE, which was still unknown to the general public, installed James Farmer as national director in January, 1961, and moved to the front rank of civil rights organizations with the famous Freedom Ride to Alabama and Mississippi that spring. Designed to dramatize the lack of transportation desegregation in those states, the Freedom Ride eventuated in a bus burning in Alabama, hundreds spending a month or more in Mississippi prisons, and partial compliance with a new order from the Interstate

Commerce Commission desegregating all facilities used in interstate transportation.

Disagreements over strategy and tactics inevitably became intertwined with rivalries between personalities and organizations. Each civil rights agency felt the need for proper credit if it was to obtain the prestige and financial contributions necessary to maintain and expand its own program. The clashes between individuals and organizations, both nationally and locally, were often very severe, and the lack of unity was often bemoaned. In actual fact, the overall effect of the competition was to stimulate more and more activity as organizations attempted to outdo each other, and thus to accelerate the pace of social change in city after city. On the other hand, even among the strictly direct-action organizations, there developed differences in style. SCLC appeared to be the most deliberate and to engage chiefly in a few major projects. From the beginning SNCC staff workers lived on subsistence allowances and appeared to conceive of going to jail as a way of life. More than any of the other groups, SNCC workers have been "True Believers."

Direct actionists often criticized the NAACP for being dominated by a conservative Black Bourgeoisie wedded to a program of legal action and gradualism. Actually, in the 1960's the NAACP's program became the most highly varied of all the civil rights organizations. It has retained a strong emphasis on court litigation. Acting in part through the Civil Rights Leadership Conference, consisting of many Negro and interracial organizations interested in promoting civil rights legislation, it has maintained an extraordinarily effective lobby at the national capitol. And it has also engaged in many direct-action campaigns. Some branches disdained direct action, but others enthusiastically adopted the tactic. In a few cases NAACP branch presidents even served as heads of SCLC affiliates.

In the absence of carefully collected empirical data, it is impossible to speak with precision about the sources of membership and leadership in either the NAACP or the other groups. Individuals of middle- and upper-class background or attainments have predominated in the leadership of all organizations, for they alone are likely to possess the necessary skills of administration and communication. This is true today, although SNCC and more recently CORE have consciously worked to create indigenous grass-roots leadership, particularly in Mississippi and Louisiana. The college students who founded SNCC and formed the backbone of the demonstrations in 1960–61 tended to be mainly from an upward-mobile lower-middle-class background, or what they themselves often described as "striving lower class." By 1962, however, SNCC had ceased to be a co-ordinator of college groups but had become a staff of activists whose field-workers stimulated direct action in Southern communities. Both SNCC community projects and SCLC affiliates have appealed mostly to working-class people rather than to the bourgeoisie. The NAACP since the 1940's has also drawn most of its members from the working class, although certain branches with a mass membership base, like the one in Chicago, have been closely allied with urban political machines, which have used the organization to siphon off protest rather than to articulate it. CORE, by 1962 and 1963, when it was turning its attention to employment problems in the Northern cities, attracted a number of blue-collar workers and even people from the chronically unemployed lower class, and during 1964–65 its Southern staff created and closely co-operated with working-class community organizations. But frequently CORE chapters, which are principally in the North and West, have leaders and members alike who are mainly middle class. In fact, in many localities the range of membership and leaders in the NAACP, in CORE, and even in the SCLC affiliates is such that one finds it hard to distinguish among them on the basis of social class. Rather, the NAACP and the more activist groups often seem to attract different personality types from roughly the same social classes.

4

Meanwhile the role of whites in the movement was changing. Instead of occupying positions of leadership, they found themselves relegated to the role of foot soldiers and followers. Negroes in the movement had come to feel less dependent on whites, more confident of their own power, and demanded that their leaders be black. The NAACP had acquired Negro leadership some years before; and both SCLC and SNCC were from the start Negro-led and Negro-dominated. CORE, having acquired a new image in 1961 after the Freedom Ride, became predominantly Negro as it expanded in 1962 and 1963. Today nearly all of its executives are Negro, and its 1965 convention adopted a constitutional amendment that officially limited white leadership in the chapters.

White liberals, Socialists, and pacifists found themselves likely to be subjected to suspicion in the activist organizations, especially if they did not endorse the most militant steps. Some of them, unenthusiastic about such techniques as school boycotts, must have felt rather like the Girondiste did when overtaken by the Jacobins. In the labor movement, black workers grew restive over the failure of even the most liberal unions to place Negroes on their international boards or to eliminate discrimination in Southern locals. Consequently the Negro-labor alliance forged during during the 1930's disintegrated. "Farewell to Liberals," as an article in *The Nation* by an NAACP vice-president was called, expressed the idea well enough.

"White liberal" thus joined "Black Bourgeoisie" and "Uncle Tom" as an epithet of opprobrium in the vocabulary of many Negro militants. The phrase "white liberal" was also employed by white revolutionary Marxists who had jumped on the direct-action bandwagon. But beginning about 1963 they too found themselves in the ranks of those being "race-baited" by their Negro colleagues in the movement.

These white radicals had been attracted to the activist cause because they regarded it as the key to a socialized America. Yet the precise role and influence of these revolutionary leftists are difficult to ascertain. Unlike the black and white Socialists in the movement, the few genuinely revolutionary Marxists have seldom identified themselves as such. Something of the rhetoric which activists have employed about the protest movement being a revolutionary one, and about the necessity of changing the basic structure of American society, may in part stem from the revolutionary Marxists (as well as from the Socialists who use the rhetoric with a different meaning). If so, it is because militant activists, for their own reasons, have come to speak in similar terms, so that their ideas appeared, superficially at least, to converge with those of the extreme leftists, or with the vague clichés of the collegiate "New Left."

5

Actually, whatever the role of the white—and Negro—revolutionary Marxists has been, purely as a result of its own dynamics the civil rights movement of the 1960's has undergone a continuous radicalization in tactics and ideology. As already noted, it was disappointment with the results of the NAACP's legal-legislative strategy that led to the triumph of direct action as a technique. Then, as lunch counters were desegregated, sit-ins and boycotts were used to secure the integration of hotels and restaurants in the South, fair housing in the North, and, most important of all, a larger share of jobs for Negroes. The rivalries among the various groups accelerated the process. As progress was made in one area, organizations looked for other forms of discrimination to attack—in part to further the battle against racism and in part to justify their own continued existence.

Large sections of the NAACP enthusiastically embraced direct action. The National Urban League, under the leadership of Whitney M. Young, Jr., appointed executive director in 1961, became outspoken and militant. The League began to speak much more firmly to businessmen whom it had previously treated with the utmost tact and caution. It was principally the new climate provided by the activists that made this change in Urban League strategy possible. As businessmen came to fear demonstrations at their doorsteps or factory gates, they listened more carefully to requests and suggestions from the Urban League.

Meanwhile, as the excitement created by the earlier demonstrations dissipated, and as it became evident that many places of public accommodation remained firmly segregated, more dramatic forms of direct action became essential. A few arrests were no longer newsworthy. To desegregate the more intransigent Southern communities, it was necessary to persuade dozens and even hundreds of people to go to jail and stay there. It became quite obvious that the unmerited suffering of the direct actionists did not bring a change in the hearts of the oppressors. Rather it was the economic pinch created by sit-ins and boycotts, the publicity obtained through mass arrests, and the national and international pressure generated by the violence of white hoodlums and police which forced social change. There followed a secularization of those Southern Negro activists who remained in the movement for any length of time. Few of them had ever been pacifists in the first place, but an important reason for the initial attraction of nonviolent direct action had been its consonance with their Christian faith. Now, instead of speaking of love and Christianity, activists began to talk in terms of power. They thought less of convincing the white man of the moral righteousness of their aspirations and more of forcing him to change his policies through the power of black bodies to create social dislocation.

A major factor leading to the radicalization of the civil rights movement was unemployment and poverty—and an important force awakening the civil rights organizations to this problem was the meteoric rise of the Black Muslims to national prominence. Paradoxically, this nationalist sect, established around 1930, reached the peak of its influence at a time when more progress toward equal rights was being made than ever before in American history. But this was also a time of deteriorating economic opportunity for the lower classes in the urban ghettos. In 1952 the average Negro family's income was 58 percent of the average white family's income; ten years later, despite the highly publicized occupational breakthroughs of a minority of Negroes, the average income of Negro families had fallen to 54 percent of that of whites. The first real spurt in the membership rolls of the Black Muslims seems to have dated from the recession of 1953–54. Due to automation and other forms of technological change, Negro unemployment rose steadily after 1958. By 1962 it was two and a half times that for whites, and in some industrial cities the differential was even greater.

More than anything else this increasing unemployment combined with the revolution in expectations created a climate in which the Black Muslims thrived. They preached an eschatological vision of the doom of the white "devils" and the coming dominence of the black man, promised a utopian paradise of a separate territory within the United States in which black men would establish their own state, and offered a more immediate practical program of building up Negro business through hard work, thrift, and racial unity. To those willing to submit to the rigid discipline of the movement, the Black Muslim organization gave a sense of purpose and destiny. Its program offered them four things: an explanation of their plight (white devils); a sense of pride and self-esteem (black superiority); a vision of a glorious future (black ascendancy); and a practical, immediate program of uplift (working hard and uniting to create Negro enterprise and prosperity). With this Puritan ethic the Muslims have appealed chiefly to an upward-mobile group of the lowest social class of Negroes. Basically, like the integrationist Negro Revolt, the Black Muslims were a manifestation of the Negroes' quest for recognition of their human dignity and their rejection of the philosophy of gradualism. In the same way that the Garvey Movement was a lower-class counterpart of the New Negro of the 1920's, so the Black Muslims were a counterpart of the *new* "New Negro" of the early 1960's. Ironically, until split by internal dissension, the Black Muslims were of distinct assistance to the civil rights organizations, for their talk of violence and their hatred of blue-eyed devils frightened white people into becoming more amenable to the demands of the integrationists. To many whites the Black Muslims sounded so extreme that integration seemed to be a conservative program.

As the direct-action tactics took more dramatic form, as the civil rights groups began to articulate the needs of the masses and draw some of them to their demonstrations, the protest movement in 1963 assumed a new note of urgency and immediatism, a demand for complete "Freedom Now!" Moreover direct action returned to the Northern cities, taking the form of massive protests against economic, housing, and educational inequities. The new mood of militance suffused the events of 1963: the fresh wave of demonstrations that swept the South from Cambridge, Maryland, to Birmingham, Alabama, and Jackson, Mississippi; the NAACP national convention, which passed a resolution calling for more direct action; the fruitless Northern street demonstrations against the discriminatory building trade unions; and, the following winter, the equally fruitless school boycotts against *de facto* segregation. The frustration of the expectations of 1963 largely accounted for the further radicalization of the most militant activists that was to begin in 1964.

At first the new militance of the early 1960's tended to propel the more "conservative" Negro community leaders, whether prominent in the NAACP or not, into a more radical tactical position. It was notable that in crisis situations engendered by mass arrests, especially if these were accompanied by obvious police brutality, temporary unity was achieved between organizations and classes—generally on the militants' terms. On such occasions only rarely did even a conservative NAACP chapter refuse aid and support. The most prominent citizens were likely to mortgage their property for bail money and, in a few cases, went to jail themselves. For example, before the Birmingham demonstration conducted by SCLC in the spring of 1963, the wealthy upper-class Negro citizens had opposed King's decision to use that citadel of segregation as the site of a direct-action campaign. But after hundreds of children had gone to jail, after the police had used their firehoses and dogs against the demonstrators, even the opponents of direct action rushed to SCLC's support.

Though a superb example of how to run a direct-action demonstration, the Birmingham project resulted in a compromise that brought the city's Negroes not "Freedom Now" but token concessions that later were not carried out. Nevertheless, the demonstration was enormously important because it compelled the United States to face the problem of Southern discrimination in a way it had never done before. For the first time in American history the President appeared before the nation and declared that race discrimination was a moral issue. Moreover, it forced President Kennedy to cease depending on mild executive manipulations as a way of advancing Negro welfare and to ask Congress for a major civil rights bill that would not only solve the public accommodations problem but would attempt to protect the Southern Negroes' political rights and provide national legislative sanction for fair-employment practices. After Kennedy's death, President Lyndon B. Johnson proved even more forceful in securing congressional action on a meaningful civil rights bill, and his manipulative skill must be counted as one of the major factors responsible for passage of the Civil Rights Act of 1964. This act, in contrast to the token and symbolic civil rights acts of 1957 and 1960, clearly declared discrimination in places of public accommodation to be illegal, instituted a modest program for protecting the Southern Negroes' right to vote, created a federal fair-employment-practices agency with mild enforcement powers, and—potentially most significant of all—gave the national Executive the power to withdraw federal funds from state and local agencies that discriminated against Negroes.

6

Although the Birmingham demonstration, and the demonstrations in numerous other cities during that spring of 1963, precipitated the shift in presidential strategy, the Civil Rights Act of 1964 would not have been passed were it not for a series of developments that converged at the March on Washington in August, 1963. Early in the year, at the suggestion of Bayard Rustin, the long-time civil rights activist, pacifist, and Socialist, A. Philip Randolph issued a call for a March on Washington in the fall, in order to dramatize the need for jobs and to press for federal action. At about the same time, the Protestant, Jewish, and Catholic churches held a conference on religion and race. Though individual Jewish and Protestant clergymen had been jailed in Southern demonstrations in 1961–62, not until 1963 did the churches officially encourage such activity. After the Birmingham demonstration, at the request of SCLC, the date for the March was advanced to the summer, and the emphasis was shifted to passage of the Civil Rights Bill. Then the churches sought and obtained representation on the March committee. Finally, though the AFL-CIO national council refused to endorse the March, thus adding to the estrangement that had been growing between the civil rights groups and organized labor, a few labor leaders and international unions did participate, and Walter Reuther of the UAW was given a place on the March committee.

With this impressive support the March had become fashionable. The President, reversing an earlier stand, welcomed the March. A quarter of a million people, about 20 percent of them white, participated. From the steps of the Lincoln Memorial, where slightly less than a quarter-century earlier Marian Anderson had sung on Easter morning, the leaders of the civil rights organizations addressed the throng. For Randolph the occasion was the culmination of a vision he had held for over two decades. Roy Wilkins, executive secretary of the NAACP, recalled the contribution of W. E. B. Du Bois. The night before, at the age of ninety-five, Du Bois had died in Ghana, a Communist, completely alienated from his native land, whose citizenship he had renounced. Martin Luther King articulated in the cadences of the old-fashioned Baptist preacher the dream of inclusion in American society that Negroes had held for centuries. It was the dream that Du Bois had had for most of his life; and before that it had been the dream of Booker T. Washington and Frederick Douglass, of Nat Turner and Harriet Tubman, of the runaway slaves and contrabands, of the bondsmen who had worked to buy their freedom and the black peasants who had sought land and education after their emancipation. After King's address, an old-line civil rights leader commented with some acerbity: "Martin had no right to say '*I* have a dream'; why, *we* have all had that dream for generations."

The March was more than a summation of the past years of struggle and aspiration. It also symbolized certain new directions: a deeper concern for the economic problems of the masses; more involvement of white moderates; and a new radicalism among the most militant, as suggested by the address of the SNCC chairman, John Lewis, who implied that only a revolutionary change in American institutions would permit Negroes to achieve the dignity of human beings and citizens.

7

The Negro revolt produced an acrid controversy over the relative merits of legal action and direct action. Historical analysis reveals that in actual fact the two approaches have complemented and reinforced each other. Legal action may be said to include not only litigation in the courts but also propagandizing and lobbying for new laws. Subsidiary to the legal-legislative approach are *nonpartisan* voter-registration campaigns designed to impress politicians with the potential power of the Negro vote. Nonviolent direct-action techniques include picketing, boycotts, sit-ins, courting arrest by disobeying unjust laws and police regulations, and filling the jails.

In the North and Far West the post-World War II nonviolent demonstrations were one of several factors leading to the enactment of antidiscrimination legislation. Although certain of these laws—those dealing with employment and housing—were to a considerable extent disobeyed, in general the new legislation not only broke down discrimination in places of public accommodation but helped to establish new patterns of socially accepted behavior. So also did the court victories being obtained by the NAACP at the same time. These new norms of behavior reduced Northern white resistance to further Negro demands, while among Negroes they created higher expectations and thereby encouraged further direct action. Neither the Northern fair-employment-practice laws nor the presidential fair-employment committees accomplished anything very striking, even among those businessmen who claimed that they followed a technically nondiscriminatory policy. Later, however, in 1963 and 1964, when direct actionists staged major demonstrations to break down employment barriers, their successes were greatly facilitated by the degree to which employers, especially those who had signed President Kennedy's "Plans for Progress," felt morally vulnerable because they had accepted the idea of equal employment practices. Negro buying power, which had been demonstrated by boycotts, was another potent influence in these campaigns, but even firms that did not manufacture or sell consumer goods began to hire Negroes, suggesting that a change in racial attitudes had been taking place.

In regard to the South we have already noted the role of litigation in securing victory for the direct-action work in Montgomery and Tuskegee. As a result of the Supreme Court ruling in the Montgomery case, several other cities quietly desegregated their buses. The public, both white and Negro, remembered not the abstruse language of the courts, but the vivid language of a Negro mass movement; and, as one might have expected, direct action, not legalism, received the credit. In 1961 the Freedom Rides tested compliance with the High Court's opinions in other transportation cases. Though the Court's views were largely respected on the main roads in the Atlantic coastal states, Alabama and Mississippi had had no intention of complying until the Freedom Riders brought the glare of national publicity and an ICC order that did much to diminish segregation in interstate bus travel. Lawyers and judges had paved the way and effected some progress; the Freedom Riders built on the foundation they had laid.

The growing number of Negro voters, an important factor in the enactment of national and state civil rights laws, was also of distinct value to the direct-action campaigns. Where Negroes voted in substantial numbers, public authorities were likely to urge compliance with Negro demands. This was true not only in the North but in the South as well. The sit-in demonstrations of the early 1960's were successful principally in places like Atlanta, Nashville, Durham, Winston-Salem, Louisville, Savannah, New Orleans, Charleston, and Dallas—cities where Negroes voted and could swing elections. Ironically, the great majority of these voters had been placed on the rolls in registration campaigns sparked by the NAACP and local affiliated groups after the white-primary decision secured by the Association's legal department in 1944.

More recently, major demonstrations in the South have been successful where employed to compel presidential action, now that the Chief Executives have become sensitive both to the aroused conscience of white people and to the Negro vote. The relationship between Birmingham and the Civil Rights Act of 1964 is a case in point. The moral indignation aroused across the nation by police brutality during that momentous week rallied white moderates as well as Negroes behind meaningful civil rights legislation—a fact dramatized by the March on Washington. But it was the tireless lobbying of that unofficial arm of the NAACP, the interracial Civil Rights Leadership Conference—along with the efforts of President Johnson—which finally led to enactment of the bill.

The Civil Rights Law of 1964 settled the public accommodations issue in the South's major cities. Its voting section, however, promised more than it accomplished. Again Martin Luther King and SCLC dramatized the issue, this time at Selma, Alabama, in the spring of 1965. Again the national government was forced to intervene, and a new and more effective voting law was passed. On this occasion even the President wrapped himself in the mantle of the civil rights movement by quoting its anthem: "We Shall Overcome" he promised, addressing Congress and a nationwide TV audience. Yet as Lyndon Johnson himself pointed out in that speech, beyond the protection of constitutional rights (for which Congress was now providing, a century after Emancipation) lay the as yet unsolved problems of the poor.

8

Where Birmingham had made direct-action respectable, the Selma demonstration, drawing thousands of white moderates from the North, made direct-action fashionable. Nevertheless, as early as 1964 it was becoming evident that like "legalism," direct action was but a limited instrument. This was the result of two converging developments.

One of these was the failure of the sit-ins of 1960–61 to desegregate public accommodations in Deep South states like Mississippi and Alabama, and the realization, first grasped by Robert Moses of SNCC, that without the leverage of the vote, demonstrations there would be failures. Beginning in 1961 Moses established SNCC projects in the cities and county seats of Mississippi. He succeeded in registering only a handful, but by 1964 had generated enough support throughout the country to enable the Mississippi Freedom Democratic Party, which he had created, to challenge dramatically the seating of the official white delegates from the state at the Democratic National Convention.

Direct action had also failed when applied to the difficult economic and social problems facing the Negroes in the black ghettos of the North. Separate and inferior schools, rat-infested slum housing, and police brutality did not prove vulnerable to an attack of this kind. Street demonstrations did compel employers, ranging from banks to supermarkets, to add many Negroes to their work force in Northern and Western cities, and even in some Southern towns where conditions were propitious and the Negroes had considerable buying power. By these successful demonstrations, and by other fruitless ones against the building trades unions, the Negro protest movement probably did more than anything else to make the nation aware of its poor. (Indeed, the civil rights organizations deserve much of the credit for the inauguration of the federal antipoverty program.) But technological innovation was leading to a steady decline in the number of unskilled jobs available, and the masses of Negroes, half of whom had not gone beyond the eighth grade, were unable to qualify for positions requiring higher skill and education. As a result, while the Negro "job-mix" changed because of new hiring policies on the part of business, the basic pattern of mass unemployment remained.

Faced with the intransigence of the Deep South and with the inadequacy of direct action to solve the problems of the slum-dwellers, the programs of the civil rights organizations diverged. The tendency toward a unity of strategy, if not between personalities, that was emerging during 1963 was dissipated. At the very time that white support for the movement was actually rising, its most militant wing felt increasingly isolated from the American scene. In contrast, the conservative wing, impressed by changes in public attitudes, now came to view its role as exercising influence within established institutions rather than fighting them from outside. Between the two poles of thought was a group who recognized the new willingness of the nation's decision-makers to move toward greater racial justice, but perceived also that powerful outside pressure would be needed to push them further in that direction. While it would be a gross oversimplification to pigeonhole Negro protest leaders and organizations, broadly speaking it can be said that the militant left wing was composed of SNCC and many individuals of CORE; that the conservative right wing consisted of Urban League officials and a substantial group in the NAACP; and that varieties of the centrist position, while found among many CORE and NAACP people, were best articulated by Bayard Rustin, A. Philip Randolph, and Martin Luther King. Upon two things, however, all segments of the movement were agreed: 1) future civil rights activity would focus on the economic and social discrimination in the urban ghettos and 2) while demonstrations would still have a place, the major weapon would be the political potential of the black masses.

People in the militant left wing of the movement were growing disdainful of American society and the middle-class way of life, cynical about the liberals and the leaders of organized labor. Any compromise, even if a temporary tactical device, had become anathema to them. They talked more and more of the necessity for "revolutionary" changes in the social structure, even of violence. They became increasingly skeptical of the value of white participation in the movement, racially chauvinistic in their insistence that black power alone could compel the white ruling class to make concessions. Yet they also dreamed of an alliance of Negroes and unorganized lower-class whites that would overthrow the "power structure" of capitalists, politicians, and bureaucratic labor leaders which exploited the poor of both races by dividing them with an appeal to race prejudice. Once this was accomplished, they would proceed to create a new society based on economic and racial justice. How much of this was vague rhetoric, and how much was genuine revolutionary and nationalist thinking would be impossible to say. Certainly at the extreme left wing of the movement Marxism and nationalism coalesced into a truly revolutionary ideology.

For the vast majority of the militant left wing, independent political action became the new credo. The first serious effort in this direction came in rural Mississippi, where the Freedom Democratic Party planned to base its power on the predominantly Negro counties of the plantation Black Belt. It was evident, however, that the future of this tactic would necessarily lie with the urban slum-dwellers. Some hoped ultimately for a new party based on an alliance of Negro political action groups and the "New Left," uniting the unorganized poor, black and white. Thus far, however, the main emphasis has been on mobilizing the political potential of the black ghetto in order to challenge the urban Democratic machines from within the party and elect officials who really represent the Negro masses.

Unlike the activists, the conservative wing, mostly an older group of individuals, appreciated the legislation of 1964 and 1965, the public stands taken by Presidents Kennedy and Johnson, and other signs of racial progress. They were keenly aware of the new opportunities in business, in government, and in the academic world for those with the training to fill them. Civil rights activity in general, and the NAACP in particular, had become so respectable that even famous protest leaders achieved high public office. The most notable example was the elevation of the brilliant NAACP chief counsel, Thurgood Marshall, first to the U.S. Circuit Court of Appeals and then to the post of solicitor general. Though the more conservative among NAACP leaders did not believe that the millennium had arrived, changed conditions prompted a reorientation of their strategy. From their vantage point, President Johnson and even many Democratic city machines were not enemies but allies. Progress therefore depended on working closely with the Democratic Party establishment and pushing from within to further the Negro's goals. With the black vote looming so large in many cities and playing such an important role in presidential elections it appeared logical to believe that the greatest progress could be achieved by working in this manner on both national and local levels. Even in Mississippi in 1965, where the strategy of the Freedom Democratic Party, backed by SNCC, was to operate as a separate organization outside of the regular state Democratic Party, the NAACP urged Negroes to work with the more moderate and progressive elements of the latter in a Mississippi Democratic conference. A comparable division in tactics also developed in Alabama. Overt protest was not, of course, ruled out in the views of the conservatives. In fact, effective publicity of Negro grievances would often be the best means of compelling reluctant public officials to take action, though the typical conservative now thought of direct action as at best a tactic of last resort.

The centrist group held that the Negro, as a dispossessed minority, could not hope to achieve its goals purely through its own actions. Its members had no illusions about alliances with the Democratic Party establishment and were highly critical of the local urban machines, though they recognized Lyndon Johnson's sensitivity to demands from the civil rights organizations. They based their strategy on a coalition of Negroes with white liberals, organized labor, and white clergy, such as had developed during the plans for the March on Washington. Negroes' interests would be most rapidly advanced by such a coalition—though it was not itself part of the Democratic political establishment— pressing the Democratic Party to progressively more comprehensive action, especially on the national level. Though this theory was not officially a part of NAACP ideology, the Association, through the Civil Rights Leadership Conference, has in effect based part of its strategy upon it. Ultimately the centrists hoped that a Negro-liberal-church-labor alliance, acting as a political force, would compel the national government to eliminate poverty in America for blacks and whites alike. Such coalition politics would admittedly involve compromises—with the national Administration and with other interest groups, and among the members of the coalition themselves. The centrists acted on the theory that realistically one must accept compromises along the way, while never compromising the ultimate goal of complete equality.* Indeed they still favored direct action—even mass civil

* When the Freedom Democratic Party challenged the seating of the Mississippi delegation at the Democratic National Convention in 1964, and was offered a compromise providing for the seating of two of its representatives as delegates at large, the Freedom Party people agreed with SNCC's no-compromise position and rejected the proposal. Rustin and King were among those urging acceptance of it, on the grounds that it

disobedience—where it was needed to create the kind of social dislocation that would bring action from political authorities. Birmingham and Selma were prototypes of this kind of strategy.

At least on specific issues, Martin Luther King, in effect, has been able to piece together such a coalition. To critics on the left King appears to be cautious, hesitant to go to jail or lead a demonstration in the streets, altogether too willing to listen to the pleas of Presidents and their emissaries. Yet to others, both Negro and white, he appears as a militant though responsible agitator. In his very willingness to make tactical compromises with the political establishment, in his very combination of militance with conservatism and caution, of righteousness with respectability, lies the secret of his success.

King articulates the dreams and aspirations of American Negroes as no other leader has done. At the same time he is easily the most effective interpreter of these aspirations to white America. His use of religious phraseology and the Christian symbols of love and nonresistance are partly responsible for this, because they are reassuring to the mind of white America. But his appeal to whites goes deeper. For one thing, he unerringly knows how to exploit to maximum effectiveness the white man's growing feelings of guilt. In this he is not unique. The novelist and essayist James Baldwin is the most conspicuous example of a man who achieved success with this formula—but unlike Baldwin and other angry young writers, King explicitly believes in the white man's salvation. Not only will the nonviolent crusade fulfill the Negro's dream, but it will help whites live up to the Christian and democratic values. If King's approach is reminiscent of Booker T. Washington it is because, like the Tuskegean, he has faith in the white man and believes that it is for the good of the white man as well as the Negro that justice be done to the black man. But Washington's career did little to influence the mainstream of historical events, whereas King's contribution has been incalculable. His occupation as a minister, his manner of speaking, and his style of operation have made him a sort of "conservative militant," able to attract an enormous range of people among both races. Indeed, it was no accident that King's

---

indicated substantial progress. For this they were criticized by SNCC militants who completely distrusted the Johnson Administration and rejected on ideological grounds the compromises inherent in the American political system.

emergence as a national symbol coincided with a pervasive religious revival among people identified with all three of the major religious faiths. Without King as its symbolic leader it is difficult to perceive how the civil rights movement would have achieved half as much as it has. It is doubtful, for example, that there would now be on the books the major civil rights legislation which nonviolent direct action brought about in 1964 and 1965.

King has also occupied a position of strategic importance as "the vital center" within the civil rights movement. Identified as militant and activist, his SCLC acts as the most deliberate of the direct-action groups. This not only gives King respectability in the eyes of whites, but also enables him to act as a bridge between the militant and conservative wings of the movement. For example, it appears unlikely that the Urban League and the NAACP would have joined the 1963 March on Washington if King had not done so. Because King participated, the March not only drew enormous support from white ministers and other middle-class white moderates, but also the numbers and money that the NAACP could bring and the respectability that accompanies Urban League endorsement.

King's evocation of the Negroes' age-old dream, the victories of the civil rights movement in the South, and the growing number of black and brown faces in the middle and upper ranks of business and government bureaucracies and in elective office lifted the expectations of the people in the urban ghettos. But, if anything, their situation was objectively worse, not better. It had become evident that while employers would hire or upgrade significant numbers of Negroes, the basic causes of structural unemployment remained. New blue-collar and white-collar jobs were opened up to Negroes as a result of the pressure exerted by the civil rights organizations, but at least as many jobs were being lost due to technological changes that eliminated the need for unskilled and semiskilled labor. The "job-mix" was changing, but the total number of job openings available seemed to be either decreasing or staying the same; in any event the tens of thousands of Negro youths dropping out of, or graduating from, high school faced a highly restricted job market.* The average Negro there-

* This book was written before the escalation of the fighting in Vietnam produced a significant decrease in U.S. unemployment, and no attempt is made here to evaluate the significance of this recent development. It should also be pointed out that the authorities have not been in

fore was on a dreary treadmill. Without education, he found it difficult to obtain a job; without a decent job and something for his children to aspire to, it was not likely that they would have the motivation to obtain an adequate education even if it were offered. The feeling of frustration, of hopelessness, was reflected in the disorders in New York, Rochester, and other cities in 1964, and in Los Angeles in 1965. Paradoxically, these outbreaks were born of a sense of powerlessness and at the same time of a sense of power derived from the knowledge that "whitey" now felt afraid or guilty and was not likely to fight back.

9

The riots of the 1960's were clearly different from those of the nineteenth and the first part of the twentieth century. What we may call the "new-style" riot first appeared in Harlem in 1935 and in 1943, where Negro attacks were mainly directed against white property rather than white people. The Detroit race riot of 1943, one of the more serious racial conflicts in American history, which brought death to nine whites and twenty-five Negroes, had affinities with both the older and more recent varieties of race warfare. As in the Chicago and certain other conflagrations of the World War I period, the Detroit riot was precipitated by Negro retaliation against mounting white hostility. White mobs kicked, beat, and shot Negroes to death, and though members of both races lost their lives, the majority of the dead and injured were Negroes. On the other hand, because the Negro mobs' major attention was directed toward destroying and looting white-owned businesses in the Negro ghetto, and because most of the Negroes who were killed were shot by white policemen, the Detroit riot bore certain striking similarities to the 1965 Los Angeles holocaust. This symbolic destruction of "whitey" through his property, characterizing the new-style riot, does not

complete agreement on the matter of the Negro unemployment rate, and that some, at least, insist that the general trend during the 1960's was for it to decline, not increase. Whether or not the problem of structural unemployment is as serious in its dimensions as other authorities and civil rights leaders maintain, it seems clear that at the very least the economic status of the mass of Negroes has not significantly improved over the last several years, at the very time that their expectations have soared.

truly fulfill James Baldwin's prediction of "the fire next time," since it does not mark a direct reversal of those conflagrations nearly half a century ago when white mobs literally hunted and killed dozens of Negroes. The modern riot does not involve white civilians at all, and policemen or national guardsmen constitute the relatively small number of white casualties.

Beyond the seething discontent among the masses in the urban ghettos that during the long, hot summers tends to erupt into overt racial warfare, the theme of retaliatory violence has cropped up in various forms in the thinking of the most militant elements in the Negro protest movement of recent years. The Black Muslims imply that Negroes should fight back against the vicious "slavemasters," and their eschatology includes a violent end to white domination. Among the individuals and tiny organizations that compose the Marxist-nationalist revolutionary fringe of Negro protest today, the most vocal is Robert F. Williams, who was dismissed as president of the Monroe, North Carolina, branch of the NAACP in 1959 for his open advocacy of violence against the oppressive white community. Now in Cuba, Williams issues a monthly bulletin which not only advocates a philosophy of violent revolution but specifically urges Negroes "to wage an urban guerrilla war of self-defense" with Molotov cocktails thrown from rooftops.

There is no evidence that the preachings of Elijah Muhammad, leader of the Black Muslims, or of Williams and other Marxist-oriented groups had any direct relationship with the riots of 1964 and 1965, though it appears that in New York, at least, genuinely revolutionary cliques attempted to take control after the unplanned rioting started. Nevertheless, both the statements of the fringe ideologists and the spontaneous actions of the masses are the product of the frustrations resulting from the growing disparity between the Negroes' status in American society and the rapidly rising expectations induced by the civil rights revolution and its successes. This feeling is reflected in the increasing use of revolutionary vocabulary and in the rising skepticism about the usefulness of nonviolence among many of the more militant people in the nonviolent direct-action organizations. By 1964 and 1965 at least some of them, especially in SNCC and to a lesser extent in CORE, were toying with the idea that retaliatory violence might be necessary. The view that "no people ever gained its freedom without some bloodshed," became a widely voiced cliché. More recently there has been considerable publicity about the Deacons for Defense, organized in Louisiana to protect Negroes and civil rights demonstrators from white attackers. CORE, without departing from its belief in nonviolent direct-action methods, has welcomed the protection offered by the Deacons, who do not engage in talk of general revolutionary violence but do assert the necessity of defending Negroes and white civil rights workers if they are attacked.

It should be pointed out that the theme of retaliatory violence has never been entirely absent from Negro thinking. This sentiment has taken various forms. Some have advocated self-defense against a specific attack—a type of action legal under the Anglo-American system of jurisprudence. Some have called for revolutionary violence. Others have predicted an apocalyptic race war from which Negroes would emerge victorious. Though seldom articulated for white ears, and only rarely appearing in print, such thoughts have been quite common. Ralph Bunche, in preparing a memorandum for Gunnar Myrdal's *An American Dilemma* in 1940, noted, "There are Negroes, too, who, fed up with frustration of their life here, see no hope and express an angry desire 'to shoot their way out of it.' I have on many occasions heard Negroes exclaim: 'Just give us machine guns and we'll blow the lid off the whole damn business.' " Thus, it would appear that the idea of violence has been a pervasive, if unpublicized, undercurrent accompanying other forms of protest.

While in no period has retaliatory violence been a central thrust in Negro protest, advocacy of violence has often been expressed more explicitly in periods of intense Negro protest activity. David Walker's and Henry Highland Garnet's calls for slave rebellions coincided with marked revivals of other kinds of militant Negro protest. A careful study of race violence during Reconstruction remains to be made, but it is clear that in some cases, at least, Negroes employed physical resistance in that period. As already noted, a major twentieth-century protest leader like Du Bois did not foreclose the possibility of revolutionary violence if and when conditions made it practicable. It is notable that in the past half-century overt discussion about the advisability of violent retaliation and actual incidents of this type of violence were most prominent during the periods of heightened militancy just after World War I and again during the past several years. In both eras a major factor leading Negroes to advocate or to adopt such a tactic has been the discrepancy between the Negroes' expectations and their objective status. We have already alluded to the rapid escalation of the expectations of the Negro masses who share Martin Luther King's dream and identify vicariously with the successes of the civil rights revolution, while their own opportunities and economic situation have not improved. A comparable situation existed during and after the First World War. The agitation of the recently founded NAACP, which more than doubled its membership between 1918 and 1919; the propaganda of fighting a war to make the world safe for democracy; and especially the Great Migration to the Northern cities, which were viewed by those who moved out of the South as a promised land—all created new hopes for the fulfillment of age-old dreams. But the Negro's new hopes collided with increasing white hostility, with overcrowded ghettos and unfriendly white workers who feared Negro competition for their jobs, with the disastrous fall in job openings following the return of peace, and with the revival of the Ku Klux Klan.

It would appear that throughout the history of American Negroes there has been a strong element of fantasy in Negro discussion and efforts concerning violent retaliation. Robert Williams talks of Molotov cocktails as the sort of device that will enable a poverty-stricken minority to engineer a social revolution, but few pay any attention to him as yet. The Black Muslims talk of violence, but the talk functions as a psychological safety valve; by preaching separation they in effect accommodate to the American social order and place racial warfare in the future when Allah in his time will destroy the whites and usher in an era of black ascendancy. Similarly, in view of population statistics and power distribution in American society, Du Bois and others who spoke of the inevitability of racial warfare and Negro victory were engaging in wishful prophecies.

James Weldon Johnson, writing in 1934, summed up the possibilities of violence in terms that would be applicable even today:

> We must condemn physical force and banish it from our minds. But I do not condemn it on any moral or pacific grounds. The resort to force remains and will doubtless remain the rightful re-

course of oppressed peoples. Our own country was established upon that right. I condemn physical force because I know that in our case it would be futile. . . . We would be justified in taking up arms or anything we could lay hands on and fighting for the common rights we are entitled to and denied, if we had a chance to win. But I know and we all know there is not a chance.

He felt that there was only one type of physical force that American Negroes should use: when confronted by a mob intent on killing, a Negro should sell his life "at the dearest price we are able to put on it." That right of self-defense is, indeed, the only type of violent retaliation that, despite the talk about violence on the part of some radical militants, is being realistically used. Even the use of self-defense in the South is made psychologically possible by the increased sensitivity of the federal government. In a less propitious era, the Deacons for Defense would have been crushed in short order.

For the most part Negroes have been nothing if not realistic about the possibilities inherent in violent retaliation. The patterns of Negro behavior in riots demonstrate this. Negro attacks on whites occurred mainly in the early stages of the riots before the full extent of the anger and power of the white mobs became evident. Where, as in the Atlanta and Washington riots, Negro attacks on whites occurred during the latter stages of the riot, it was upon whites who had entered the Negro ghetto, where they were in a minority. One of the remarkable things about the riots of 1964 and 1965 was that, in spite of their having been marked by particular resentment at police brutality, Negro destruction was aimed at "whitey's" property rather than his life. In part this may be due to psychic conditioning and the fear of white authority, but this behavior is consistent with the pattern of action that includes the extolling of passive resistance and the Christian virtues, the minor part violence has played historically in Negro protest activities, and the tendency to talk and dream of violence rather than to practice it. Today, the economically impoverished Negroes are pressing as far as they realistically can; and one reason for the explosions of the summers of 1964 and 1965 was the awareness that whites are to some degree in retreat, that white mobs in the North no longer organize to attack, and that to a large degree the frustrated Negroes in slums like Watts can get away with acts of violence.

10

The number of middle-class Negroes has been growing as economic opportunities in business and government open up for those fortunate enough to have obtained an adequate educational background. There has been in very recent years at least some token residential dispersal of members of the Negro middle and upper classes into white neighborhoods and suburbs. Yet the future of Negroes and of American race relations will revolve around the question of what happens in and to the ghetto. The plantation system has all but disappeared; with the continued mechanization of both tobacco and cotton agriculture it will vanish completely in the next few years. In the cities the political strength of the black ghetto is growing, both in the North, where an increasing number of Negroes are being elected to local, state, and national office, and in the South, where in very recent years a thin but significant trickle of Negroes have appeared in a few municipal councils and state legislatures. Will the civil rights organizations be able to harness this political potential and thus help the black masses in the ghetto to secure for themselves the power with which to compel society to provide them with adequate employment, education, and housing? If this should be achieved, will the ghetto, like the plantation, disappear as the locus of Negro life, or will it remain as a cohesive community, at the core of the nation's largest cities, shaping the texture and spirit of American life?

SELECTED BIBLIOGRAPHY

THIS BIBLIOGRAPHICAL ESSAY lists significant works, chiefly secondary sources, which are readily available to the general reader and the college student. No attempt is made to include most of the materials on which this book is based. A few important doctoral dissertations are included; microfilm copies of these are easily obtained from University Microfilms, Ann Arbor, Michigan.

GENERAL WORKS

The leading and most detailed general survey is John Hope Franklin, *From Slavery to Freedom* (2nd ed., New York, 1956), and it includes excellent and comprehensive bibliographical notes. Benjamin Quarles, *The Negro in the Making of America* (New York, 1964) is an admirable shorter survey. J. Saunders Redding, *The Lonesome Road* (Garden City, 1958), and Arna W. Bontemps, *One Hundred Years of Negro Freedom* (New York, 1961) also have material of value. The two major sociological works are Gunnar Myrdal, *An American Dilemma* (2 vols., New York, 1944) and E. Franklin Frazier, *The Negro in the United States* (New York, 1957). Both contain considerable historical material and good bibliographies. The best introduction to Negro ideologies is Ralph J. Bunche, "Conceptions and Ideologies of the Negro Problem," a research memorandum prepared for the Carnegie-Myrdal Study of the Negro in America (available on microfilm from the New York Public Library). The leading magazines devoted to Negro studies are *Journal of Negro History* (Washington, 1916–   ), *Journal of Negro Education* (Washington, 1932–   ), whose scope of articles is far broader than its title implies, and *Phylon* (Atlanta, 1940–   ). Louis R. Harlan's pamphlet *The Negro in American History* (Washington, 1965) is an excellent critical essay discussing the most recent books and interpretations in the field of Negro history. The historical changes in white America's attitudes toward Negroes are best described in David Reimer's account of *White Protestantism and the Negro* (New York, 1965).

253

CHAPTER I

There is as yet no satisfactory history of the American Negroes' attitudes toward Africa. Suggestive treatments are to be found in George Shepperson, "Notes on Negro American Influence on the Emergence of African Nationality," *Journal of African History,* I, 2 (1960); John A. Davis, ed., *Africa from the Point of View of American Negro Scholars* (Paris, 1958, a special issue of the magazine *Présence Africaine*); and Harold R. Isaacs, *The New World of Negro Americans* (New York, 1963). W. E. B. Du Bois' major work dealing with African history and culture is *Black Folk: Then and Now* (New York, 1939), an expanded version of his earlier book, *The Negro* (New York, 1915). Carter G. Woodson's views are to be found in his *African Background Outlined* (Washington, 1936). Also pertinent is Louis R. Harlan, "Booker T. Washington and the White Man's Burden," *American Historical Review,* LXXI (January, 1966).

George Peter Murdock's controversial reconstruction of early West African cultural development is to be found in his *Africa: Its Peoples and Their Culture History* (New York, 1959). It should be supplemented with the critical article by Christopher Wrigley, "Speculations on the Economic Prehistory of Africa," *Journal of African History,* I, 2 (1960). The only general history of West Africa south of the Sahara is J. D. Fage, *An Introduction to the History of West Africa* (3rd ed., London, 1962). Edward W. Bovill, *The Golden Trade of the Moors* (London, 1958) is a brilliant history of the western Sudan. An analysis of the characteristics of Sudanese kingship is to be found in Joseph Greenberg, "The Negro Kingdoms of the Sudan," *Transactions of the New York Academy of Sciences,* Series II, II, 4 (1949). Thomas Hodgkin, ed., *Nigerian Perpectives: An Historical Anthology* (London, 1960) sheds valuable light on the history of an important section of the slaving area.

Useful studies of the peoples who were the sources of the New World Negro population include: Robert S. Rattray's *The Ashanti* (Oxford, 1923), *Religion and Art in Ashanti* (Oxford, 1927), and *Ashanti Law and Constitution* (Oxford, 1929); K. A. Busia, *The Position of the Chief in the Modern Political System of Ashanti* (London, 1951); Melville J. Herskovits, *Dahomey* (2 vols., New York, 1938); Elliott P. Skinner, *The Mossi of the Upper Volta* (Stanford, 1964); Jacob Egharevba, *A Short History of Benin* (3rd ed., Ibadan, 1960); C. Daryll Forde, *The Yoruba-Speaking Peoples of South-Western Nigeria* (London, 1951); Samuel Johnson, *The History of the Yorubas* (Evanston, 1964); C. Daryll Forde and G. I. Jones, *The Ibo and Ibibio-Speaking Peoples of South-Eastern Nigeria* (London, 1950). A recent discussion of West African sculpture will be found in William Fagg and Eliot Elisofon, *The Sculpture of Africa* (London, 1958).

The standard reference on African survivals in American Negro culture is Melville J. Herskovits, *Myth of the Negro Past* (New York, 1941). Much of the basis for the conclusions reached in that study will be found in the published accounts of his own field research, but these should be supplemented with James G. Leyburn's extraordinary volume, *The Haitian People* (New Haven, 1941) and Lorenzo D. Turner's pioneering *Africanisms in the Gullah Dialect* (Chicago, 1949). In somewhat popular fashion, Zora Neale Hurston's *Mules and Men* (Philadelphia, 1935) deals with "hoodoo" cults in the United States.

Herskovits' most articulate critic was E. Franklin Frazier, whose views on the subject are summed up in the opening chapter of his *Negro in the United States.* For Frazier's influential thesis about American Negro family structure see his sociological classic *The Negro Family in the United States* (Chicago, 1939).

CHAPTER II

Though written for a popular audience, Basil Davidson, *Black Mother: The Years of the African Slave Trade* (Boston, 1961) is the best general account of the slave trade and its influence on African societies available, and includes a superior bibliography. The role of the Western powers can be best studied in John W. Blake, *European Beginnings in West Africa, 1454–1578* (London, 1937) and in the introductions of the four volumes of Elizabeth Donnan's *Documents Illustrative of the History of the Slave Trade to America* (Washington, 1930–35). A most illuminating and pioneering description of the workings of the slave trade from the African end is the second chapter of K. O. Dike, *Trade and Politics in the Niger Delta, 1830–1885* (London, 1956). Eric Williams, *Capitalism and Slavery* (Chapel Hill, 1944) is a provocative interpretation of the impact of the slave trade on the British imperial economy.* The

* Not readily available, but an important contribution, are the three critiques of Eric Williams' volume by Roger Anstey, John Hargreaves, and C. Duncan Rise, in *The Transatlantic Slave Trade from West Africa* published by the Centre of African Studies, University of Edinburgh (Edinburgh, 1965).

activities of British merchants are described in George F. Zook, "The Company of Royal Adventurers Trading in Africa," *Journal of Negro History,* IV (April, 1919); the model monograph by K. G. Davies, *The Royal African Company* (London, 1957); and Gomer Williams, *History of the Liverpool Privateers and Letters of Marque, with an Account of the Liverpool Slave Trade* (London, 1897). The best eye-witness accounts written by Europeans who participated in the traffic are William Bosman, *A New and Accurate Description of the Coast of Guinea* (trans. from the Dutch, London, 1705); J. Barbot, *A Description of the Coasts of North and South Guinea* (trans. from the French, London, 1746); William Snelgrave, *A New Account of Some Parts of Guinea and the Slave-Trade* (London, 1754); and Alexander Falconbridge, *Account of the Slave Trade on the Coast of Africa* (London, 1788).

For varying views on the nineteenth-century illicit slave trade see W. E. B. Du Bois, *Suppression of the African Slave Trade to the United States, 1638–1870* (Cambridge, Mass., 1896); Harvey Wish, "The Revival of the African Slave Trade in the United States, 1856–1860," *Mississippi Valley Historical Review,* XXVII (April, 1941); and Warren S. Howard, *American Slavers and the Federal Law, 1837–1862* (Berkeley, 1963).

Practically all of the volumes dealing with slavery in the English mainland colonies are hopelessly outdated. The principal exception is Lorenzo J. Greene, *The Negro in Colonial New England* (New York. 1942). A very recent study is Edgar J. McManus' *A History of Negro Slavery in New York* (Syracuse, 1966). The most satisfactory analysis of the evolution of slavery out of indentured servitude in Virginia is Carl N. Degler, "Slavery and the Genesis of American Race Prejudice," *Comparative Studies in History and Society,* II (October, 1959). For a contrary point of view see Oscar Handlin, *Race and Nationality in American Life* (Boston, 1950), Chapter 1. On Negro participation in the exploration of the New World see especially Richard R. Wright, "Negro Companions of the Spanish Explorers," *Phylon,* II (Fourth Quarter, 1941), reprinted from *American Anthropologist,* 1902.

The role of Negroes in the American Revolution is best described in Benjamin Quarles' scholarly *The Negro in the American Revolution* (Chapel Hill, 1961). There is no over-all study of the attitudes toward the Negro and slavery exhibited by the founding fathers. Monographs of interest in this connection are Thomas C. Drake, *Quakers and Slavery in America* (New Haven, 1950); George Livermore, *An Historical Research Respecting the Opinions of the*

Founders of the Republic on the Negroes as Slaves, as Citizens, and as Soldiers (Boston, 1862); and Walter H. Mazyck, *George Washington and the Negro* (Washington, D.C., 1932). A recent book, Robert McColley, *Slavery and Jeffersonian Virginia* (Urbana, Ill., 1964) argues that plantation slavery remained highly profitable in the Upper South during the late eighteenth century, and that there was little sentiment for emancipation among Virginia slaveowners.

The best general description of the institution of slavery in nineteenth-century America is Kenneth Stampp, *The Peculiar Institution* (New York, 1956). This should be supplemented with Lewis C. Gray, *History of Agriculture in the Southern United States to 1860* (2 vols., Washington, D.C., 1933); the description of the technology of Southern agriculture in Ulrich B. Phillips, *Life and Labor in the Old South* (Boston, 1929); John Hebron Moore, *Agriculture in Ante-Bellum Mississippi* (New York, 1958); Frederic Bancroft, *Slave Trading in the Old South* (Baltimore, 1931); and Carter G. Woodson, *Free Negro Owners of Slaves in the United States in 1830* (Washington, D.C., 1925). For an excellent description of Southern slavery in all its variety by a contemporary observer see Frederick Law Olmsted, *The Cotton Kingdom* (2 vols., New York, 1861; new one-volume edition, New York, 1953).

For the varied views on the slave's adjustment under slavery see, in addition to the Stampp book cited above, Ulrich B. Phillips, *American Negro Slavery* (New York, 1918); Herbert Aptheker, *American Negro Slave Revolts* (New York, 1943); Stanley M. Elkins, *Slavery: A Problem in American Institutional Life* (Chicago, 1959). Earlier discussions of slave revolts, containing less detail than Aptheker but arriving at similar conclusions without his Marxist bias, are Harvey Wish, "American Slave Insurrections before 1861," *Journal of Negro History,* XXII (July, 1937) and Joseph C. Carroll, *Slave Insurrections in the United States, 1800–1860* (Boston, 1938). For suggestive statistical analysis of distribution of slave revolts see Marion D. de B. Kilson, "Towards Freedom: An Analysis of Slave Revolts in the United States," *Phylon,* XXV (Summer, 1964). On the comparison of Latin-American and United States slavery see, in addition to Elkins, Frank Tannenbaum, *Slave and Citizen* (New York, 1947) and the new and boldly revisionist Marvin Harris, *Patterns of Race in the Americas* (New York, 1964). Recent interpretations of the nature and history of United States slavery are sharply questioned in the highly controversial Eugene D. Genovese, *Political Economy of Slavery* (New York, 1965).

CHAPTER III

Richard C. Wade's *Slavery in the Cities* (New York, 1964) opens up a new area and offers some challenging interpretations.

For the ante-bellum free Negro there is no general survey, and most of the older monographs and articles are outdated, biased, or amateurish. Among the more recent studies of value are John Hope Franklin, *The Free Negro in North Carolina, 1790–1860* (Chapel Hill, 1943); Luther P. Jackson, *Free Negro Labor and Property Holding in Virginia, 1830–1860* (New York, 1942); William R. Hogan and Elmer A. Davis, *The Barber of Natchez* (Baton Rouge, 1951); E. Horace Fitchett, "The Origin and Growth of the Free Negro Population of Charleston, South Carolina," *Journal of Negro History,* XXVI (October, 1941), and Fitchett, "The Traditions of the Free Negro in Charleston, South Carolina," *Journal of Negro History,* XXV (April, 1940); Richard C. Wade, "The Negro in Cincinnati, 1800–1830," *Journal of Negro History,* XXXIX (Jan., 1954); Emma Lou Thornbrough, *The Negro in Indiana* (Indianapolis, 1957); Leon F. Litwack, *North of Slavery: The Negro in the Free States, 1790–1860* (Chicago, 1961); Leo H. Hirsch, Jr., "New York and the Negro from 1783–1865," *Journal of Negro History,* XVI (October, 1931); and J. Merton England, "The Free Negro in Ante-Bellum Tennessee," *Journal of Southern History,* IX (February, 1943). An older but stimulating article is Dixon Ryan Fox, "The Negro Vote in Old New York," *Political Science Quarterly,* XXXII (June, 1917). Constance Green's *Washington: Village and Capital, 1800–1878* (Princeton, 1962) is an urban history unique in its careful attention to the Negro community. Two surveys by Carter G. Woodson, *The Education of the Negro Prior to 1861* (New York, 1915) and *The History of the Negro Church* (Washington, D.C., 1921) contain much useful material, as do the opening chapters of Charles H. Wesley, *Negro Labor in the United States, 1850–1925* (New York, 1927) and of Abram L. Harris, *The Negro as Capitalist* (Philadelphia, 1936). Specialized articles of value are Edward N. Palmer, "Negro Secret Societies," *Social Forces,* XXIII (October, 1944) and Dorothy B. Porter, "The Organized Educational Activities of Negro Literary Societies, 1828–1846," *Journal of Negro Education,* V (October, 1936).

Carter G. Woodson, ed., *The Mind of the Negro as Reflected in Letters Written During the Crisis, 1800–1860* (Washington, D.C., 1926) and the first half of Herbert Aptheker, ed., *A Documentary History of the Negro People in the United States* (New York, 1951), both contain many documents which illustrate the history and thinking of ante-bellum free Negroes, though Aptheker underplays the importance of colonization movements. A specialized work of considerable interest is William H. and Jane H. Pease, *Black Utopia: Negro Communal Experiments in America* (Madison, Wis., 1963). The ante-bellum convention movement is best studied through the unpublished dissertation of Howard H. Bell, "A Survey of the Negro Convention Movement, 1830–1861," Northwestern University, 1953.

There is no satisfactory account as yet of the role of the black abolitionists in the antislavery movement. The three general works on the abolitionists which have the most material on Negro participants are Dwight L. Dumond, *Anti-Slavery: The Crusade for Freedom in America* (2 vols., Ann Arbor, 1961); Louis Filler, *The Crusade Against Slavery, 1830–1860* (New York, 1960); and Martin Duberman, ed., *The Antislavery Vanguard* (Princeton, 1965). The best discussion of the racial attitudes of the white abolitionists thus far in print is to be found in William H. Pease and Jane H. Pease, "Antislavery Ambivalence: Immediatism, Expediency, Race," *American Quarterly*, XVII (Winter, 1965). Charles H. Wesley has written two helpful articles: "The Negroes of New York in the Emancipation Movement," *Journal of Negro History*, XXIV (January, 1939) and "The Participation of Negroes in Anti-Slavery Political Parties," *Journal of Negro History*, XXIX (January, 1944). David Walker's *Appeal* has recently been reprinted (New York, 1965). Frederick Douglass may be studied through Benjamin Quarles's biography, *Frederick Douglass* (Washington, D.C., 1948); Douglass' own recollections, *The Life and Times of Frederick Douglass* (rev. ed., 1893; reprinted several times since); and Philip S. Foner, ed., *The Life and Writings of Frederick Douglass* (4 vols., New York, 1950–55).

The career of another noted abolitionist is outlined in Arthur Huff Fauset, *Sojourner Truth: God's Faithful Pilgrim* (Chapel Hill, 1938). Unfortunately there is no satisfactory biography of Harriet Tubman. On the Underground Railroad generally see Larry Gara's *The Liberty Line* (Lexington, Ky., 1961), a fresh and provocative reinterpretation. It should be supplemented with Dorothy B. Porter, "David M. Ruggles, An Apostle of Human Rights," *Journal of Negro History*, XXVIII (January, 1943); the recollections of William Still, entitled, *The Underground Railroad* (Philadelphia, 1879); and the best of the fugitive slave memoirs: Lunsford Lane, *The Narrative of Lunsford Lane* (2nd ed., Boston, 1842), Henry Bibb, *The Narrative of the Life and Adventures of Henry Bibb* (New York, 1849), William Wells Brown, *Narrative of William Wells Brown, A Fugitive Slave* (Boston, 1847), and Samuel Ringgold Ward, *Autobiography of a Fugitive Slave* (London, 1855), as well as Douglass' auto-biography cited above. A helpful analysis and useful selection from fugitive slave materials is to be found in Charles H. Nichols, *Many Thousand Gone: The Ex-Slaves' Account of Their Bondage and Freedom* (Leiden, 1963).

CHAPTER IV

The Civil War is perhaps the phase of Negro history that has been studied most adequately. Leading monographs are Benjamin Quarles, *The Negro in the Civil War* (Boston, 1953) and Dudley T. Cornish, *The Sable Arm: Negro Troops in the Union Army* (New York, 1956). They can be supplemented with Thomas W. Higginson, *Army Life in a Black Regiment* (Boston, 1869; also available in several reprints); James M. McPherson, *The Negro's Civil War* (New York, 1965) and *The Struggle for Equality: Abolitionists and the Negro in the Civil War and Reconstruction* (Princeton, 1964), an exceed-ingly important book, although it minimizes the racial ambivalence of the white abolitionists; and Bell Irwin Wiley, *Southern Negroes, 1861–1865* (rev. ed., New York, 1953). Two contemporary docu-ments of interest are A. Hunter Dupree and Leslie H. Fishel, Jr., eds., "An Eye-Witness Account of the New York Draft Riots, July, 1863," *Mississippi Valley Historical Review*, XLVII (December, 1960) and Ray A. Billington, ed., *The Journal of Charlotte L. Forten* (New York, 1953).

Two useful general recent surveys of the Reconstruction period are Kenneth Stampp, *The Era of Reconstruction, 1865–1877* (New York, 1965) and John Hope Franklin, *Reconstruction After the Civil War* (Chicago, 1961). The only general account of the Negro during Reconstruction is W. E. B. Du Bois, *Black Reconstruction in America* (New York, 1935), which gathered together all the data available on the subject and attempted a Marxist analysis of the period. It is still the best single source of information for the activities of Negroes during Reconstruction. The best monographs on the Negro in individual states are Willie Lee Rose, *Rehearsal for Re-construction* (Indianapolis, 1964), a superb account of the Sea Island Negroes of South Carolina during the Civil War; Joel William-son, *After Slavery: The Negro in South Carolina During Reconstruc-tion, 1861–1877* (Chapel Hill, 1965); A. A. Taylor, *The Negro in the Reconstruction of Virginia* (Washington, D.C., 1926); Vernon Lane Wharton, *The Negro in Mississippi, 1865–1890* (Chapel Hill, 1947). The best monograph on educational efforts among the freed-men is the unpublished dissertation of Richard B. Drake, "The American Missionary Association and the Southern Negro, 1861–1888," Emory University, 1957. Five significant articles are LaWanda Cox, "The Promise of Land for the Freedmen," *Mississippi Valley Historical Review,* XLV (December, 1958); Louis R. Harlan, "Segregation in New Orleans Public Schools During Reconstruction," *American Historical Review,* LXVII (April, 1962); Leslie H. Fishel, Jr., "Northern Prejudice and Negro Suffrage, 1865–1870," *Journal of Negro History,* XXXIX (January, 1954); James M. McPherson, "Abolitionists and the Civil Rights Act of 1875," *Journal of American History,* LII (December, 1965); and Patrick W. Riddleberger, "The Radicals' Abandonment of the Negro During Reconstruction," *Journal of Negro History,* XLV (April, 1960).

CHAPTER V

General works dealing with the Negro in the period between Reconstruction and the First World War include C. Vann Woodward, *Origins of the New South, 1877–1913* (Baton Rouge, 1951); Woodward, *The Strange Career of Jim Crow* (rev. ed., New York, 1965); Rayford W. Logan, *The Negro in American Life and Thought: The Nadir, 1877–1901* (New York, 1954); August Meier, *Negro Thought in America, 1880–1915* (Ann Arbor, 1963); Gilbert T. Stephenson, *Race Distinctions in American Law* (New York, 1910). Ray Stannard Baker's *Following the Color Line* (New York, 1908; reprinted New York, 1964) is an interesting contemporary analysis by a leading journalist. State and local studies of value include Charles E. Wynes, *Race Relations in Virginia, 1870–1902* (Charlottesville, 1961); George B. Tindall, *South Carolina Negroes, 1877–1900* (Columbia, S.C., 1952); Frenise Logan, *The Negro in North Carolina, 1876–1894* (Chapel Hill, 1964); John Daniels, *In Freedom's Birthplace* (Boston, 1914), on Boston Negroes; and Mary White Ovington, *Half a Man: The Status of the Negro in New York* (New York, 1911). A valuable source of material on the changing status of Northern Negroes is Leslie H. Fishel, Jr., "The North and the Negro, 1865–1900," doctoral dissertation, Harvard University, 1953.

The problems of Negro labor are treated in Sterling D. Spero and Abram L. Harris, *The Black Worker* (New York, 1931) and Bernard Mandel, "Samuel Gompers and Negro Workers," *Journal of Negro History,* XL (January, 1955). Aspects of Negro education in the South are illuminated by Louis R. Harlan, *Separate and Unequal: Public School Campaigns and Racism in the Southern Seaboard States, 1901–1915* (Chapel Hill, 1958); Willard Range, *The Rise and Progress of Negro Colleges in Georgia, 1865–1949* (Athens,

Ga., 1951); Louis D. Rubin, ed., *Teach the Freeman: The Correspondence of Rutherford B. Hayes and the Slater Fund for Negro Education* (2 vols., Baton Rouge, 1959); Horace Mann Bond, *Negro Education in Alabama* (Washington, D.C., 1939); and Kelly Miller, "Education of the Negro," Chapter XVI of *Report of Commissioner of Education for 1900–1901* (Washington, D.C., 1902). For varying views on the Negro and the agrarian revolt see the works by Woodward cited above; Jack Abramowitz, "The Negro in the Populist Movement," *Journal of Negro History*, XXXVIII (July, 1953); Helen G. Edmonds, *The Negro and Fusion Politics in North Carolina, 1894–1901* (Chapel Hill, 1951); and V. O. Key, *Southern Politics in State and Nation* (New York, 1949), pp. 530–40. A valuable mine of information on the Negro community during the late nineteenth and early twentieth centuries is to be found in W. E. B. Du Bois, ed., *Atlanta University Publications* (1897–1915). An illuminating picture of the Negro in Southern politics is contained in the dissertation by Clarence Bacote, "The Negro in Georgia Politics, 1880–1908," University of Chicago, 1955.

Booker T. Washington's outlook is expressed best in his *The Future of the American Negro* (Boston, 1899) and the autobiography, *Up From Slavery* (New York, 1901). There is as yet no adequate biography of the Tuskegean, and his place in American history is best approached through Hugh Hawkins, ed., *Booker T. Washington and His Critics* (Boston, 1962). See also Meier, *Negro Thought in America, 1880–1915,* cited above. For Du Bois and the radicals see his volume of essays, *Souls of Black Folk* (Chicago, 1903), his autobiography, *Dusk of Dawn* (New York, 1940), and two recent biographies: Francis L. Broderick, *W. E. B. Du Bois: Negro Leader in Time of Crisis* (Stanford, 1959) and Elliott M. Rudwick, *W. E. B. Du Bois: A Study in Minority Group Leadership* (Philadelphia, 1960). The best representative of the middle-of-the-road point of view is Kelly Miller, *Race Adjustment* (3rd ed., New York, 1910).

CHAPTER VI

For a general survey of Negro migration to the North see Arna Bontemps and Jack Conroy, *Anyplace But Here* (New York, 1966).

For the wartime and postwar migration the best works are still those written by contemporaries: Thomas J. Woofter, *Negro Migration* (New York, 1920); Emmett J. Scott, *Negro Migration During the War* (New York, 1920); and Charles S. Johnson, "How Much Is Migration a Flight from Persecution?" *Opportunity,* I (September, 1923). Two of the riots that followed upon the wartime migration are given extended analysis in the Chicago Commission on Race Relations, *The Negro in Chicago* (Chicago, 1922) and in Elliott M. Rudwick, *Race Riot at East St. Louis, July 2, 1917* (Carbondale, Ill., 1964). On the development of the urban ghetto and its subculture, see Robert C. Weaver, *The Negro Ghetto* (New York, 1948); Claude McKay, *Harlem: Negro Metropolis* (New York, 1940); Roi Ottley, *New World A-Coming* (Boston, 1943); Gilbert Osofsky, *Harlem: The Making of a Ghetto* (New York, 1966); that classic study of the Negro community in Chicago, St. Clair Drake and Horace Cayton, *Black Metropolis* (New York, 1945); the forthcoming volume of the Chicago ghetto by Allan Spear; and Kenneth Clark, *Dark Ghetto* (New York, 1965). The problem of residential segregation is explored in Davis C. McEntire, *Residence and Race* (Berkeley, 1960); Luigi Laurenti, *Property Values and Race* (Berkeley, 1960); and Karl E. and Alma F. Taeuber, *Negroes in Cities: Residential Segregation and Residential Change* (Chicago, 1965).

On the economic aspects of life in the ghetto see Abram L. Harris, *The Negro as Capitalist;* Sterling D. Spero and Abram L. Harris, *The Black Worker;* Horace Cayton and George S. Mitchell, *Black Workers and the New Unions* (Chapel Hill, 1939); F. Ray Marshall, *The Negro and Organized Labor* (New York, 1965); Brailsford R. Brazeal, *The Brotherhood of Sleeping Car Porters: Its Origin and Development* (New York, 1946). On the impact of urbanization on the Negro family see E. Franklin Frazier, *The Negro Family in the United States.* On the political role of Negroes in Northern cities see Harold F. Gosnell, *Negro Politicians: The Rise of Negro Politics in Chicago* (Chicago, 1935); James Q. Wilson, *Negro Politics: The Search for Leadership* (Glencoe, Ill., 1960); and John A. Morsell, "The Political Behavior of Negroes in New York City," doctoral dissertation, Columbia University, 1951. For a broad analysis of the Negro in politics in the period between the two world wars, both in the North and in the South, see Ralph J. Bunche, "The Political Status of the Negro," unpublished memorandum for the Carnegie-Myrdal Study, 7 vols., 1940 (available on microfilm from the New York Public Library). Aspects of religious life are treated in Arthur Huff Fauset, *Black Gods of the Metropolis: Negro Religious Cults of the Urban North* (Philadelphia, 1944); Robert A. Parker, *The Incredible Messiah: The Deification of Father Divine* (Boston, 1937); and Benjamin E. Mays and Joseph W. Nicholson, *The Negro's Church* (New York, 1933).

All these matters are also dealt with most perceptively in Drake and Cayton, *Black Metropolis,* as is the subject of social stratification. For a controversial essay on the Negro class structure see E. Franklin

264   SELECTED BIBLIOGRAPHY

Frazier, *Black Bourgeoisie* (Glencoe, Ill., 1957). This discussion should be supplemented by two studies of Southern communities: John Dollard, *Caste and Class in a Southern Town* (New Haven, 1937) and Allison Davis and Burleigh and Mary Gardner, *Deep South* (Chicago, 1941). Also of considerable interest and high quality is a more recent study of Negro life in a piedmont town, Hylan G. Lewis, *Blackways of Kent* (Chapel Hill, 1955).

The best introductions to the Harlem Renaissance are Alain Locke, ed., *The New Negro* (New York, 1925) and Langston Hughes's autobiography, *The Big Sea* (New York, 1940). Incisive analyses of Negro literature are to be found in Sterling Brown, *The Negro in American Fiction* (Washington, D.C., 1937) and *Negro Poetry and Drama* (Washington, D.C., 1937); and in Robert Bone's controversial, *The Negro Novel in America* (New Haven, 1958; rev. ed., 1965). The best historical survey of the Negro in artistic and theatrical life is to be found in James Weldon Johnson, *Black Manhattan* (New York, 1930). The outstanding biography of Ira Aldridge is Herbert Marshall and Mildred Stock, *Ira Aldridge: The Negro Tragedian* (New York, 1958). The finest anthology of Negro literature is Sterling Brown, Arthur P. Davis, and Ulysses Lee, eds., *The Negro Caravan* (New York, 1941). Also useful are James Weldon Johnson, ed., *Book of American Negro Poetry* (New York, 1922); James Weldon and J. Rosamond Johnson, eds., *Books of American Negro Spirituals* (New York, 1925, 1926); Arna Bontemps and Langston Hughes, eds., *Poetry of the Negro, 1746–1949;* Alain Locke, *Negro Art: Past and Present* (Washington, D.C., 1936); and James A. Porter, *Modern Negro Art* (New York, 1943).

Outside of a few articles, the Negro and the New Deal is a subject that still remains to be explored by historians. Gunnar Myrdal, *An American Dilemma* is still the best source of material on the subject. Leslie H. Fishel, Jr., has written a suggestive account in "The Negro in the New Deal," *Wisconsin Magazine of History,* XLVIII (Winter, 1964–65). On one topic of concern during the New Deal period, Southern farm tenancy, there are a number of volumes. Among them are Charles S. Johnson, Will Alexander, and Edwin R. Embree, *The Collapse of Cotton Tenancy* (Chapel Hill, 1935); Charles S. Johnson, *Shadow of the Plantation* (Chicago, 1934); Arthur F. Raper, *Preface to Peasantry* (Chapel Hill, 1933); Raper and Ira DeA. Reid, *Sharecroppers All* (Chapel Hill, 1941). The replacement of cotton agriculture by animal husbandry during the years after the Second World War is lucidly described in Morton Rubin's description of Wilcox County, Alabama: *Plantation County* (New Haven, 1963).

The historical research done on twentieth-century Negro protest movements and organizations is thin. The useful volumes are Edmund D. Cronon, *Black Moses: The Story of Marcus Garvey and the U.N.I.A.* (Madison, Wis., 1955), which should be supplemented with the relevant chapters in the books by McKay and Ottley, cited above; the amateurish Robert L. Jack, *History of the NAACP* (Boston, 1943), which sketches the main outlines; a not altogether clear account of the NAACP's legal accomplishments, Jack Greenberg, *Race Relations and American Law* (New York, 1959); Wilson Record, *The Negro and the Communist Party* (Chapel Hill, 1951); Herbert Garfinkel, *When Negroes March: The March on Washington Movement in the Organizational Politics for FEPC* (Glencoe, Ill., 1959), a perceptive volume; and Clement E. Vose, *Caucasians Only: The Supreme Court, the NAACP and the Restrictive Covenant Cases* (Berkeley, 1959), which is the sort of specialized study badly needed for other phases of the NAACP's work. A survey of the legal restrictions which the NAACP was fighting during the New Deal era is to be found in Charles S. Mangum, *The Legal Status of the Negro* (Chapel Hill, 1940). For critical analysis of the programs of Negro organizations during the 1930's, see Ralph J. Bunche, "The Programs, Ideologies, Tactics and Achievements of Negro Betterment and Interracial Organizations," unpublished memorandum for the Carnegie-Myrdal Study, 4 vols., 1940 (available on microfilm from the New York Public Library). A summary of his conclusions is available in Bunche, "A Critical Analysis of the Tactics and Programs of Minority Groups," *Journal of Negro Education,* IV (July, 1935). For illustrative documents see Francis L. Broderick and August Meier, eds., *Negro Protest Thought in the Twentieth Century* (Indianapolis, 1966).

CHAPTER VII

Francis L. Broderick and August Meier, eds., *Negro Protest Thought in the Twentieth Century* and August Meier and Elliott M. Rudwick, "Come to the Fair?" *Crisis,* LXXII (March, 1965), the latter a description of Negro protest at international expositions between 1893 and 1940, both deal with the changes in the character of the civil rights movement during the twentieth century. Benjamin Muse, *Ten Years of Prelude: The Story of Integration Since the Supreme Court's 1954 Decision* (New York, 1964) and Anthony Lewis and the New York *Times, Portrait of a Decade* (New York, 1964) summarize the major events in race relations and civil rights.

Sketches of the histories of CORE and SNCC are to be found in

James Peck, *Freedom Ride* (New York, 1962) and Howard Zinn, *SNCC: The New Abolitionists* (Boston, 1964), respectively. Martin Luther King's point of view can be best studied in his *Stride Toward Freedom* (New York, 1958) and *Why We Can't Wait* (New York, 1964). A discussion of the way in which King functions in the civil rights movement is August Meier, "On the Role of Martin Luther King," *New Politics,* IV (Winter, 1965). Louis Lomax's *The Negro Revolt* (New York, 1962) is superficial and distorted, but provocative. A different point of view is taken in August Meier, "New Currents in the Civil Rights Movement," *New Politics,* II (Summer, 1963). Two illuminating case studies, one on the Tuskegee Civic Association and the other on the student nonviolent movement in Atlanta, have been published under the auspices of the Eagleton Institute of Politics. They are Charles V. Hamilton, *Minority Politics in Black Belt Alabama* (New Brunswick, N.J., 1960) and Jack L. Walker, *Sit-Ins in Atlanta: A Study in the Negro Revolt* (New Brunswick, N.J., 1964). The changed viewpoint of the Urban League is cogently expressed in Whitney M. Young, Jr., *To Be Equal* (New York, 1964). Two fine studies of the Black Muslims are C. Eric Lincoln, *The Black Muslims in America* (Boston, 1961) and E. U. Essien-Udom, *Black Nationalism: A Search for an Identity in America* (Chicago, 1962). James Farmer, *Freedom—When?* (New York, 1965) is indispensable for an understanding of recent tendencies among militant civil rights activists.

The economic problems of the black masses and their meaning for the civil rights movement are discussed in A. Ross and H. Hill, eds., *Employment, Race, and Poverty* (New York, 1967), and in Nat Hentoff, *The New Equality* (New York, 1964). A scholarly explanation of the increasing militance among Negroes is Thomas F. Pettigrew, *A Profile of the Negro American* (Princeton, 1964). Elizabeth Sutherland, ed., *Letters from Mississippi* (New York, 1965) is illuminating on the way in which Northern white youth functioned in the Mississippi Summer Project of 1964. Probably the best case study of a local civil rights movement is one about Chapel Hill, North Carolina: John Ehle, *The Free Men* (New York, 1965).

Among the most perceptive analyses of trends in the civil rights movement are three articles by Bayard Rustin: "The Meaning of Birmingham," *Liberation,* VIII (June, 1963), "The Meaning of the March on Washington," *Liberation,* VIII (October, 1963), and "From Protest to Politics," *Commentary,* XXXIX (February, 1965). For a presentation of the views of the nationalist-Marxist advocates of violence see Robert Williams, *Negroes with Guns* (New York, 1962). An incisive and provocative analysis of one aspect of the dynamics of the civil rights movement is Lewis Killian and Charles Grigg, *Racial Crisis in America: Leadership in Conflict* (Englewood Cliffs, N.J., 1964). A superb sampling of recent Negro writing reflecting the contemporary outlook is Herbert Hill, ed., *Soon, One Morning: New Writing by American Negroes, 1940–1962* (New York, 1963). A collective study of the current status of the Negro community, including the impact of the civil rights revolution, will be found in two issues of *Daedalus,* XCIV (Fall, 1965) and XCV (Winter, 1966), entitled "The Negro American," which contain contributions by a number of prominent scholars.

INDEX

Abolitionist movement, Negro role in, 97–98, 101–18; *see also* Antislavery movement

Abyssinian Baptist Church, 78

Accommodation, 60–63 *passim,* 83, 92, 93, 134, 156–57, 165, 172, 178, 179–82, 183, 186–88, 196, 205, 222, 250

Adams, Abigail, 43

AFL-CIO, 214, 237

Africa: attitudes of American Negroes toward, 2–4, 21–22, 200, 206, 209, 223, 226; West, history and culture of, 5–16, 34

African Benevolent Society of Newport, 84

African Civilization Society, 122, 142

African Free School of New York, 84, 89

African Methodist Episcopal Church, 76–77, 78, 85, 88, 142, 146

African Methodist Episcopal Zion Church, 77, 78, 114, 146; *see also* Rush, Christopher

African survivals in American Negro culture, 3, 16–22, 62, 206

African Union Society of Newport, 75

Africanisms in the Gullah Dialect, 17

Afro-American Council, 172, 182

Afro-American Industrial Insurance Society of Jacksonville, 174

Agricultural Adjustment Administration (AAA), 210–11, 212–13

Alabama, 48–50, 57, 68, 78, 112, 124, 143, 157, 160, 162, 163, 191, 229, 241

Albany, N.Y., 106

Aldridge, Ira, 208

Alexandria, Va., 142

Allen, Richard, 76, 81, 82, 96, 97

Allen University, 147

All-Negro communities, 92, 201–02

Almoravids, 8

American and Foreign Anti-Slavery Society, 101, 104, 106, 107, 111, 142

American Anti-Slavery Society, 79, 98, 100, 101, 103–07, 110–11, 113, 115, 132

American Colonization Society, 95–98, 102, 121

American Federation of Labor (AFL), 168–69, 196, 213; *see also* AFL-CIO; Trade unions

American Missionary Association, 142, 143; *see also* Congregational Church

American Moral Reform Society, 100

American Revolution, Negroes in, 45–46

American Society for African Culture (AMSAC), 21

Amherst College, 88

Anderson, Charles W., 181

Anderson, Marian, 211, 237

Angola, 4, 9, 25, 26, 30, 34

Antislavery movement, 42–44, 46, 69, 95, 97–98; *see also* Abolitionist movement, Negro role in

Aptheker, Herbert, 62

Arkansas, 48–49, 152, 157, 159, 189

Armed forces, Negroes in, 45–46, 123–32 *passim,* 170, 192–94, 217, 218

Armstrong, Samuel C., 178

Aro Chukwu oracle, 30

Arthur, Chester A., 73, 169

Ashanti, 9, 10, 11, 13, 14, 25, 34

Ashmun Institute, 88

Asiento, 27

269

Tilden, Samuel J., 155
Tillman, Benjamin R., 159
Timbuktu, 7, 9, 25
To Secure These Rights, 220
Togo, 26
Toomer, Jean, 209
Tougaloo College, 143, 145, 178
Townsend, Willard, 214
Trade unions, and Negroes, 167–69, 196–97, 199, 213–14, 237, 244; see also American Federation of Labor; Congress of Industrial Relations
Trotter, William M., 182, 185
True Reformers' Bank, 175
Truman, Harry S, 219, 220
Truth, Sojourner, 110, 116, 149
Tubman, Harriet, 112, 116, 238
Tulsa, Okla., 195
Turner, Henry M., 152, 202
Turner, Lorenzo, 17
Turner, Nat, 61, 78, 238
Tuskegee, Ala., 218, 225, 239
Tuskegee Civic Association, 225
Tuskegee Institute, 178, 179, 186, 199, 218, 221

Uncle Remus tales, 17
Underground Railroad, 112–15
Union Relief Association of Israel Bethel Church of Washington, 142
United Automobile Workers (UAW), 213, 214, 237
United Mine Workers, 213
Upward mobility, 1, 21, 145, 147, 176, 202, 205, 235; see also Social stratification
USSR, 216, 217

Van Vechten, Carl, 207
Vardaman, James K., 163, 170
Vesey, Denmark, 61, 78
Vicksburg, Miss., 52, 131, 137
Villard, Oswald Garrison, 185, 186
Virginia, 28, 36–40 *passim*, 43, 45, 46, 48, 50, 51, 53, 56, 58, 66, 77, 78, 79, 97, 124, 136, 142, 143, 144, 147, 154, 157, 163, 174, 175, 177, 182
Virginia Union University, 147

Wade, Richard C., 61 *n.*
Wald, Lillian, 186
Walker, A'Leila, 207
Walker, George, 208
Walker, Madame C. J., 176
Walker, Quok, 42
Walker's Appeal, David, 96, 98, 118

Wangara, 7, 25
War of 1812, 49, 125, 131
Ward, Samuel Ringgold, 106, 115, 119, 122
Washington, Booker T., 147, 165, 169, 178–88, 193, 196, 199, 204, 221, 225, 238, 245
Washington, George, 43, 45
Washington, D.C., 66, 79, 82, 83, 86, 127, 128, 142, 143, 156, 175, 190, 191, 194, 195, 211, 251
Watkins, William, 97, 98, 104
Watson, Tom, 160, 161
Weaver, Robert C., 212, 228
Weld, Theodore D., 101, 106, 107, 108, 115
Welles, Gideon, 124
Wells-Barnett, Ida, 182, 185
West Indies, 16, 19, 26, 27, 28, 33, 35, 36, 47, 62, 201 *n.*
Western Colored Baptist Convention, 78
Wheatley, Phillis, 42
Whigs, 69, 119
Whipper, William J., 100
White, George H., 161
White, Walter, 210, 214, 216
White Citizens' Councils, 226
White primaries, 157, 198, 215, 226, 240
White working classes, and Negroes, 70, 90, 192, 242; see also Populism, Trade unions
Whitney, Eli, 47, 48
Whydah, 29, 31
Wilberforce University, 88
Wilkins, Roy, 237
Williams, Bert, 208
Williams, Peter, 79, 103
Williams, Robert F., 248, 250
Wilmington, N.C., 157, 161, 164
Wilson, Woodrow, 170, 185, 188
Winston-Salem, N.C., 240
Wisconsin, 86
Wood River Baptist Association, 78
Woodson, Carter G., 3, 4, 16, 206
Woolman, John, 44
World War I, 191–94, 217, 250
World War II, 217–18, 219
Wright, J. J., 152
Wright, Richard, 210
Wright, Theodore S., 104, 105, 106, 108, 114, 115

Yoruba, 9, 10, 11, 25, 122
Young, Charles, 193
Young, Whitney, Jr., 233